THE FAITH AND FIR

IN MEMORY OF THE MEN OF HEXHAM
WHO FELL IN THE GREAT WAR

by
Alan Isaac Grint

ERGO
PRESS

Publishing for Northumberland

THE FAITH AND FIRE WITHIN

IN MEMORY OF THE MEN OF HEXHAM WHO FELL IN THE GREAT WAR

First published 2006
©Alan Isaac Grint 2006

Published by ERGO PRESS

ISBN: 0-9552758-1-4
ISBN: 978-0-9552758-1-4

Printed by Robson Print Ltd, Hexham

**ERGO
PRESS**
5, St Mary's Chare
Hexham
Northumberland
NE46 1NQ

ergo.press@yahoo.co.uk
www.ergopress.com

Written, published and printed in Northumberland

Cover Graphics: Harriet McDougall

CONTENTS

ACKNOWLEDGEMENTS

This book would not have been written without the help and loving support of Julia, my wife, who has endured endless discussions about trenches and soldiering, and who has been a sympathetic companion on several visits to the battlefields of France, Belgium and Turkey. I would also like to acknowledge the kind help that I have received from the enthusiasts who respond to questions posted on the forum of the *Long Long Trail* website. The breadth and depth of their knowledge is staggering. Thanks are due also to Colin Dallison, who kindly allowed me to use his catalogue of Hexham's war memorials undertaken for the 1989 National War Memorials Project. In particular I would like to thank the local people who took the trouble to visit Cogito Books to bring me what personal information they had – photographs, papers and indeed childhood memories. Such details have helped to bring colour and humanity to enhance this volume which I earnestly hope is a fitting tribute to the men of Hexham who died in the Great War.

Editor's Note

This was a massive undertaking. If I had included every bit of information researched by the author the book would have been too large to handle... It was decided quite early in the process of putting it all together that the reader should be offered a fairly simple and concise overview of the various theatres of war, followed by (where possible) finer details of where the men were when they died. I hope that the resulting format is clear and helpful.

FOREWORD

The history and the moral meaning of our nation, of our Empire and indeed of the continent of Europe can be 'read' in the lapidary texts of war memorials. They are at the same time intensely local, as Alan Grint shows in his book about the Hexham war memorial, and of broad historical significance. Men from small towns and villages assembled in their regiments and found themselves (probably for the first time!) in Europe, facing foreign troops consisting of young men similarly recruited. War memorials are profoundly religious, expressing the centrality of the sacrificial in Christian teaching, and profoundly male, replete with actual and symbolic statements regarding the duties of men as protectors, through self-sacrifice, of their communities. This of course is particularly true of the Great War, when the vast majority of casualties were soldiers, and where the civilian and female losses were proportionally very small. Dr Grint's study tells of young men dutifully going to war. Of all of the ways in which The Great War was 'remembered' – poetry, novels, films – none more accurately represents what the war meant to soldiers, their families and their communities than war memorials such as that in Hexham's Abbey Gardens.

The memorial at Hexham is no more than any other war memorial a proclamation of belligerency. They represent the ordinary chivalries of ordinary men, and the deaths they record express the tragedy, as well as the necessity, of duty and self-giving. This memorial, as was the case with so many others, was paid for by public donation. Cynics who regard such memorials as nothing more than 'propaganda in stone' totally fail to understand the deep need felt by the communities from which these men came to accord proper and permanent respect for what they did. In creating the memorial, in the initial dedication ceremony, and in the annual re-dedications, the people of Hexham (as the people of villages and towns all over Britain and Europe) marked out in the company of their dead the grim and terrible history of the Twentieth Century.

In the best tradition of historical research, Alan Grint tells the story of that century through the lives of the men whose names are to be found on one Northumbrian war memorial. It is the case, though, that these memorials are a common European symbol, a symbol understood by all involved. War memorials, and their associated war cemeteries, can be found all over Europe, and indeed in Africa, India, the Middle East, Canada and Australia. They mark out the ebb and flow of our world. The memorial at Hexham sums up that world.

Dr Jon Davies

CHAPTER ONE

IN MEMORIAM

'My subject is War and the Pity of War'
Wilfred Owen

Britain and its Empire paid a terrible price for its participation and ultimate victory in the Great War. By the end of hostilities in 1918 there was hardly a family in the land not intimately associated with someone who had died during this worldwide conflict. The title of this book comes from Thomas Hardy's poem *The Men Who March Away*, in which those who went to fight did so believing that 'victory crowns the just', hence 'the faith and fire within' each soldier. For the families left grieving and miserable when their men died – sons, fathers, brothers, uncles – the crown of victory may well have seemed hollow and unwanted. However much their country needed them, so did their families. To the modern ear, some of the words written to inconsolable wives seem curiously callous, if well meant:

> *"Do not think of your husband as dead, but just passed over into – and entered upon – a higher, a happier more perfect life. I feel sure that our heavenly Father is looking down with infinite mercy and regard upon all these noble sacrifices, nobly made, and that the way of sacrifice (the way His own dear Son followed) is a way that meets his fullest approval."*

> *(See Chapter 8, letter written by his Army Chaplain to the widow of Michael Irwin.)*

This book honours those fallen ones and the families who waved them goodbye. When the people of Hexham stand in silence at the foot of their War Memorial each November, they

1

do 'remember them'; they acknowledge that victory has a price, and that the chiselled names on the memorial represent the torn bodies and minds of the men who marched away.

Many of us associate the Great War with the horrors of the Western Front, with the slaughters at the Somme and at Passchendaele for the English, Verdun for the French. However, in the small town of Hexham the war memorial in the Abbey Grounds records also the deaths of men killed in other, less well-known theatres of war such as Salonika, Gallipoli, Palestine, Italy, and Russia; Mesopotamia, too, saw many casualties, as did East Africa. As well as the multitudes that died on land, there were countless others that died at sea; others came home to die of injuries sustained on land or at sea. Nearly a million men from Britain died in the Great War and the vast majority died abroad, many being buried in the wonderful cemeteries found in countries all over the world, cared for by the Commonwealth War Graves Commission.

However there were still a significant number of men who lost their lives and have no known grave and whose names are etched not on gravestones but on magnificent monuments across the battlefields of the Western Front. To see them one needs to visit the Menin Gate (Ypres), Tyne Cot (Flanders), Arras, Thiepval (Somme) and more exotic locations in Istanbul, Iraq, Egypt and Pakistan. On the 21 March 1918 – the first day of the German offensive on the Somme – of the seven thousand five hundred men killed fewer than a thousand have known graves.

Given that every city, town and village erected a war memorial, their presence altered the landscape of post-war Britain. There was no governmental direction about their erection; the memorials were bred of the grief and respect of local people who wished to remember those who had gone to war. Thus, the shape and form of memorials vary across the country as does the style of presentation of names for remembrance. Virtually every local community built one, therefore the vast majority of the dead are recorded. After the war, further memorial tablets were installed in churches, sports clubs, schools and places of work, replacing many of the temporary shrines which had been hastily built in churches and in the streets all over Britain, Ireland and the British Empire. Many names are found on both centrally placed civic memorials and on the other kind. In Great Britain, at the last count, there are over 36,000 memorials to the dead of the Great War.

The process of remembrance began even as the war persisted, with the development of small street shrines and rolls of honour. Many of the volunteers in the early part of the war were known as Pals because they were friends that had volunteered en masse from tightly knit communities or even from sporting clubs. Because these 'teams' joined up together, battles such as the first day of the Somme left many of their communities devastated, leaving neighbourhoods full of families without fathers and in some cases children who would never even see their fathers. Although Hexham did not raise any of these Pals Battalions, it did have a local Territorial Battalion which had fearsome losses at Ypres (April 1915), the Somme (September 1916), Passchendaele (1917) and the Aisne (1918).

The lack of any prescriptive template for memorials has resulted in the country being embroidered with a plethora of monuments of countless different styles, many of which have a dark and haunting beauty.

Some are simply a list of names of the dead, usually incorporating their ranks, whilst others also incorporate regimental information. Unsurprisingly, the year of death is also a common feature. Some war memorials incorporate the names not only of those who lost their lives, but also of all the local people who served their country and lived to tell the tale. The names to be included on the central memorial would be compiled from the responses to a public advertisement calling for families and friends to submit details; the advert was usually placed by a committee who had taken on the task of securing the fund to build the memorial and to devise its shape and form.

Given the sheer quantity of people and information involved, it was inevitable that errors would be made when the final selection was made. In a number of cases, initials were confused, one simple reason for this being that the hero might have been commonly known by his nickname. Thus soldier Bob 'Robert Everyman' might be transcribed as soldier 'B. Everyman'.

Those who submitted the names also supplied the details of many of the regimental affiliations. During the course of the war the 'where?' and 'which?' of a man in service could change considerably. If he were wounded and then returned to the Front after treatment, it was not always the case that he went back to the battalion and regiment of original enlistment; he may have been sent into another battalion of the same regiment or even to another regiment altogether. It is hardly surprising that in many cases his details were out of date by the time he died.

Further, during the course of the war, battalions that were devastated in action were sometimes amalgamated with others to make them viable. If battalions were lacking a core of experienced men, then men from battalions who had more than their share would be ordered to transfer a number of men. In early 1918 the army was so desperately short of manpower that the brigade system was modified; the number of Front Line infantry battalions contained by each brigade was reduced from four to three. Thus, a soldier's service record was not always easy to trace.

During my extensive research in writing this book on the Hexham men, I have come upon a number of inconsistencies, where the data on the war memorial is not consistent with that found in public records and the newspapers. Further research has proved that the error always lies with the war memorial. At first I was tempted to pursue a crusade to correct all of the anomalous details – perhaps even to have some inscriptions on the Hexham memorial re-carved. This idealism was short-lived, not least because there was a mountainous region of bureaucratic landscape to be crossed.

More importantly, however, I was touched by an entry in Colin Dallison's extensive catalogue of the war memorials of Hexham relating to Private John Kirkland. His name is on a private memorial on the west wall of the church hall of the West End Methodist Church, Leazes Terrace. This building initially opened in 1905 and was used as the United Methodist church, until the present church was opened in 1936. When the new church was built the family requested that the plaque be left in the old building, now the church hall, because this was the building that John knew. Families have long accepted that details are wrong, places have changed – it seemed hubristic on my part to want to change what the years have settled. Let it all rest.

In this book I have attempted to pay homage to men who gave their lives in the Great War by integrating some facts about their private lives and what was going on in the theatre of war at the time they died. My first list of men came from the War Memorial in the Abbey Gardens. It soon became apparent that not all of the names were of men who lived and worked in Hexham. Some were included simply because they had been born in the town and were remembered because close relatives still lived in Hexham, as was the case with the Canadians and Australians. After looking at the other memorials in the town (twenty eight of which have survived the rigours of time) it became obvious that a selection process was required. Thus, there are a few men, mentioned on the other memorials, whose connection with Hexham was too tenuous to warrant their inclusion in this volume.

CHAPTER TWO

FOR KING AND COUNTRY

'What greater glory could a man desire?'
Siegfried Sassoon, *Memorial Tablet*

Overview

In the years of the twentieth century leading up to the Great War, the British army was regarded as a Police Force for Britain's extensive empire. It was recognised as a highly professional force, but its continental neighbours dwarfed it: France had 2.75 million men and Germany had 3.7 million men at arms. In comparison the British Army was regarded as second to its Navy and had a total strength of fewer than 250,000 men, half of whom were based overseas. When the British Expeditionary Force landed in France in 1914 it could muster only 5 Divisions; in comparison the Germans could count on 72 Divisions and even Belgium could muster 6 Divisions.

From 1908, in the years leading up to the war, the British Army gained its recruits from three sources: professional soldiers, part time members of the newly established Territorial Force and soldiers of the Special Reserve.

A man enlisting in the regular army could do so as long as was able to pass a number of physical tests, was taller than five feet three inches and was aged between nineteen and thirty-eight. He would join up either at the Regimental Depot or at the local recruiting office and could choose the regiment in which he would like to serve. At the end of the man's time in service he was assigned to the National Reserve and could be called back to make up the numbers of his regiment. At the beginning of the war over 350,000 men were on the National Reserve list, and many of these reserves rejoined the army immediately, most of them without waiting to be called.

In 1908 the Territorial Force came into existence as a result of the reorganisation of the earlier militia forces and other voluntary bodies. This new force followed closely the models of the regular army, but was composed of volunteers who would train as soldiers part time and could give up a night or two for training. They were also required to attend an annual military camp. The majority of county regiments supported up to four battalions of Territorials with associated support units such as transport, medical and artillery. The physical criteria for joining the Territorials were similar to that of the regular army but with the lower age limit of eighteen. Territorial soldiers were not obliged to serve overseas, but their enthusiasm for the war in the early days was measured by the fact that vast numbers signed up for active service overseas as soon as they were able. Initially, these were sent to the Western Front, as individual battalions, but eventually they served as entire Divisions. The Hexham Territorials (1/4th Northumberland Fusiliers) went to Europe as part of a Division (50th Northumbrian), entirely made up of Territorial Battalions from Northumberland, Durham and North Yorkshire. Territorial battalions could always be recognised by their unique numbering system such as '1/4th' coming before the county appellation. Many areas produced further territorial battalions bearing a '2' prefix.

Recruitment Poster
(Hexham Courant)

It was with regular soldiers, reservists, territorials and troops from the colonies that the battles in the early months of the war were fought.

In early August 1914, Field Marshall Earl Kitchener, Minister for War, issued orders for the expansion of the Army. Against popular opinion he was convinced that the war would *not* be 'over by Christmas'. This expanded army was to be composed of volunteers, who would sign up for three years or for the duration of the war, and could be sent to fight anywhere.

"Your King and Country need you. A call to Arms" was published on 11 August 1914, calling upon 100,000 men to enlist, a figure which was achieved in two weeks. Army Order 324 created six new divisions from these volunteers, numbered Divisions 9 to 14, and referred to as 'K1'. Men in these new divisions were transported to France in May 1915 or to Gallipoli in August of that year.

On 28 August, Kitchener asked for another 100,000 volunteers and by Army Order 382 created a further six divisions numbered Divisions 15 to 20 and referred to as 'K2'. A third 100,000 came forward and formed yet another six divisions numbered Divisions 21 to 26, and referred to as 'K3'.

Regimental Recruitment Poster (Evening Chronicle 1914)

9

More volunteers came forward to form reserves and by December 1914 orders were given to create another six Divisions, eventually numbered 30 through to 35 and referred to as 'K4'. Most of units of 'K4' were locally raised and often referred to as *Pals*. All the volunteer units used the word 'service' after their unit number. This indicated that they were there only for the duration of the war.

By the Spring of 1915 voluntary recruitment was recognised to be at a level which was not going to provide the numbers of men required by the armed services and so on 15 July the Government passed the National Registration Act as a step towards stimulating recruitment and to discover how many men between the ages of 15 and 65 were working, and engaged in what trade. The results of this census became available in the middle of September 1915.

On 11 October 1915, Lord Derby was appointed as Director-General of Recruiting and within a week had instigated a scheme, referred to as the Derby Scheme, for increasing the numbers of men available for military service. This scheme is mentioned in Siegfried Sassoon's *Memorial Tablet*, which begins:

> Squire nagged and bullied till I went to fight
> (Under Lord Derby's scheme). I died in hell –
> (They called it Passchendaele); my wound was slight,
> And I was hobbling back, and then a shell
> Burst slick upon the duck-boards; so I fell
> Into the bottomless mud, and lost the light.

This typically ironic poem ends with the bitter words, 'What greater glory could a man desire?' Under the scheme, men between the ages of 18 and 41 could continue to enlist voluntarily, or could *attest*, which carried the obligation to respond to being called up; Sassoon's poem suggests that a great deal of pressure was probably exerted here and there by those with local influence.

All men who registered under the Derby Scheme were classified into either married or single, and both groups were sub divided into twenty-three classes, based on age. At the same time, a War Pension was introduced to entice men who were worried about supporting their dependents. 15 December was the date chosen for the closing of the Derby Scheme and by this point a further 215,000 men had enlisted and 2,815,000 had attested under the scheme, many of whom were sent home until their call-up came. However, it was estimated that over 615,000 unmarried men had evaded the call up.

First to be called up were the twenty-three groups of unmarried men, from youngest to eldest, followed by the married men.

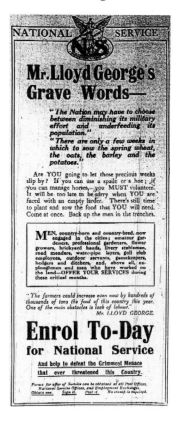

Enrolment invitation for National Service (Hexham Courant)

The Military Service Act introduced on 27 January 1916 concluded that all British males between the ages of 18 and 41, residing in Great Britain and unmarried or widowers on November 15th 1915, should by now have enlisted in the armed forces. In effect, they were conscripted. The Act was extended to married men on 25 May 1916, and from September 1916 men were assigned to training battalions before going to Front Line units.

Initially, the Act delivered only a further 43,000 men for service; another 93,000 failed to appear and were chased through the courts, whilst another 750,000 claimed some form of exemption in addition to the 1,400,000 already serving in war occupations such as coal mining and munitions work. Others were deemed to be too ill to serve.

A series of tribunals was established to hear the cases of men who believed that they were exempt from military service on the grounds of ill health, occupation or conscientious objection. The reports mentioned below relate to one of many tribunals held in Hexham to hear such cases.

On Saturday 20 January 1917, The Hexham Herald reported that forty-six appeals had been heard at Hexham involving the call up of agricultural workers, butchers and grocers.

The Appeals Tribunal was presided over by Colonel Fenwick of Higham Dykes, with Mr C Riddell of Swinburne Castle, Mr John Robson of Newton, Bellingham and Mr James T Robb of Hexham in attendance. Lieutenant Kinsley Taylor appeared as the military representative with Mr A W Hoyle (Prudhoe Military Representative) and Mr George H Waddilove (Hexham Military Representative) and Mr A M Allgood (Agricultural Representative). Mr Jasper Gibson acted as clerk.

A Hexham Grocer's Appeal

The exemption of a grocer's assistant manager aged 30, was appealed for by a Hexham grocer who stated that he had now only two men left in his shop, and one of them was going to join up on the 30 January 1917. The man for whom he was appealing was classed as B1. Conditional exemption was granted.

[The 'B' signified that the man was 'free from serious organic disease, able to stand service on lines of communication in France or in garrisons in the tropics'. The '1' further meant that he was 'able to march 5 miles, see to shoot with glasses and hear well'.]

Not a Job for Women

Mr M Green applied for exemption (until the end of February) for two cartmen employed by Tynedale Coal Company. The men were engaged in leading coals all over the town and if they could be retained in their present employment until the end of February it would help [Tynedale Coal and its customers] over the worst part of the cold season. At the time they had only six cartmen, men being very difficult to get.

Mr Robson asked if women could not be got for this work, since women were doing all sorts of work at Bellingham. Mr Green replied that this class of work was beyond women – it was much too heavy.

Exemption was indeed granted till 1 March, when the men would have to join up.

Grocer to act as a substitute.

A man employed in a Newcastle brush factory, but who was a grocer by trade, appealed for exemption on domestic grounds.

Replying to a question put by Lieutenant Taylor, the appellant stated that he understood the grocery business.

Lieutenant Taylor relied that in the circumstances he should serve as a substitute for some general service man in the grocery trade. "I am told there are general service men employed in the trade in Hexham. You will get notice which shop to go to".

A Wagon man to serve

A Hexham haulage-contractor appealed for the exemption of one of his employees whom he stated had been engaged in hauling timber for twelve years. He was a single man, 35 years of age and passed for C1.
Conditional exemption was granted.

13

[The 'C' signified, 'free from serious organic diseases, able to stand service in garrisons at home'. The '1' further meant that he was 'able to march 5 miles, see to shoot with glasses and hear well'.]

An Allendale Farmer's Dilemma

An Allendale farmer applied for the exemption of his son, a married man of twenty-nine years of age, who acted as his shepherd and was also employed as a postman in the district. The only other man he had on the farm was his younger son, a lad of twenty-two, who had been shot through the lungs and discharged from the army. It was impossible for a lad in his condition to assist in shepherding on such exposed territory as his Northumbrian farm.

Lieutenant Taylor said he had been told that the Postmaster had a man available for the post work.

Appellant: 'But this man is my shepherd and I have no one else.'
The Chairman: 'The appeal is dismissed; he will have to serve.'
Appellant: 'I don't know what to do with the sheep.'

Conditional Exemption for Diary Farmer

Application was made for the exemption of a young man of thirty-eight who had passed for general service but who was managing a dairy farm for his father, the latter being in failing health. There was only the father and this young man and a delicate housekeeper on the farm, which was a holding of 136 acres. It was a dairy farm with contracts to supply milk to the Workhouse and to the Sanatorium. To find a substitute would be a most difficult matter.

Conditional exemption was granted.

A further extension to the Act was made on 10 April 1918 to offset a serious political crisis concerning the provision of men to the services.

By the end of the war, 8.5 million men had been recruited from Britain, and the British Army had become the most effective fighting force on the Western Front.

CHAPTER THREE

1914
GREAT EXPECTATIONS
'WAR OVER BY CHRISTMAS'

And he is dead who will not fight;
And who dies fighting has increase.

Julian Grenfell, *Into Battle*

Overview

Germany declared war on both France and Russia in early August, in the aftermath of the assassination of Archduke Franz Ferdinand in Sarajevo earlier in June 1914. Germany declared war on both France and Russia in early August. Germany also invaded neutral Belgium, prompting Britain to declare war on 4 August. In France a week later, Britain landed an Expeditionary Force of 103,600 men which was under the control of Field Marshall Sir John French. Of this force, Kaiser Willhelm II decreed:

> "*It is my Royal and Imperial Command that you concentrate your energies and the valour of my soldiers to exterminate the treacherous English and walk over General French's contemptible little army*"

Thus the name *Old Contemptibles* was coined for this force of regular soldiers, which advanced northwards and met hugely superior German forces at *Mons*. Along the Front both the British and French forces were compelled to retreat, but in September at the *First Battle of the Marne* (5 – 10 September), the German advance was checked. After the subsequent *Battle of the Aisne* a system of trenches was built by both sides; each army tried to outflank the other as the

17

battle moved progressively westwards towards the sea.

By this time, the Germans had attacked Russia and its ally Austria Hungry, and were therefore fighting on two Fronts. At the end of October, Turkey had entered the War on the German side, declaring a Jihad. The much-misunderstood Arabic word jihad means 'struggle', and in the Qur'anic context of war means the defensive action of Muslims against any non-Muslim threat towards Islam. Perhaps this is why the other Arab nations failed to support Turkey's involvement in the Great War.

In the autumn, Allied troops were sorely tested during the *First Battle of Ypres* (14 Oct – 22 Nov), where they barely held the line but managed to inflict tremendous losses on the Kaiser's troops. British casualties were high and in many cases artillery batteries were counting their last few shells because of manufacturing inadequacies at home – there weren't enough being produced.

In August 1914 the 3rd Battalion Coldstream Guards was part of the 2nd Division, which landed in France at the start of the war. They saw action at *Mons* and were part of the subsequent retreat. They were involved in the famous rearguard action at *Villers Cotterets* following the retreat from *Le Cateau*. At this action the Guards Regiments are reported to have fired a minimum of fifteen rounds per minute, wreaking havoc on the advancing Germans thereby protecting the rear of the retreating forces.

During the *Battle of the Marne*, the British Expeditionary Force played only a small part in this clash of the Titans, but their presence caused the Germans to abandon the field of battle and retreat northwards to the valley of the River Aisne. The Germans entrenched themselves along the north bank of the river and along the steep slope leading up to the Chemin des Dames Ridge.

The subsequent battle, the *First Battle of the Aisne*, began on 13 September when both French and British Troops launched a frontal attack.

The 3rd Battalion Coldstream Guards were involved in the action near Soupir, which lies on the north bank of the river. The Guards' position on 15 and 16 September was shelled heavily. One shell hit a hollow which was being used as a hospital, killing twelve soldiers including the battalion medical officer, and wounding at least fifty others. The next day, a further eight men were killed and thirty-nine wounded. The following day, 18 September, the battalion was relieved in the trenches and returned to Soupir, only to be recalled to the Front during the early morning of the next day. They stayed in the line for a further two days until relieved by a battalion of the Royal Fusiliers.[1]

Private Edward Baty, aged 29
3rd Battalion Coldstream Guards
Died 21 September 1914

Edward Baty had been in the Coldstream Guards for seven years before the outbreak of war. He was born in Hexham and was the son of John and Mary Baty of Hexham and the nephew of William Baty of Haugh Lane. Edward's brother worked for William Baty. Before he joined the army he had worked on the North Eastern Railway. He was known in the Guards both as a fine swimmer and a good boxer.

He travelled to France with the Guards Brigade. This body of troops was involved in some of the heaviest

fighting of the earliest days of the War. In dispatches, Sir John French mentioned five non-commissioned officers and five men of the 3rd Coldstream Guards for distinguished conduct in the field. Private Baty was one of these gallant men. [2]

Edward died of his wounds, which were complicated by the onset of pneumonia.

He is buried in Soupir Churchyard, which is situated twelve miles east of Soissons.

Following the battles of *Marne* and *Aisne*, both sides attempted to outflank the other by moving north and west in a series of attacks known as the 'Race to the Sea', which ended at the North Sea coast, and which resulted in the development of a continuous trench system to the Swiss Border.

The Northumberland Hussars, a Territorial yeomanry regiment, left Southampton on October 5, arriving on the continent at Zeebrugge. After a number of days in retreat they arrived at the looted town of Ypres and on the following day (8 October) they clashed with German cavalry. During the *First Battle of Ypres* (19 October – 22 November), the Hussars spent much of the time in general reserve although they did see some action at *Ledegham* on 19 October. On 22 October they saw further action near *Hooge Chateau*, whilst the following day they were involved in checking a German breakthrough. As the Front Line gave way, a gap appeared in it. The Hussars were brought up quickly from reserve and filled the depleted Front Line trenches. In tandem with the Scots Guards they charged the enemy, forcing them to retreat and averting a very serious breakthrough. The next day (25 October) near *Polygon Wood* the Hussars, together with the 2nd Royal Warwicks, prevented another breakthrough of the

British line although a section of the wood was lost. This section was regained later in the day by a bayonet charge from the Worcestershire Regiment. [3, 4]

On 7 Nov, The Hexham Herald printed a letter from Corporal Civil (of Wark) of the Northumberland Hussars which included under the heading, '25th October, Ypres':

> *"How are things going over the channel: not so warm as it is here with shrapnel shells and bullets flying around you like a swarm of bees. We have covered a lot of country since we came down here yesterday (Saturday). We were called out at a minute's notice and while we were advancing across some fields we met an infantryman coming up on a bike. His remark as he passed was 'There is hell on down there.' When we arrived the Germans had broken through the line and were coming up the wood in droves, which I believe we turned and saved the position: but I can tell you I would not like to go into same if I knew it. This is the third scrap we have had and the worst so far. We have had several wounded, but the North Tyne lads are all to the front as yet...."*

Until 5 November, when they were withdrawn from the area, the Hussars were involved in the desperate defence of Ypres salient. They were sent to an area around the towns of Bailleul and Meteren.

Trooper William Metcalfe, aged 21
'A' Squadron Northumberland Hussars
Died 6 November 1914

William was born in Stockton on Tees and was the son of Jonathan and Isabella Metcalfe of Prior Terrace, Hexham. Two of his brothers, Arthur and Jonathan, also served in the forces during the war. Both were wounded during their service for the

King, and Jonathan was discharged because of the amputation of a leg from wounds received in action.

The Hexham Herald on Saturday 7 November published a letter sent to his parents by William, under the date 24 October (no place specified).

"Just a short line to let you know things are quite all right at this side. We are living in great style – poultry pork chops, veal, etc. Of course, I may say the Government does not supply these. We have been billeted out at a farm for about a week. The owner left on account of the firing, so of course we help ourselves so far as the foodstuffs go. You can imagine we are living like lords; so long as we stay here we are quite A1. The heavy guns are busy all day long, and we never know when we are to move. We have had two moves already, but always come back here again. Only one thing is missing, that is smokes. So would you mind sending me as soon as possible some Woodbines? English cigarettes are very scarce; you can buy what you call English, but they are not the same as you get at home, so will look forward to you sending some. We have very little news here, except that our fellows have killed hundreds of Germans, but as quick as they are killed others come up. However I don't think it will be long before this business is finished. I hope so, as it is a terrible business. I am still keeping in the best of health, so don't worry about me."

William's death was reported in a letter sent from France by Trooper C Liddle and published in the Hexham Courant on 21 November:

"We are now resting for a few days, several miles in the rear of our last position and now we can only faintly hear the sound of the guns. I do not have to keep moving for the nearest bullet-proof cover.....

... I am sorry to say we lost three of our comrades on Nov. 6. They were killed by a shell bursting in a stable whilst they were asleep. The bodies of Trooper Thwaites and Trooper G Stevenson were identified and it appears that Trooper Metcalfe of Hexham was buried in the debris.

Trooper Metcalfe was seen in the stable a few minutes previously, but has not since been seen. ....."

In the early autumn of 1916 the Hexham Courant reported that one of William's brothers had been wounded in the left leg and face by gunshot and as result the leg had to be amputated. It also notes that a further two brothers were serving in the forces.

William is commemorated on the Menin Gate Memorial in Ypres, which contains the names of more than 54,000 officers and men whose graves are not known.

The Menin Gate Memorial
Opened 1927

Designed by Sir Reginald Blomfield, the Menin Gate is, by any standards, a remarkable place to visit and is one of the most cherished memorials on the Western Front. Long before the war the ancient Menin Gate, which was part of the ramparts of the original fortified town of Ypres, had been demolished to widen the road. After the war there was talk of making the whole site of Ypres – by then completely demolished – into a memorial for the British and Empire participation in the struggle. However, the people of Ypres were determined to rebuild their town and offered the British the Menin Gate site to build their memorial to those who had died and whose bodies had no known graves. This was necessary because, in spite of real efforts made to mark and remember where men were buried, after more than four years of war on the same ground many bodies were lost and never found.

There is a passage in Sebastian Faulk's magnificent novel, *Birdsong*, that makes reference to the Thiepval memorial on the Somme which, like the Menin Gate, offers a shocking visual reminder of the number of men whose bodies, even if

23

buried, eventually became part of the mangled soil of the battlefield, and whose families have therefore never had the solace of a proper grave to visit:

> *As she came up to the arch Elizabeth saw with a start that it was written on. She went closer. She peered at the stone. There were names on it. Every grain of the surface had been carved with British names; their chiselled capitals rose from the level of her ankles to the height of the great arch itself; on every surface of every column as far as her eyes could see there were names teeming, reeling, over surfaces of yards, of hundreds of yards, of furlongs of stone.*
> *She moved through the space beneath the arch where the man was sweeping. She found the other pillars identically marked, their faces obliterated on all sides by the names that were carved on them.*
> *'Who are these, these ...?' She gestured with her hand.*
> *'These?' The man with the brush sounded surprised. 'The lost.'*
> *'Men who died in this battle? [The Somme]*
> *'No. The lost, the ones they couldn't find. The others are in the cemeteries.'*
> *'These are just the unfound?' ...*
> *When she could speak again, she said, 'From the whole war?'*
> *The man shook his head. 'Just these fields.' He gestured with his arm.*

Every night of the year, whatever the weather, visitors can attend a moving ceremony at the Gate. Since it is a busy thoroughfare, through which traffic and pedestrians pass continually, the road needs to be closed for the duration of the ceremony. The length of the ceremony varies according to the number of those visiting and who wish to lay special memorial wreaths.

The trumpeted 'Last Post' resonates around the huge arches which have etched upon them the names of 54,896 officers and men who died in the locality and who have no known graves. Astonishingly, in spite of its size, there was not enough room for all of those lost near Ypres; those who died between 16 August 1917 and the end of the war – a further 34,984 men – are recorded instead at Tyne Cot near Passchendaele.

❦ ❦ ❦

On 6 December 1914 the 1ˢᵗ Battalion Royal Irish Rifles were returning to the Front Line trenches near Estaires for a three-day tour of duty, relieving the Lincolnshire Regiment. The Battalion opted to change its approach to the Front so as to avoid Laventie Station, (3 miles southeast of Estaires) which was under heavy artillery fire. They arrived under the cover of darkness and during the change over Captain Allgood was shot whilst taking his men into the trenches.[4]

Captain Bertram Allgood, aged 40
1st Battalion Royal Irish Rifles
Died 6 December 1914

Bertram Allgood was born in February 1874. He was the second son of Elizabeth and Major-General Allgood, C.B., Indian Army, and latterly Chief Constable of Northumberland. He was educated at Eton, and received his commission in the Royal Irish Rifles in May 1897, becoming a Lieutenant in the following year and a Captain in 1904. He served in India and in Belfast until retiring in February 1914, when he joined the Reserve of Officers. Bertram was married in April 1913, to Isa Cochrane, daughter of the late Arthur Bayley and Mrs Herbert Lyde. (sic) He was also the father of a daughter, born in August 1914.[6]

At the outbreak of war Bertram was called up for service, eventually joining his old battalion.

Colonel G B Laurie wrote in his diary: [7]

"I had ordered everyone to return, (to the trenches), wished them good luck, and was waiting to see that they were all in whilst the Germans were sniping at us, when someone came and reported to me that a man had been shot through the shoulder by the same bullet which I afterwards heard was believed to have killed Captain Allgood. The stretcher bearers brought the latter in, and I sent for the doctor at once, but he could only pronounce him to be dead also! He was shot through the heart, and fell down remarking: "I am hit, but I am all right", and never spoke or moved again. He leaves one little daughter and a young wife....He looked so peaceful lying on the stretcher."

On 19 December, the Hexham Courant published the details of a memorial service held in St John Lee for Captain Allgood. Bertram is buried in Estaires Communal Cemetery, Nord, France.

Urged on by the French, who had totally misunderstood the strength of the German Army, a series of divisional actions took place in December 1914 even though both the French and British armies were severely under strength following the *First Battle of Ypres*.

The first action was planned to capture the village of Wyschaete and a wood called Petit Bois using units of the French army and the British 3rd Division, which had been severely ravaged during *First Ypres*, losing more than 8,000 men in a few days. The attack was made by the 1st Gordon Highlanders and the 2nd Royal Scots.

The diary of Billy Congreve (an onlooker) describes the attack with an acid tone.[7] Billy was the son of Brigadier-General Congreve and later in the war he won the VC before being killed on the Somme.

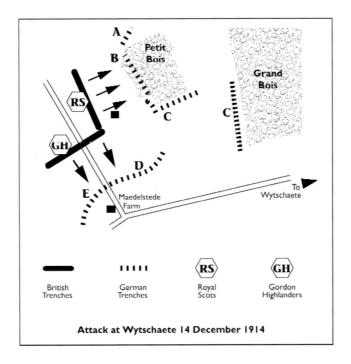

Attack at Wytschaete 14 December 1914

15 December 1914

> *"Yesterday we made an attack and, as we only put two battalions into it, the attack naturally failed. We had about 400 casualties. It was very depressing. I should have thought that we had learned our lesson at Neuve Chappelle (October 1914) about unsupported attacks, but it seems not.*
>
> *The truth of the matter is this I believe: Sir John French wanted to see the army on the offensive, so an attack on the Petite Bois was arranged. Then later, for some other reason or other, it was decided to also attack Maedelstede Farm. Sir John, Sir H Smith-Dorrien, HRH the Prince of Wales and many other lights of the Gilded Staff sat about on the Scherpenberg and watched the preliminary bombardment of ours (3rd Division artillery) and the 5th Division artillery - and then saw these two unfortunate battalions go to more or less certain failure...*

27

A, B, C, D and E (see Billy's sketch map) are the German trenches – B in Petit Bois and D round Maedelstede Farm. What happened was that for half an hour our guns gave the German trenches a very heavy and accurate fire with shrapnel and a smaller amount of HE... The effect of field gun shrapnel on trenches is almost nil and there was too little high explosive to do any good.

The Royal Scots actually got into B taking two machine guns and some prisoners, but they were then so heavily enfiladed from A... which held up their attack making further advance impossible. ... Proper reconnaissance would have made sure that A was detected and shelled, the Germans were able to shoot our fellows down one after another.

The Gordons left their trenches to attack D and E and fared even worse. The mud on the ploughed field, which they had to attack over, was so bad that they could just move out of a walk. On leaving the trenches they came under a terrible rifle and machine gun fire from C, D and E. Imagine sending a battalion alone to attack a strongly wired position up a hill and over mud a foot deep, under frontal and enfilade fire. It was a regular Valley of Death. The losses were of course very heavy .... They lost 7 out of 9 officers and 248 out of 550 men ...

Next day, I read in the paper 'British troops hurl back Germans at Wyschaete'.
A beautiful epitaph for those poor Gordons who were little better than murdered."

Casualties for the engagement were (killed, wounded or missing):
1ˢᵗ Gordon Highlanders: seven officers and two hundred and forty eight men
2ⁿᵈ Royal Scots: six officers and ninety-seven men.

Private John Robert Wallace, aged 27
1st Battalion Gordon Highlanders
Died 14 December 1914

John was born in South Shields, Durham in 1888 and was the son of Henry Wallace, a well-known local builder who lived in Wylam at the outbreak of war. When the war began, John joined the famous Highland regiment, the Gordon Highlanders, enlisting in Edinburgh. Previously he had seen service with the navy, and was therefore sent to the Front in early November.

He was 'a universal favourite' during the years he lived in Hexham, according to a report in the Hexham Courant. He was a keen football player associated initially with the Northern Star club. He then played for Hexham Athletic, captaining the 'A' team, which in the season 1913 – 14 won the West Tyne Clayton Charity Cup.

John is commemorated on the Ypres (Menin Gate) Memorial, which commemorates men who have no known grave.

As the year ended, the men in many sectors of the Front, who had witnessed so much carnage, declared an unofficial truce on Christmas Day against the firm orders of their masters. This fraternisation, which has become the stuff of legend because of the famous football match, was never to be repeated.

References

1. WO 95/1342. *War Diary, 3rd Battalion Coldstream Guards.*

2.	*The Old Contemptibles, Honours & Awards*
	Pub: J B Hayward, 1915.

3.	Pease, H. *The History of the Northumberland (Hussars) Yeomanry.*
	Pub: Constable and Company Limited, 1924.

4.	Ascoli, D. *The Mons Star*
	Pub: Birlinn Limited, 2001.

5.	WO 95/1730. *War Diary, 1ˢᵗ Battalion Royal Irish Rifles.*

6.	Clutterbuck, Col L. A. *The Bond of Sacrifice, Volume 1*
	Originally Pub: 1915, Reprinted Naval & Military Press 2002.

7.	Taylor, J. *The 1ˢᵗ Royal Irish Rifles in the Great War*
	Pub: Four Courts Press, 2002.

8.	Ed. Norman,T. *Armageddon Road: A VC's Diary 1914-1916 Billy Congreve*
	Pub: William Kimber & Co, 1982.

CHAPTER FOUR

1915
SECOND YPRES

'If ye break faith with us who die
We shall not sleep, though poppies grow
In Flanders Field'

John McRae, *In Flanders Fields*
Written during the Second Battle of Ypres

Overview

During 1915 the war persisted along the Western Front, with Allied and German armies both enduring limited and ineffective attacks in Artois and Champagne. The Germans attempted to break this deadlock by using a new and inhumane weapon: chlorine gas. Although the Hague Convention of 1907 had banned the use of chemical warfare, the Germans used chlorine gas near Ypres in April. The method of dispersing the gas was primitive: it was carried by the wind passing over pipes leading from large cylinders buried beneath the soil near the Front; natural forces were thus used to carry and deliver this deadly poison. Within seconds of inhaling its vapour the victims' respiratory organs were destroyed. For a graphic account of the effects of chlorine gas, the reader might read Wilfred Owen's poem *Dulce Et Decorum Est*, in which he describes the 'froth-corrupted lungs' of dying soldiers. Later in the year the British also used chlorine, during their attack at Loos.

In February the Germans began to inflict submarine attacks on Allied and neutral shipping, in an attempt to blockade Britain. A month later the British blockaded German ports.

31

The war continued on the Eastern Front.

The British and French mounted a disastrous landing on the Turkish Gallipoli Peninsula in April 1915. The intentions of this landing were threefold: to break down the deadlock on the Western Front, to make the Ottoman Empire sue for peace and to establish a supply route to help Russian allies.

Italy entered the war on the Allied side and attacked Austro-Hungarian Troops at Isonzo. After some initial success in the East, the Russians were beaten by the Germans, who then went on to capture Warsaw.

Another Front was opened by the Allies at Salonika in Greece; the war was now spreading to become a global conflict with action in Belgium, France, Greece, Turkey, Mesopotamia and Africa. On the Western Front after the calamitous *Battle of Loos*, Sir Douglas Haig replaced Sir John French as commander of the British Expeditionary Force (the BEF).

Overall, 1915 proved to be a disappointing year for the Allies and a correspondingly positive one for the Germans and their allies.

The Second Battle of Ypres

The Second Battle of Ypres was not a Bosworth Field, over in a day. It lasted for well over a month and is an 'umbrella' title for a number of smaller battles, some of which have official recognition as battles in their own right as seen below.

By the end of 1914 the Germans had secured Hill 60 to the south of the village of Zillebeke and only 2^1/$_2$ miles southwest from the centre of Ypres, Belgium. Hill 60, an important military position, was merely a low ridge about 180 feet high, formed from the earth moved when constructing a cutting for the Ypres to Comines railway. In such a flat landscape, troops that commanded its summit had uninterrupted views of this sector of the battlefield, directing their artillery onto any troop movements.

By 1 April 1915, a Canadian division had arrived in France; two weeks later they had replaced French troops in the "bulge" at the Front Line. To their left was the 45th Algerian Division and beyond them the French 87th Territorials, Reserve formations both.

The Battle of Gravenstafel, 22 – 23 April 1915

At 1700 hours on 22 April the Germans released 160 tons of chlorine, which drifted with the wind onto the French lines occupied by French colonial troops of the 45th (Algerian, Zouaves) Division. At low concentrations chlorine causes extreme irritation to the eyes and lungs; at higher levels it causes the lungs to fill with liquid which causes the victim to drown. The French either fled or died and thirty minutes later the whole of the north side of the salient, from Langemarck to Steenstraat, was open to the German advance.[1]

> " ...the German soldiers simply walked forward through the allied (sic) line, over the bodies of the dead, lying sprawled out, faces discoloured and contorted in the grimaces of agony. Within an hour the Germans had advanced more than a mile and they had hardly needed to fire a shot."

In desperation, the Canadians and a small contingent of French Zouaves created a new defensive line north of St Julien. As news of the gaping hole in the Front Line reached headquarters, whatever troops were available were rushed to the Front to stem the gap. The 1st Canadian Division fought magnificently and at midnight mounted a counterattack on Kitchener's wood, but, unsupported on the right by the

33

French, they had to withdraw. However, a new line was formed on its southern edge.

On 23 April another disparate force (known as the Geddes Force) was quickly assembled and ordered to fill the gap between the French and the Canadians west of St Julien. The attack failed, partly owing to the French not being able to commit any troops as they were needed further west near Steenstraat. At a meeting in Cassell between the French General Foch and Sir John French it was agreed to make an attempt to regain all the ground lost in the last few days. As a result, the three brigades of the 50th (Northumbrian) Division were attached to General Sir Horace Smith-Dorrien's Second Army.

The Battle of St Julien, 24 April – 4 May 1915

Early in the morning of the 24 April, the Germans attacked the Canadians again with a mixture of chlorine gas and high explosive shells. The Canadians fought bravely but they had to yield ground to the advancing German forces; by early evening the Germans had captured St Julien and the Front was under increasing pressure.

On 25 April another scratch force was mobilized which tried to recapture St Julien and Kitcheners Wood. It was stopped by a larger German force, although the action did succeed in stabilising the Front to a certain extent.

The next day, 26 April, further plans were set in motion to regain the lost ground. The scheme involved a large attack by the French using their 152nd Division and parts of their 5th and 18th Divisions, with significant forces in reserve.

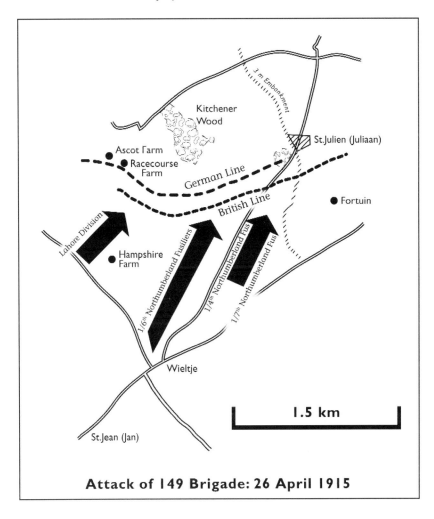

Attack of 149 Brigade: 26 April 1915

The Lahore Division, newly arrived from India and already tired after marching thirty miles from Béthune, would attack northwards from St Jean and reoccupy the ridge west of St Julien. The attack would also involve elements of the 149th Brigade, also newly arrived in France, and the 10th Canadian Brigade, which would be on their right. The 1/4th Battalion Northumberland Fusiliers had landed in France as part of the 149th Brigade (50th Division) on the evening of 20 April.

On the morning of 26 April the 1/4th Northumberland Fusiliers found themselves in good trenches to the east of

Wieltje, but were under heavy artillery bombardment as German spotter plans flew unmolested overhead.[2, 3]

Early in the afternoon, the 1/4th, 1/6th and 1/7th Northumberland Fusiliers were moving forward in order to take up positions for an imminent attack.

This attack was to take place in a north-easterly direction following the road between Weiltje and St Julien. The 1/4th Battalion moved forward on the right hand margins of the road, whilst the 1/6th progressed on the left. The 1/7th battalion was held in reserve. As they reached their attacking positions the battalions came under heavy shelling, machine-gun fire and rifle fire. As the men passed through the narrow gaps in the protective wire in front of the British defences, they tended to bunch up – they were easy targets.

In his diary, Lieutenant Bunbury wrote: [4]

> *"Practically from the moment that we started off we had to face a perfectly hellish shelling, which increased in intensity as we advanced. Shells of every description literally raining upon us from our front, right and rear, while it seemed to me in the excitement of the advance that our artillery was giving no support whatever.*
>
> *The line of our advance lay for about a mile over open ground and after we had gone a short way, in addition to the inferno of shells in which we were, we became exposed to a very heavy rifle and machine gun fire from the German trenches, which were directly in front of us near a wood at the top of some rising ground, and in such a position that they could fire right over what turned out to be our advanced trench, down on to us. The small arm fire was intense and the nearest thing I can liken it to is a gigantic swarm of angry bees buzzing around one. Men were falling on every side, and I felt an intense excitement, but there was no time for thinking ..."*

By 2.45pm, what was left of 1/4th and 1/6th Northumberland Fusiliers had reached the trenches that formed the Front Line, where surprisingly a few 2ⁿᵈ Seaforth Highlanders were found to be in occupation. Some of the 1/6ᵗʰ managed to enter the southern part of St Julien before being driven back. Later, the brigade's commander, Brigadier-General Riddell, moved up to the Front in order to get a greater understanding of what was going on and was shot in the head (see *Splendid Gallantry of County Territorials,* below). Lieutenant-Colonel Foster, the next senior officer and battalion commander of the 1/4ᵗʰ, replaced him. By 7.30pm the brigade was ordered to retire and spend the night near Wieltje.

In an article published in the Hexham Courant on 29ᵗʰ May 1915, an officer of the 1/4ᵗʰ Northumberland Fusiliers wrote:

> *"After the attack it was a strange sight when darkness fell that night. Although quite close to the German trenches both sides seemed to be tired of fighting for the present, and we were able to get up and walk about with comparative safety and get the Battalions and Companies sorted up ready for everybody else. We had a busy time after that gathering in the wounded and burying the dead, and there were many things I saw that night I should be glad to forget. What disgusted me most I think was the way they fired on the wounded crawling back to shelter. There was a farm about half way up used as a dressing station, and this they shelled continuously and any party of stretcher bearers leaving it always came in for a hot time".*

During that afternoon's work, more than fifty fusiliers from the 1/4ᵗʰ Battalion were killed or died later of wounds received that day. Detailed below are the men killed in this action whose names appear on Hexham's Memorial in the Abbey Grounds:

Private George Pearson, aged 26
1/4ᵗʰ Battalion Northumberland Fusiliers
Died 26 April 1915

37

George was the eldest son of Annie and the late William Pearson, who had been a Hexham butcher. Before enlisting with the Fusiliers at the outbreak of hostilities, George worked in the butchery trade for Mr William Teasdale.

Private Kavanagh, a stretcher-bearer with the Dublin Fusiliers wrote to Mrs Pearson telling her of the death of her son:

"You can always feel proud of the fact he died a hero's death. He was advancing with his regiment on the German trenches north of Ypres when he met his death."

George is commemorated on the Menin Gate Memorial in Ypres.

Lance Corporal William Ernest Woodman, aged 23
'E' Company 1/4th Battalion Northumberland Fusiliers
Died 26 April 1915

(William) Ernest Woodman was the second son of Mr W H Woodman who lived at Abbotsford Terrace, Newcastle upon Tyne. He was educated at the Royal Grammar School and Giggleswick. After leaving school he entered his father's business, Messrs Wilson and Woodman, wool and skin brokers in Newcastle and Dublin. When his father bought the Hexham-based business of John Riley Wool Merchant and Chemical Manufacturer, Ernest

came to Hexham in order to run the enterprise. He joined the regiment at the outbreak of war and during training was recommended for a commission. This did not come through before he was called to the Front.

Captain Robinson wrote to Ernest's father:

"He was a gallant soldier. He was at the time of his death carrying a message to the General."

The Hexham Courant reported on Saturday 6th June that Lance-Corporal Woodman had been mentioned in dispatches by Colonel Foster:

"On April 25th carrying a message from Major B. D. Gibson to the Brigadier over 1000 yards under heavy shell fire. He was killed in action the following day, when he showed great coolness."

Captain Bunbury, who in his letter arranged to meet Ernest's father and to show him where the body of his son was buried, wrote:

"Your son was shot in the head so death was instantaneous. He was buried that night in his uniform near where he fell"

The Hexham Courant of Saturday 1 May 1915 recorded the words of a close friend of Ernest:

"He has done his bit. What do the shirkers think when they read of the sacrifices of the gallant heroes, which are recorded daily. Can they say that their conscience does not prick them and do they not think that now is the time to do their bit."

Ernest is commemorated on the Menin Gate in Ypres

Private John Thompson, aged 21
1/4th Battalion Northumberland Fusiliers
Died 26 April 1915

John Thompson was a son of Mr T Thompson of Quatre Bras, Hexham. He worked as a road foreman for the County Council and had been a member of the Abbey Choir.

Captain F Robinson wrote to his father in order to tell him that his son met his death under circumstances that reflected the highest honour:

> *"Private J Thompson was killed yesterday morning while taking a man to the dressing station. He was a fine lad and a brave one at that. On the previous day he brought in wounded men all the afternoon under heavy fire."*

A further letter to his father from Captain Plummer explains that John was doing his duty as a stretcher-bearer at the time of his death:

> *"They have to expose themselves to a great extent whilst tending to the wounded and make very good targets from the brutes who are termed snipers, who do not refrain from firing on our wounded."*

John is commemorated on the Menin Gate Memorial in Ypres.

Drummer William Gilles Pearson, aged 21 years
'A' company, 1/4th Northumberland Fusiliers
Died 26 April 1915

William was the only son of William John and Margaret Pearson, and was a grandson of the late William Pearson who was a grocer in the town. Three sisters also mourned the death of their brother.

William had been in the Territorials for about three years before the outbreak of war. Although he was buried by his companions on the night he died, as was the case with Ernest Woodman (above), his body was lost.

William is commemorated on the Menin Gate Memorial in Ypres.

Sergeant Victor Elton Scott, aged 37
'A' Company, 1/4th Battalion Northumberland Fusiliers
Died 26 April 1915

Mrs Bertha Scott, of Garden Terrace, Hexham received a letter from Captain F. Robson saying that her husband had been missing since 26 April. He had last been seen on that afternoon in a trench outside St Julien. Weeks later his death was confirmed. Victor had previously served in the Boer War with the Northumberland Hussars. He was the brother in law of George Pearson who, by a curious and tragic coincidence, died on the same day. Before the war, he worked for a Mr Price of Dilston.

Victor, also, is commemorated on the Menin Gate Memorial for men who have no known grave.

Private James Smith, aged 19
1/4th Battalion Northumberland Fusiliers
Died 26 April 1915

SMITH J. 1185
SMITH J. 4030
SMITH J. 8597

James was born in Hexham, the son of Mr and Mrs Smith of St Mary's Chare (Back Street). He was initially reported missing, but later the Army Council confirmed his death through the Territorial Records Office, York. His father was serving as a Staff Corporal, stationed at York.

James, also, is commemorated on the Menin Gate Memorial for men with no known grave.

🌺   🌺   🌺

Private Isaac Hopper Whitaker, aged 29
'A' Company 1/4th Battalion Northumberland Fusiliers
Died 26 April 1915

Isaac was born in Hexham and was the son of Mrs Jane Whitaker of Hencotes.

On 29 May, the Hexham Courant reported that Private Whitaker was missing, presumed dead. Reference to his death can be found on the Commonwealth Grave Site under the name of Whittiker (sic).

In August 1916, after over a year, the Territorial Force Records Office in York confirmed to his wife Elizabeth Whitaker of 5, Market Street that Isaac had died in action.

Isaac is commemorated, again under the name Whittiker (sic), on the Menin Gate Memorial at Ypres.

🌺   🌺   🌺

Private Joseph Cunningham, aged 20
1/4th Battalion Northumberland Fusiliers
Died 26 April 1915

Joseph was the son of Edward and Bridget Cunningham of Gilesgate Bank. He was unmarried and was a blacksmith by trade, working for Mr W Baty of Haugh Lane. Even though he was only twenty he had served in the Territorial Regiment for over two years.

Although his commanding officer reported that he had been buried, Joseph is commemorated on the Menin Gate Memorial for men who have no known grave. Presumably his body, too, had been lost in the mire and destruction of the battlefield.

Private John Grierson, aged 25
1/4th Battalion Northumberland Fusiliers
Died 27 April 1915

John was born and bred in Hexham and was married to Ellen, of Gilesgate Bank, Hexham. He died leaving his wife with three small children. His parents, Arthur and Jane Grierson, lived in Pimlico, London. Before joining the Territorials at the outbreak of the war, he worked at Tynedale Colliery. He played both football for the 'Pats' and rugby for Tynedale. Research shows that he died of his wounds.

John is buried in Boulogne Eastern Cemetery.

Private William Donnelly, aged 32
'C' company, 1/4th Battalion Northumberland Fusiliers
Died 27 April 1915

William Donnelly was the son of Phillip and Esther Donnelly of Gilesgate, Hexham. He was married to Annie Donnelly and lived on Haugh Lane. He left his widow and no fewer than eight children, the eldest being about eleven years old. Before going off to war he was employed by Mr Bland, a Hexham builder.

A letter to his wife from a companion at the Front reported that he had been killed in action.

William, with other Hexham men, is commemorated on the Menin Gate Memorial in Ypres

Private George Watson, aged 26
1/4th Battalion Northumberland Fusiliers
Died 7 May 1915

On Saturday 22 May 1915, the Hexham Courant reported that George, the eldest son of Joseph and Ellen Watson of 4 Haugh Lane had been admitted to No. 13 General Hospital suffering from shell wounds to leg, hand and head. A week later the newspaper records that he had subsequently died in hospital in France.

Although not a territorial soldier before the war, he enlisted soon after mobilization. He was a keen footballer, who played regularly in the local football leagues. He was playing for Hexham Argyle when they won the West Tyne League (second division) and he also played for North Star and Hexham Athletic.

44

George is buried in Boulogne Eastern Cemetery. Boulogne, and nearby Wimereux, were centres for major hospitals during the war.

Splendid Gallantry of the County Territorials

On 29 May 1915, The Hexham Courant under the heading **Splendid Gallantry of the County Territorials**, printed extracts from national daily papers, quoting reports sent from their war correspondents in France:

North Mail

"Of the performances of the Territorial battalions engaged it is impossible to speak too highly. In some cases the units had only been in the country a bare week before they had their first experience of trenches and yet they faced the enemy's gruelling fire like hardened veterans and never gave an inch. Every officer that I have spoken to of the subject expresses the same opinion and many are the stories of unflinching bravery displayed by these units."

The Times

"The hardest task, perhaps, fell to the men of North England. The others for the most part had been some time in the field and had been broken in gradually to war. But these had arrived from home only a short time before."

"The Northumberland men were employed in an attack on St Julien on the 26th. There was no time to reconnoitre the position: they got into wire and were faced with a terrific shelling. Their 6th Battalion managed to advance 250 yards beyond our front trenches, but they could not maintain their position and had to retire in the evening. Brigadier-General Riddell falling with many gallant officers

and men."

"Consider what is meant by the fight of these Northern Territorials. Men only lately out from home, most of whom had never before seen a shot fired in battle, were flung suddenly into the most nerve-racking kind of engagement. They had to face some of the worst artillery bombardments of the war and the new devilry of the poison gas. There was no time for adequate staff preparation, the whole a wild rush, a crowding up of every available man to fill the gap and reinforce the thin lines. They were led by officers who a year ago had been architects and solicitors and business men. The result was a soldier's battle like Albuera where we escaped the annihilation which by all rules was our due, by the sheer dogged fighting quality of our men and their leaders. The miners of the north are a sturdy race in peace both in work and sport. The second battle of Ypres has proven them to be one of the finest fighting stocks on earth."

London Daily Express

"Equally gallant was the work of certain Northumberland Territorial Battalions during the bombardment of the 26th-27th. They attacked St Julien on the afternoon of the 26th and after advancing steadily isolated parties of the 6th Battalion got 250 yards forward of the first line and occupied some small trenches that the enemy had abandoned. These they held until dusk when they retired to the first line."

"Brigadier-General Riddell who was in command of these operations was killed about half past three. He was on his way to a farmhouse to get in closer touch with his men, and while walking along an exposed road was hit by a rifle bullet."

"One German attack was frustrated by a battalion of Northumberland Fusiliers. The bombardment had been intensified – the usual prelude to a bayonet attempt – and when it suddenly ceased to allow the infantry to come on, our waiting reserves were rushed into the weakened first line."

46

"'You should have seen the Northumberland Fusiliers come tumbling into the trenches' says an eye witness, 'turning their machine guns on the enemy almost at the same moment and cutting great swathes in their ranks. The disordered column turned tail and sought cover again'."

"Thus we held what was seemingly an impossible line day after day, while men were being blown out of trenches and dying in hundreds on all sides."

On 25 April, the 1/9th Battalion Durham Light Infantry received orders to move forward through the village of Verlorenhoek and to advance to high ground. The War Diary reports that, during this operation, Second Lieutenant Little was killed and seven others were wounded. One of the wounded, Captain Fenton, died within hours. During the previous night, the wood in which they had sheltered had been under artillery attack and two men had been killed. Later the battalion was ordered to entrench to the east and south of Verlorenhoek, after which the war began to take its toll on the battalion, which had just arrived at the Front with a strength of 31 officers and 1026 other ranks.[5]

Second Lieutenant Andrew (Drew) Little, aged 28
1/9th Battalion Durham Light Infantry
Died 25 April 1915

Drew Little was the second son of Andrew and Sarah Little of Oakfield, Hexham. He was educated at Bilton Grange, Harrogate and subsequently entered the family milling business. He joined the Forces at the outbreak of war and received his commission in November 1914 whilst stationed

at Gateshead.   He was a noted hockey player, representing Northumberland on many occasions. [6]

Drew is commemorated on the Menin Gate Memorial in Ypres.

The Hexham Courant records on Saturday 8 May 1915 that a memorial service for Drew took place in the Presbyterian Church. The pastor, Reverend J E McVitie, chose for his text that day "Be thou faithful unto death and I will give thee a crown of life", (Revelations II: 10).

In a letter to the Hexham Herald published on 15 May 1915, Lieutenant R E Atkinson of the 1/9th Battalion Durham Light Infantry (who was killed on the 29 February 1916) gave a graphic account of his experiences at the Second Battle of Ypres, in which he mentioned Drew Little:

> *"News came through that the Germans had broken through and we had to be hurried up. We started at dark. Ypres was three or four miles off, and we marched in with no mishap. Hardly were we in the town when the first shrapnel screamed overhead and fell about forty yards from our column. It was a dreadful moment of fear, which was in no way subdued by our surroundings. Ypres was a mass of ruins. What once was a beautiful city was smashed to pieces. On the streets lay dead horses in trams, making the air loathsome with their stench, while here and there dead men lay as they had fallen, struck by shrapnel or overcome by wounds. The air was laden with the fumes of shells, that smell so peculiar to burned houses (sic). Through this place we ran in silence, tripping over masonry and large holes in the streets. Scarcely were we safely across the canal when the Germans started to bombard it in earnest, and it lay burning a fierce furnace behind us. By this time shells were dropping around us frequently, but we reached our destination without any casualty. Our destination was a wood called Potige, where our men rested. I dug myself in with a man called Selby Cain and together we spent a fearful night. The soil was clay, the weather was bitter and*

*it rained heavily. However, although quite numb all over I slept quite soundly and felt refreshed the next morning. On Sunday we were bombarded at intervals. We heard how the battle for our lost trenches was going, how they were retaken and then again lost. The 8th, 6th and 7th D.L.I. all went up and as you know suffered heavily. At last in the evening we were told to advance. We marched in fours to Velorenhoek and from there advanced N.W. across country. We went off a company at a time in lines of platoons in fours. Then we got up into the "blob" formation and quickly extended. The whole thing was done like a drill. Taube (name given to German observation aircraft) gave us away and we got the attention of the German artillery. **The second shell burst at the head of a platoon, wounding several and instantly killing Drew Little.** Capt. Alf. Raine was blown off his feet but unhurt. The artillery fire enfiladed us, and how we escaped as we did with so few casualties is a marvel. We have certainly been lucky up till (sic) now. One shell moved the cap on my head in passing and burst a few yards away nearly deafening me. Had I not had my head well down I would not have been writing this now. Well, we got up to some clear ground and pulled ourselves together. The Germans must have been waiting for us to come over the crest of the hill, but just then orders came for us to retire. We had I presume achieved our objective by diverting the attention of the enemy".*

The Battle of Frenzenburg: 8 – 13 May 1915

From the 8 – 13 May, the two opposing armies fought for the Frezenberg Ridge situated between St Julien and Hooge. The Germans won the battle, although the lines in front of Ypres held.

The Battle of Bellewaarde: 24 – 25 May 1915

On 24 May at 2am the Germans attacked along a four and half mile front, using chlorine once again, and succeeded in capturing Bellewaarde Ridge and 'Mouse Trap' Farm.

49

At the time of the attack, the 1/4th Northumberland Fusiliers were occupying dugouts near Chateau des Trois Tours, near Brielen, and were immediately moved into a reserve position near the canal three miles from the Front. Even in this position, the threat from the gas was formidable. At 10am they were ordered into the line west of the St Jean to Wieltje road. During all of this time, gas shells were falling amongst the fusiliers. Late that night the Northumberland Fusiliers were instructed to deploy to the right of the road and "to stick at it at all costs".

During 25 May the Battalion was moved all along the Front to try and stem the German attacks. Although they were not directly involved in any fighting, exposure to non-stop shelling and gas resulted in the death of six fusiliers.[2]

Private John Robson, aged 20
'B' Company, 1/4th Battalion Northumberland Fusiliers
Died 25 May 1915

John was the eldest son of Mr and Mrs John Robson of North Terrace, who also had two other children, a boy and a girl. After leaving school he was employed by the Post Office. He was based mainly at Hexham but spent time at Woodburn. During this time he played football for Woodburn AFC and helped them to win the North Tyne League in 1913/14 season. He was educated at Beaumont Street Wesleyan School. Captain Dixon, his commanding officer, reported that he was killed in action and that he was buried close behind the firing line.

John is commemorated on the Menin Gate Memorial.

What follows is an extract from a Letter from Private J Moody published in the Hexham Courant (17th June 1915). It refers to the action in which John Robson died.

"On Sunday night a terrific bombardment started, and early on Monday morning (24th May) we got the order to leave our dugouts and advance. The Germans were using those gases so we had to use our respirators. I do not know how we could have come on without them, and we passed a lot of unfortunate soldiers making their way back, some very badly gassed. The effects of gas are too awful for words. The sweat was teeming down the men's faces and they were gasping for breath. Thanks to my respirator I was able to go on although I thought my head was going to split. Once as we advanced towards some trenches a German machine gun started to play on us and Lt Bunbury, one of our officers was wounded. Whenever we crossed a field it was ploughed up by 'Jack Johnsons'.*

They were bursting all over, and how we got so far up with so few casualties is little short of a miracle. When night fell we went forward again and took our place in the firing line. Things were pretty quiet just then, only a few stray bullets flying about, but we had to keep a sharp lookout, as the German trenches were only 500 yards in front of us. We were only in the front line for two days and are now back in some reserve trenches not far behind the front line. I expect we will be going further back for a rest shortly and will give you further news then".

* Jack Johnson was an Afro-American boxer who held the world heavyweight championship until 5th April 1915 and whose name was used as slang for a heavy German artillery shell that gave off a lot of black smoke.

Just after midnight on the morning of 25 May, elements of the 80th and 84th Brigades were detailed to attack on a Front between the Menin Road and the railway line to the north, to regain lost ground. The 80th Brigade deployed the 4th Rifle Brigade against the Menin Road with the 3rd King's Royal Rifle

Corps on its left (northwards). In the light from a full moon, the attack moved forward and initially met no German fire; the Germans knew about the attack and were waiting until it was difficult to miss them. Little ground was gained by this counter-attack and there were a growing number of casualties. However, a gap was plugged in the Front between 2nd Cavalry Brigade and 85th Brigade.

Rifleman James William Banks, aged 23
3rd Battalion King's Royal Rifle Corps
Died 25 May 1915

James was born in Hexham and was the son of Mrs Elizabeth Bathgate (sic) of Haugh Lane. He was an active member of the *Church Lads Brigade*. After leaving school he worked for R and R Phipps before becoming a Regular Soldier in 1908.

At the start of the war his battalion was stationed in India and returned to England in November 1914. The 3rd Battalion was attached to the 80th Brigade, part of the 27th Division, seeing action at St Eloi on 14 and 15 March before its involvement in the Second Battle of Ypres.

James is commemorated on the Menin Gate Memorial.

The End of the Second Battle of Ypres

By now the Germans had succeeded in capturing all of the high ground around Ypres. This was to be the status quo for the next two years, a dangerous situation indeed because it afforded the Germans uninterrupted observation of troop movements inside the salient. Their gunners were able to do their worst. To use a well-worn cliché, it was a 'damned close run thing'.

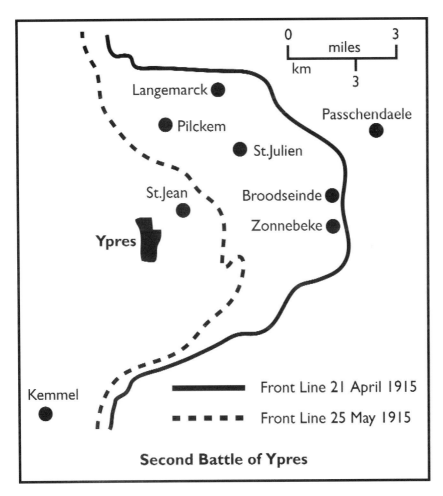

Second Battle of Ypres

It is well that, when the Germans called off their attack on the 25 May, they were not in a position to know the state to which they had reduced the Allied defences. The Allied artillery reported that they only had 272 rounds of HE (high explosive) remaining, and no shrapnel shells; the remnants of the infantry were exhausted and there were *no* credible reserves available.

References

1. MacDonald, L *1915 The Death of Innocence*
   Pub: Penguin 1997

2. WO 95/2826 *War Diary 1/4th Battalion Northumberland Fusiliers.*

3. Wyrell, E. *The Fiftieth Division, 1914-1919*
   First published 1939, reprinted Naval and Military Press 2002.

4. Bunbury, W. J. *A Diary of an Officer with the 4th Northumberland Fusiliers in France and Flanders.*
   Pub: J Catherall & Co, 1915, Courant Office Hexham

5. WO 95/2840 *War Diary 1/9th Battalion Durham Light Infantry.*

CHAPTER FIVE

THE GALLIPOLI CAMPAIGN

"If I should die, think only this of me:
That there's some corner of a foreign field
That is for ever England"

Rupert Brooke, d. 23 April 1915, *The Soldier*

Overview

By early 1915 progress on the Western Front had stagnated
and Winston Churchill, First Lord of the Admiralty, was keen
to push for a new Front in the East. Turkey, allied to
Germany, was fighting against the Russians in the Caucasus
and against the British in the Middle East. Churchill devised
a naval attempt to win the Dardanelles Straits, allowing a
bombardment of Constantinople (Istanbul since 1930),
which would, he hoped, lead to Turkish surrender.
Furthermore, this would allow a passage along the
Bosphorus from Istanbul for the supply of food and
ammunition to Russia.

Churchill set a date of 19 February for the opening of the first
bombardment of the Dardanelles. A combined British and
French fleet including a battleship, HMS Queen Elizabeth,
four battlecruisers, sixteen predreadnoughts and a range of
smaller ships were involved. In spite of this force, the long-
range bombardment proved to be ineffective.

Another bombardment at closer range began on 25 February,
but again this proved to be unsuccessful. Marines seized the
outer forts on both sides of the straits but they were unable
to silence a number of mobile Turkish batteries protecting an

elaborate minefield guarding the Narrows. Without neutralising the minefields, the fleet could not force its way through the Narrows.

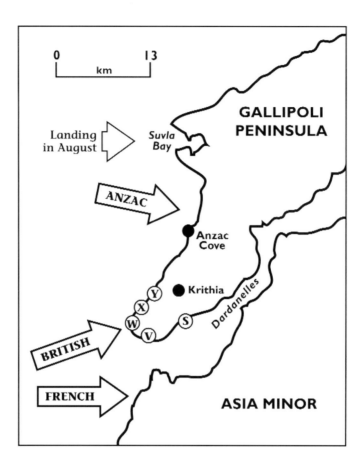

Gallipoli Peninsula

This did not deter Churchill, who *ordered* Sir Sackville Carden to capture the Dardanelles Straits. The Dardanelles Straits are about forty miles long and roughly four miles wide, with one significantly narrow section called the Narrows; it is worth getting out an atlas to see how this part of Turkey relates to Istanbul and the rest of the country. The name Gallipoli is taken from the Turkish *Gelibolu*, a small town on the eastern coast of the peninsula close to where the Dardanelles widen out to become the Sea of Marmara, north of the area shown on this map. The attack was launched on 18 March, five days after the beginning of a campaign of disastrously ineffective mine-sweeping. This renewed attack by a flotilla of sixteen battleships and many other smaller ships was a disaster, due to the presence of an undetected floating minefield. Five Allied battleships were sunk or disabled: the British ships Inflexible, Irresistible and Ocean and the French ships Bouvet and Gaulois.

At this point the Navy insisted that no further attempt could be made until ground troops had landed and captured the high ground above the Narrows. It was the admission that the naval attack had failed that brought about Churchill's political demise.

Even before the failure of the naval attack, preparation had begun for an Anglo-French landing on the Gallipoli Peninsula. Lord Kitchener appointed General Sir Ian Hamilton as regional Commander in Chief in charge of a force of 75,000 men, consisting largely of untested Australian and New Zealand troops. The landing on 25 April would be centred on two localities: Helles Point, where five landing sites were selected, called S, V, W, X and Y Beaches (using British troops from the 29th Division) and Gaba Tepe using Australians and New Zealanders, known collectively as Anzacs.

At X Beach the 2nd Royal Fusiliers landed, meeting minimal resistance, and after securing the beach and cliff top were reinforced by men from the 1st Border Regiment and 1st Inniskilling Fusiliers. Regrettably, instead of moving inland, they dug in and waited for orders, which unfortunately did not come.

At W Beach, which was better defended, the Lancashire Fusiliers suffered terrible losses, but thanks to the considerable bravery of those involved they were able to secure their position and were awarded six Victoria Crosses 'before breakfast'. As a result of outstanding courage Hill 114 was captured, allowing a link up with the troops on X Beach, as was Hill 138, allowing link up with Y Beach.

At V Beach the Dublin Fusiliers were massacred as they reached the shore, with only a few survivors making it to the relative safety of a low ridge of sand. Disembarking from the River Clyde, a specially adapted freighter, the Munster Fusiliers met a similar fate. By the afternoon the gentle waves lapped red on the shore and only nightfall brought some respite from the slaughter.

At S Beach, the South Wales Borderers easily captured the lightly defended beach, but again the troops made no attempt to move inland.

The northernmost landing site on Cape Helles, Y Beach, was allotted to the 1st Kings Own Scottish Borderers, supported by a company from the 2nd South Wales Borderers together with the Plymouth Battalion of the Royal Marine Light Infantry. The landing site had been chosen because of its narrow beach and high cliffs, hence this laconic verse penned by Winston Churchill's younger brother, John (known as Jack).

> Y Beach, the Scottish Borderer cried,
> While panting up the steep hillside,
> Y Beach!
> To call this thing a beach is stiff,
> It's nothing but a bloody cliff,
> Why beach?
>
> Major J Churchill

Jack was serving as an officer with the Mediterranean Expeditionary Force and later in the campaign, on July 3, he wrote what was on the whole a fairly optimistic letter to his father, the Duke of Marlborough – "I think a big success will be achieved before the autumn" – but in this letter he also admitted that:

> *"The losses are awful ... wherever you are on the peninsula you come under shell fire. The troops have had a terrible strain – there is nowhere to rest. If you come out of the advanced trenches you cannot get away from the shells."*

Interestingly, Jack had some admiration for the enemy, remarking that "[t]he Turk is fighting splendidly, and behaving like a gentleman – letting wounded men save themselves etc." This contrasts markedly with the comment made in a letter from a relative of Arthur Patterson who died in the Second Battle of Krithia (see below).

Notwithstanding the difficult terrain, the landing from rowing boats was trouble free, encountering fire from only four Turks. By 5.45am the entire force had landed with no casualties and by 6.20am the cliff top had been secured. Confusion about orders resulted in the British forces pushing inland to the outskirts of Krithia only to withdraw again to the cliff edge and to begin to dig a defensive position, which proved difficult with the tools available. In the afternoon, when the Turks attacked in strength, they had managed to achieve only shallow scrape holes; the line was, *faut de mieux*, reinforced using only the men's packs. The Turks attacked in strength on a number of occasions during the course of the evening and many times were within ten yards of the defensive line. It is reported that in one case a German officer (the Turkish army in this sector was led by German officers) walked up to the trench and said, 'You English surrender, we ten to one (sic)'. He was thereupon hit on the head with a spade.

On a number of occasions the Turks were beaten off by the use of naval bombardments; unfortunately, however, many shells fell short, killing a number of King's Own Scottish Borderers.

The Turks renewed their attacks on the morning of 26 April, which resulted in heavy casualties and by 7am the left flank of the defensive line broke, forcing troops to withdraw down the cliff face. The troops in the centre were forced to counter-attack, incurring heavy casualties. By 3pm the order to evacuate the beach had been received.

Within twenty-nine hours of arriving the troops had withdrawn from Y Beach; it took until July 1915 to regain this land. [1]

Second Lieutenant, James Thomas Redpath, aged 29
1st Battalion King's Own Scottish Borderers
Died 25 April 1915

James was the eldest son of the late James A Redpath (Northumberland Constabulary) and Hannah R Taylor of Abbey House, Hexham. He was born in 1887 at Heddon on the Wall and educated at Morpeth. He enlisted in 1903, serving in the ranks of the 1st King's Own Scottish Borderers, spending time in both India and Africa. He was gazetted 2nd Lieutenant in February 1915 and was posted to the 1st Battalion. Only hours after landing at Y Beach, James was wounded twice. He returned to the Front after treatment but was killed shortly afterwards. He was married to Agnes McMillan MacDonald and was the father of two children, a son born in 1909 and a daughter born in February 1915. [2]

James is buried in Pink Farm Cemetery, Helles, where this photograph was taken by the author.

My Help Cometh of God
Who Preserveth Them
That are true of Heart

Because of mismanagement, the Anzacs landed about a mile and a quarter from their intended landing site. Instead of disembarking on a flat beach with gently undulating landscape beyond as they expected, they were faced with shrub-covered cliffs with deep gullies running into them. The troops quickly stormed the lightly defended heights, but lamentable disorganization prevented a greater number of them from penetrating further into the peninsula. By late evening the Turks had put together a number of counter-attacks; the Anzac force was reduced to fighting a number of disparate and uncontrolled battles. It was a terrible situation and many of the commanders on the ground pressed for withdrawal.

Sir Ian Hamilton replied: [3]

" ...*Make a personal appeal to your men and Godley's to make a supreme effort to hold their ground. P.S. You have got through the difficult business, now you have only to dig, dig, dig, until you are safe.*"

The next day, as daylight dawned, it was found that their beachhead was a mere 700 yards deep and 1 $^1/_4$ miles long.

The First Battle of Krithia

On 28 April, parts of the 29th Division to which the 1st Battalion Border Regiment belonged were dispatched to capture Krithia, together with recently landed French troops.

The 1st Border Regiment and the 1st Inniskilling Fusiliers reached the southern end of Gully Ravine, securing it and the beach with no resistance. The advance continued with the Borderers proceeding along the top of the gully that became known as Gully Spur. However, by mid-day the advance had lost momentum and was described as 'hopelessly disorganised'. Under pressure from the Turks, who made a counterattack with bayonets, the Borderers broke ranks. The position was stabilized when HMS Queen Mary used its guns to annihilate this massed Turkish offensive. As the smoke and dust settled the Borderers rallied and a line was re-established. This battle was to become typical of the whole Gallipoli campaign: asking too much of troops with limited artillery support against enemies who were defending their homeland. [4]

Captain Reginald Head, aged 30
'A' Company, 1st Battalion Border Regiment
Died: 28 April 1915

Reginald was the only surviving son of Mr Jack Oswald Head (who had died in July 1914) and Mrs Head of Hackwood, Hexham. He was born in 1885 and educated at Harrow and Sandhurst. He received his first Commission in 1906 and served with the Border Regiment in both India and Burma. He was promoted to Captain in December 1914. He married Margaret Waller of Suffolk and left a child called Pamela, whom he was never to see. [2]

A letter from a fellow officer gave his widow the following account of his death:

62

"He died a most gallant death after holding an exposed position against overwhelming odds for the best part of two hours. During the whole time he displayed the greatest pluck and coolness, and did everything that was possible under the most trying circumstances. He fell mortally wounded, with a bullet through the body, just before we were forced to evacuate. His body was recovered and buried by Captain Moore the following day".

Hexham Parish Magazine for June 1915 recorded the loss of Captain Head.

Reginald is commemorated on a special memorial at Pink Farm Cemetery, Helles. A further tribute, commissioned by his mother Dorothy, can be seen in Hexham Abbey.

*Memorial to
Captain Reginald Head
Hexham Abbey.*

The Second Battle of Krithia, 6 – 8 May 1915

Early in May, Turkish forces were massing on Gallipoli. As a result the Allies needed to push on with haste if they were to make any progress up the peninsula; this required the capture of Krithia and the heights of Achi Baba. Forces were assembled to attack the Turkish line. The right of the attack was given to French forces supported by a brigade of the Royal Naval Division; in the centre were the 87th and 88th Brigades, whilst to the left was the 125th Brigade of the 42nd Territorial Division.

Minutes after leaving their trenches on 6 May the troops were greeted by heavy Turkish fire, making any real progress impossible. The following day, after a preliminary bombardment from the fleet, the Allies made a second attempt with even less success than the day before, suffering heavy losses.

On 8 May the New Zealanders took the place of the 88th Brigade and met a similar fate, gaining less than 100yds at the price of enormous human sacrifice. Later in the day the Australians were called up and again were met by withering Turkish fire.

From this point until the inglorious retreat from the peninsula, the Gallipoli campaign turned into trench warfare, as in Europe.[4]

Private Arthur Patterson, aged 25 years
Portsmouth Battalion, Royal Marine Light Infantry
Died 6 May 1915

Before enlisting, Arthur was employed as a clerk by Messrs William Fell and Company Limited of Haugh Lane. He was active in many sports within the town, and played regularly for Tynedale Rovers Rugby Football Club, for whom he acted as secretary. He was also a member of the Church Lads' Brigade, where he held the rank of Staff Sergeant. In his younger days he was a member of the Abbey Church Choir. His younger brother, Stanley, served with the 2nd Dragoons (Queen's Bays). His family received information of his death from a relative, also serving in the Dardanelles, who stated that:

"Arthur was killed on the morning of the 6th May"

He went on to say, in contrast to the favourable comments made by Jack Churchill, mentioned above:

"the Turks were very cruel to our wounded, but this was not the case with Arthur, who was killed outright".

Arthur is commemorated on the Helles Memorial to the missing.

The Third Battle of Krithia, 4 – 6 June

In preparation for the third attempt at the village of Krithia and Achi Baba (a prominent hill which gave the Turks a panoramic view of the Allied landings), a number of limited night advances were made during late May which moved the Front forwards by half a mile with fewer than fifty casualties; by contrast, the three quarters of a mile gained during the *Second Battle of Krithia* had cost the lives of some six thousand men.

The attack began on 4 June – a sunny, breezy day – using troops from the 29th Division on the left, the 49th Division in the centre and the Royal Naval Division to the right with French Troops on the extreme right of the attack. The attack was preceded by an ineffective bombardment. Some progress was made in the centre by the troops of the 42nd Division, but those on the flanks, particularly the French, made very little progress. Instead of exploiting the gains in the centre, the British and French commands committed their reserves to the flanks.

The Royal Naval Division committed men from the Howe, Hood, Anson and Collingwood Battalions for the initial attack. By the afternoon Hawke Battalion, which had been in reserve, was ordered to go towards the Front, near Backhouse Post. Throughout the night wounded men streamed from the field of battle. Early in the morning of 5 June, Hawke Battalion went up to the line to relieve the remnants of the four battalions already committed. A company of Drakes was dispatched immediately to maintain a junction between the Naval Division and the 42nd Division who were clinging on to their gains on the immediate left. Hawke Battalion stayed in the line until the night of the 7/8 June. [4, 5]

Stoker 1st Class William Wilson, aged 23 years
Hawke Battalion, Royal Naval Division
Died 6 June 1915

William Wilson joined the Royal Naval Volunteer Reserve soon after the outbreak of war and after initial training at Crystal Palace was sent out to the Dardanelles. The only son of Mr and Mrs Thomas Wilson of Sele Terrace, he was a painter by trade. As a youth he was a member of the Church Boys Brigade and served as a Sunday School teacher at the Abbey. An account of William in the Parish Magazine described him thus:

> *"He was the type who gives encouragement to clergymen, for he was a good man from head to toe".*

William is commemorated on the Helles Memorial to the missing.

The 1/5th Battalion Manchester Regiment was a territorial battalion. It arrived in Gallipoli in early May at W Beach and was involved in the *Third Battle of Krithia* in early June, where the first objective was taken with little opposition. However, the second objective was a lot tougher to achieve and could not be held because of enfilade fire. By 6 June the battalion was withdrawn to Army Corps Reserve and then to the Greek island of Imbros for rest and consolidation. The 1/5th arrived back at Helles on 21 June and on 29 June were sent to the Krithia Nullah sector to relieve the 1/6th Manchester regiment.[6]

Lieutenant Frank Taylor Iveson, aged 30 years
16t[h] Battalion, Durham Light Infantry
Attached to the 1/5th Manchester Regiment
Died 30 June 1915

Frank was the youngest son of Mr and Mrs William Iveson of Tynedale House, Hexham. Mrs Iveson did not live to know about the death of her son, having died in March 1915. Before the war Frank was a chartered accountant in partnership with his brother. Interested in all kinds of sport he was a noted and successful tennis player and for several years filled the post of secretary to the Tynedale Athletic Association's lawn tennis tournament. He also played hockey for Tynedale.

Along with his brother, Harry, he joined the Officers Training Corps at Newcastle shortly after the onset of hostilities and soon afterwards enlisted in the University and Public Schools Battalion. In October 1914 he was gazetted to a commission in the Durham Light Infantry. He was subsequently attached to the 1/5th Manchester Regiment and left England for the Dardanelles on 16 May. Letters home state that he arrived in Turkey some time after 21 June, meeting his death after only a few days at the Front.

Frank is buried in Redoubt Cemetery, Helles, where the author took this photograph.

Suvla Bay

By August, the Allied leadership, still certain of the importance of gaining control of the Dardanelles, hatched a plan for breaking out of Anzac Beach-Head and capturing the heights of Sari Bair Ridge. At this stage a force of 100,000 men was available, but it was necessary to find a suitable place to land them on the peninsula because conditions in Anzac Cove were very cramped. The coastline at Suvla was selected. Its main feature was a large bay and the Suvla Plain, a flat area lending itself to the deployment of troops. New flat-bottomed landing craft were to be used. The landing was to be made by troops of 10th 11th and 53rd Divisions under the leadership of Sir Frederick Stopford, an elderly, conservative general with no previous battle experience.

On 3 July, 8th (Service) Battalion Northumberland Fusiliers left England as part of 34th Brigade 11th Division aboard the Aquitania with 26 officers and 839 other ranks. The War Diary reports that on 4 August a German submarine attacked the Aquitania; fortunately, its torpedo missed its target.

On 6 August at 10pm the 11th Division began landing on 'A' Beach in Suvla Bay and on B and C beaches to the south. To the south the landings were a success, with the capture of Lala Baba. However, the Northumberland Fusiliers met with calamity: the landing vessels grounded too soon and when the men jumped out of the vessels they found themselves up to their necks in water. To make matters worse, they came under fire from Hill 10 and began to suffer casualties.

On the day after the landing the defenders of Hill 10 were successfully driven out. However, Allied troops were not meeting objectives because of the lack of coherent leadership. Astonishingly, it was not until 8 August that a start was made on making inroads into the interior; by this time Turkish reinforcements had arrived from Bulair and were entrenched on Tekke Tepe, a strategic objective for the

British. The British advanced but they were driven back
immediately.   On 10 August the 53rd Brigade tried again
without success, and on 12 August men of the 54th Brigade
were unable to leave their starting position. Within four days
the Suvla Bay adventure was over.

The following is a transcript of the War Diary of the 8th
Battalion Northumberland Fusiliers covering the days of the
Suvla Bay landings and the deaths of Privates Henderson,
Kirsopp and Pigg.[7]

5 August.   In bivouac, 6 officers and 214 other ranks
                     inoculated for cholera (1st injection)

6 August.   Battalion embarked on two destroyers at
                     4pm and left for Suvla Bay, Gallipoli
                     peninsula at 7.30pm, arriving about 11pm.
                     Enemy opened shrapnel and rifle fire,
                     disembarked at 3.30am under fire. Adjutant
                     wounded. Battalion took part in attack on
                     Turkish trenches, which was successful.

7 August.   Continuous   fighting   until   7am.
                     Commanding Officer and three other
                     officers wounded.   Remained on beach.
                     Major Williams took over command.

8 August.   Battalion in divisional reserve.

9 August.   Battalion ordered to support attack, took
                     over firing line, 3 officers killed, 1 missing, 4
                     wounded.

10 August.   Battalion remained in firing line and
                     consolidated position.

11 August.   Still in same position relieved in evening
                     and returned to Lala Baba Hill for a rest.

12 August. Spent day having a rest in trenches and moved up to fire trenches in evening – this time in centre of line – spent rest of night carrying out further entrenchments.

13 - 14 August. Still in fire trenches – certain amount of sniping – one man killed and several wounded

15 August. Relieved in evening and returned to reserve trenches – Received mail today.

16 August. In reserve trenches. Shelled now and then. One man killed and two wounded.

17 August. Marched out 8pm and occupied front trenches relieving 5th Dorset Regiment. Heavy rifle fire during the night from the enemy.

18 August. In Front Line trenches all day. Casualties 17/18th 4 other ranks killed, 11 wounded

19 August. Ordered to attack entrenched position about 700 yds in front of our line and 1000 yds south of W. Hill. Moved out 4 am, X and Z companies front line, W and Y companies in support. Advanced almost up to enemy trenches, unable to capture position owing to heavy fire of machine guns and rifles, occupied a gully. There caught in close order at dawn by shrapnel. Had to retire. Commanding Officer (Major E E Williams D S O) and 2 other officers killed, 5 wounded and 3 missing: other ranks 23 killed 141 wounded and 90 missing. Marched back to reserve trenches.

20 August. In reserve trenches

Private William Anthony Henderson, aged 30 years
8ᵗʰ Battalion Northumberland Fusiliers
Died 7 August 1915

William was born in Crawcrook, Co Durham and was the son of Mrs Margaret Henderson of Wallsend. He was married to Jane Isabella Henderson and was the father of five children. They lived in Back Row, Hexham. Before enlisting he was employed to work on the roads by Northumberland County Council.

William is commemorated on the Helles Memorial to servicemen who have no known grave.

Private William Kirsopp, aged 34 years
8ᵗʰ Battalion Northumberland Fusiliers
Died 8 August 1915

William was born in Hexham. He was reported missing on 8 August, and little is known of him other than that he was the father of one child, and that it was his sister who, a year later, was told officially of his death.

William is commemorated on the Helles Memorial, where this photograph was taken by the author. Note that his name is spelled in the same way as it is on the Commonwealth War Grave Commission database. For this book the name used is that which appears on the Hexham War Memorial in the Abbey Grounds.

Stoker 1st Class William Wilkinson, aged 23 years
Drake Battalion, Royal Naval Division
Died 16 August 1915

William was the son of Mr Wilkinson who worked as an engine driver at Hexham for the North-Eastern Railways. Before living in Hexham the family lived in Gateshead. On leaving school William was employed as a cartman with Gateshead Co-operative Society; following this he worked for two years for Mr Peart of Gateshead as a farm labourer. After this he joined the Navy, signing up for twelve years. After six years he left as a reservist and returned to Hexham where he was employed as a postman for Humshaugh. At the start of war he was mobilized and joined Drake Battalion and was involved in the ill-fated defence of Antwerp in 1914, for which he was awarded the 1914 Star.

Records show that William died of typhoid fever and is buried on the Greek island of Lemnos in East Mudros Military Cemetery.

The difficult terrain and the closeness of the trenches did not allow for the burial of the dead; flies and other vermin flourished in the heat, resulting in wide scale epidemic sickness, chiefly dysentery, diarrhoea and enteric (typhoid) fever.

By August 1915, 80% of the men at Anzac Cove and Helles were suffering from dysentery.[3]

Private Thomas Pigg, aged 35 years
8th Battalion Northumberland Fusiliers
Died 20 August 1915

Thomas was born in Hexham and was the eldest son of George Pigg. He was well known in the area, working as a roadman for Northumberland County Council. He was unmarried. Thomas enlisted in Newcastle in January 1915 and after some months in training was sent out to the Dardanelles. In the official correspondence from the War Office to his brother Cecil Pigg, it was reported that Thomas had died of his wounds.

Thomas is commemorated on the Helles Memorial, which stands at the tip of the Gallipoli Peninsula. This memorial serves as a record for the whole of the Gallipoli campaign and is a place of commemoration for many men who have no known graves.

In August it was decided that the beachheads of Suvla Bay and Anzac Cove, about three miles apart should be connected. The plan required that a number of hilltops to the east and north of Suvla Bay be attacked and the Turkish positions called W Hills be captured. Further south, Scimitar Hill would also be attacked. This series of coordinated attacks was scheduled for 15 August 1915.

Australian and New Zealand forces attacked Hill 60 on 21 August from Anzac Cove, although a force of only 3000 men could be mustered. The attack brought heavy casualties from Turkish machine gun fire and as a result it achieved no notable gains. On 27 August the attack was renewed and after 36 hours of constant fighting the trenches around the hill were captured. However, owing to the lack of proper reconnaissance, Turks from a hitherto unknown second line of trenches were able to open fire on the depleted Anzacs.

Later in the day the attack was called off; there were over 2,500 Allied casualties.

The 29th Division, which had been dispatched from Helles, conducted the attack on Scimitar Hill; the attack initially succeeded in its aims but was ultimately repelled. Reserves sent to help were also badly mauled.

The attack on W Hills also failed when the attacking forces lost their bearings.

Private Joseph William Robinson, aged 25 years
D Company 19th Battalion Australian Infantry
Died 30 August 1915

Joseph Robinson was the youngest son of Mr and Mrs George Robinson of Quatre Bras, Hexham. After leaving school he served his apprenticeship as a baker with Messrs T Lishman and Sons of Battle Hill and afterwards worked in partnership with his brother George running a grocery, bakery and confectionary business on Gilesgate Bank. George was a keen rower and was a member of the Hexham Amateur Rowing Club; he won the club's Confined and Open Handicap in 1912. Indeed, the Rowing Club has named its Rowing Club Championship after him. He was also a keen footballer, playing a number of times for Hexham Wesleyan Club. In 1913 both brothers decided to emigrate to Australia, working as bakers. His brother, who also joined the forces, survived the war, returning to Australia. [8]

In a letter to his parents, Sergeant- Major Marshall wrote:

"Joseph has been killed in action on Hill 60 and was buried there by his comrades."

Today Joseph is commemorated on the Lone Pine Memorial, which serves as a memorial to over 4900 Anzac servicemen who have no known grave.

A tribute to Private Joseph William Robinson from the Botany Citizens Association

Private Walter Turnbull, aged 35 years
D Company, 24th Battalion Australian Infantry
Died 21 September 1915

Walter Turnbull was the eldest son of Mr and Mrs E Turnbull of Orchard Place, Hexham. He was educated at the North Eastern School, Barnard Castle, and emigrated to Australia in 1912. When war broke out he was living in Bayswater, Victoria, and was employed on a fruit farm. Before this, when living in Hexham, Walter had been a member of the Territorial Army.[8]

Walter joined the Forces in March 1915 and left Melbourne in May aboard HMAT Euripides. After an initial stopover in Egypt, the Australian Force arrived on the Gallipoli Peninsula; a little over three weeks later, Walter was wounded near Lone Pine.

His parents received a letter from the Reverend A J Nisbet Wallace, chaplain to the forces in the Dardanelles. The letter dated 21 September was from HM Hospital Ship Guildford Castle. It stated that:

"Walter was brought aboard seriously wounded on the 19th and died in the afternoon of the 21st."

Walter is commemorated on the Lone Pine Memorial, which commemorates men who have no known grave or who were 'buried' in Gallipoli waters.

Because of the limited space and opportunity for burial on land, many Allied soldiers were 'buried at sea' during the Gallipoli campaign. There are a number of small cemeteries on the peninsula, but these are nowhere near as big as those found on the Western Front.

After the dismal failure of the Allied attacks at Scimitar Hill and Hill 60 in August (with the aim of linking Anzac cove with Suvla Bay) the credibility of Sir Ian Hamilton as Commander in Chief for the Mediterranean Forces was in tatters. In early September he was informed of a proposal to evacuate the peninsula; his angry response was to estimate that evacuation would result in casualties of more than fifty percent. Sir Charles Munro, who replaced Hamilton, toured the beachheads of Helles, Anzac Cove and Suvla Bay as his first task; he recommended an immediate evacuation of the Allied forces. This was not to Kitchener's liking, who travelled to the region to assess the situation – he quickly altered his opinion.

The evacuation was initially set for 7 December but a heavy blizzard set in, making the operation hazardous. Between 10

– 20 December the evacuation of 105,000 men and 300 guns took place from Anzac Cove and Suvla Bay beachheads. Evacuation of men from the Helles site began in late December, when over 35,000 men were shipped from the beaches. During this period only three casualties were reported; many devious tricks were used to deceive the Turks into believing that the movement of Allied forces was not one of withdrawal.

In all, 480,000 Allied troops (from Britain, the Empire and France) played their part in the Gallipoli Campaign. Casualties for the British and the Empire were 115,000 killed, missing or wounded and 90,000 evacuated sick.

> *"Perhaps as the years roll by we will be remembered as the expedition that was betrayed by jealousy, spite, indecision and treachery. The Turks did not beat us – we were beaten by our own high command". Soldiers always say that, [but] this time it was probably true.* [8]

In 1934, Kemal Ataturk, who had fought on the peninsula and who was now president of the new Turkey spoke the following words, described by Robert Fisk the journalist as 'the most compassionate ever uttered by a Muslim leader in modern times'. They are inscribed on a marble plaque at Anzac Cove:

> *Those heroes that shed their blood and lost their lives ...*
> *you are now lying in the soil of a friendly country.*
> *Therefore rest in peace.*
> *There is no difference between the Johnnies and the*
> *Mehmets to us,*
> *where they lie, side by side here in this country of ours.*
> *You, the mothers, who sent their sons from far away*
> *countries, wipe away your tears.*
> *Your sons are now lying in our bosom and are in peace.*
> *After having lost their lives on this land they have become*
> *our sons as well.*

This is from a man who, when sending his troops to do battle, told them that he did not expect them to win, he expected them to die.

References

1. *The Old Front Line.*
    http://battlefields1418.50megs.com

2. Clutterbuck, Col L. A. *Bond of Sacrifice Volume 2*
    Originally printed 1915, Reprinted Naval and Military Press 2002.

3. Carlyon L. A. *Gallipoli*
    Pub: Bantam Books 2003.

4. Chambers S. *Gully Ravine*
    Pub: Pen & Sword Books 2003.

5. Jerold, D. *Hawke Battalion, Some Personal Records of Four Years, 1914-1918*
    Pub: Naval and Military Press, 2002.

6. Westlake, R. *British Regiments at Gallipoli*
    Pub: Leo Cooper 1996.

7. WO 95/4299. *War Diary, 8th Battalion, Northumberland Fusiliers.*

8. *Australian War Memorial.*
    www.awm.gov.au

CHAPTER SIX

THE BATTLE OF LOOS AND
THE WESTERN FRONT

They took my boy to Loos …
The boy we carved out of heaven's breath,
A boy with the powder of love
Now just a breath of lead, smell of steel.

Edna J Lacey, *Loos*

Overview

Between 25 September and 19 October 1915, the British army fought an offensive action known as the *Battle of Loos*. Compared to the earlier, small-scale offensives of 1915, (*Battle of Neuve-Chapelle* in March, *Battle of Aubers* 9 – 10 May and the *Battle of Festubert* 15 – 25 May), this attack used six divisions and was at the time referred to as the 'Big Push'.

The battle plan was ill-conceived, taking place as it did before plentiful supplies of ammunition and artillery had been stockpiled in France. Furthermore, the battleground was not chosen by the British army. The opening of the battle is noteworthy as it marks the first use of poison gas by the British army, which ironically caused a significant number of British deaths.

Even though initial casualties were considerable, the British achieved success on the first day by breaking deep into German positions near Loos and Hulluch. However, as reserve soldiers were held a long way from the Front, this success couldn't be exploited. In the following days the battle raged with only minor gains achieved for enormous loss of life.

The 95th Field Company Royal Engineers was attached to the 7th Division. The Division took part in the initial assault on 25 September, north of the Vermelles-Hulluch road, facing the Quarries and a series of strong points. Unfortunately, they suffered badly from the British gas cloud which was not carried on towards the enemy by the gentle breeze as had been intended; many men were wounded or killed by German machine gun and artillery fire. Nevertheless, the Division seized the Quarries and only just failed to take the enemy's third defensive line. During this operation their Divisional Commander, Major-General T Capper died of wounds received in action.[1, 2]

Sapper Ernest Batey, aged 26
95th Field Company, Royal Engineers
Died 27 September 1915

Ernest was the eldest son of Mr and Mrs Thomas Batey of Leases Crescent, Hexham. Before the war he spent some time in America, returning in December 1914 to join the Royal Engineers.   He arrived in France in August – merely six weeks or so before his death – so it is probable that Ernest died in his first action.

Ernest is commemorated on the Loos Memorial for men who have no known grave.

His name is spelled wrongly (E Baty R.E.) on the memorial in the Abbey Gardens. His name also appears on the memorial in St Aidan's United Reformed Church on Battle Hill, but in this instance as Batey.

On the afternoon of 27 September the Guards Division was ordered to attack Hill 70. However, two hours before the attack its objectives were scaled down because of problems along the whole Front. The 2nd Irish Guards, with the 1st Scots Guards on its right, led the attack. This attack necessitated crossing 1000 yards of ground before reaching the German trenches. The attack began at 4.00pm following a ninety-minute bombardment by the British. At this stage the 1st Scots Guards suffered few casualties. However, as they approached their objective, Puits No 14 (winding gear for a coal mine), they came under heavy fire; hundreds of men were mown down in the murderous crossfire.[2, 3] Lieutenant John Kipling of the Irish Guards, son of Rudyard Kipling, was one of those killed here. It is reported that a small party led by Captain J H Cuthbert reached the Puits. For a time they fought on, their strength increased by a platoon of Grenadier Guards, but without further support Cuthbert's men had to fall back. Initial reports from the Front stated that Cuthbert had been wounded and was missing in action.

The Hexham Courant reported this extract from the Daily Mail, written by Mr G Valentine Williams, a special correspondent in France:

The Guards were ordered to attack at 4pm on the Monday, September 27th. The Irish guards advanced down the valley, calm and cool and in good order, and gained the lower edge of the wood about the chalk pit without many casualties. It was the baptism of fire of this battalion. Behind them came the Coldstreamers. The Irish men established themselves in the wood and with their machine guns and rifles opened a heavy covering fire against Pit 14a, to check the enemy and to enable the Scots Guards to reach Pit14a, which was their objective.

With their scrap of red Stewart tartan on their caps as their distinguishing badge, the Scots Guards advanced. A perfect inferno of fire was loosed from machine-guns which could not be seen, but which rapped out their nerve racking note high above the thunder of the guns. The Scots guards suffered heavily, their Colonel was wounded and other officers dropped, but "the Kiddies" as they call them in the army kept on. Pit 14a was ours to all intents and purposes. Captain Cuthbert, D.S.O. of the Scots Guards, who displayed splendid gallantry went boldly in among the houses round about the pithead, leading a party of his men in the desperate hand-to-hand struggle with bomb and bayonet against the Germans still residing there.

Brave men all, Scots Guards and Grenadiers hung on in the position they had won with their dead and dying comrades all around them. Men were falling fast. Rain came on as the shades of night crept over. Cuthbert and Ritchie held on to Pit 14a until practically no-one was left, waiting for the support which is was impossible to send them owing to the deadly German machine-gun fire in enfilade. It must have been with bitterness in their hearts that they recognized that the position was untenable.

In this desperate and bloody fighting in which the Guards Division made its heroic debut fitly carrying on the high traditions already established by the Guards in this war, many gallant officers fell. Captain Cuthbert, D.S.O., who so distinguished himself in the attack on Pit 14a, is missing. He was last seen to enter a house with some men. It is feared that he was killed by a shell.

Most of the other special correspondents who deal in detail with the special work of the Guards Brigade speak of the splendid leadership and bravery of Captain Cuthbert.

Captain James Harold Cuthbert DSO, aged 39 years
1st Battalion Scots Guards
Died 27 September 1915

James Cuthbert of Beaufront Castle was born on 21 July 1876 in South Africa. He was educated at Eton and Sandhurst. Joining the

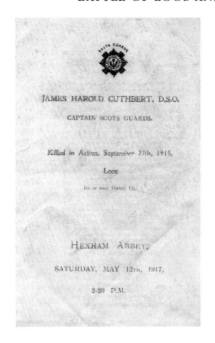

Scots Guards in August 1896, he served as a Lieutenant in South Africa 1899-1902. During the Boer War he was involved in the advance on Kimberley, and was present at the actions of Belmont, Enalin, Modder River and Magersfontein. He held the Queen's and King's medals with eight bars. His DSO was awarded in recognition for services during operations in South Africa in 1901, after being mentioned in dispatches. James won the Army shooting championship in 1902 and served as High Sheriff of Northumberland in 1904. He also wrote a definitive history of the 1st Battalion Scots Guards in South Africa, 1899-1902. He married Anne Dorothy Frederica Byng, the third daughter of the Earl of Strafford in September 1903, who died in January 1907. James was married again in October 1909, to Kathleen Alice Straker of Stagshaw, in Hexham Abbey. He was recalled to the Colours from the reserve officers' list in 1914 and went to France in April 1915. He left a wife, three sons and a daughter. [4]

At the end of a Memorial Service in Hexham Abbey held by Rector Canon Savage the organist played 'O rest in the Lord'. During the afternoon a muffled peal was rung on the Abbey bells.

James is commemorated on the Loos Memorial for men who have no known grave. In Hexham, his death is recorded on the Rolls of Honour in the Abbey and at the War Memorial Hospital and at Hexham Golf Club.

On hearing about this book, James' grandson wrote to the author about his grandfather. It is his understanding that his grandfather was last seen carrying the dead or dying John Kipling (Lieutenant 2nd Battalion Irish Guards, son of Rudyard Kipling), but then he disappeared amidst the German shelling. Rudyard Kipling used to visit Beaufront Castle after the war to talk to James's wife about her husband and to honour his courageous act of comradeship towards his much loved son. A grave in St Mary's ADS Cemetery, Haisnes, was ascribed to young Kipling (aged 18) although no trace of Cuthbert's body could be found.

The 2nd Battalion Gordon Highlanders (as part of the 20th Brigade, 7th Division) saw action under Major-General Capper at the Battle of Loos. The Highlanders were in the initial phase on 25 September when the 20th Brigade attacked, advancing along the Hulluch Road. When chlorine gas was released they found that their protective helmets were worthless. This is described in a passage from the War Diary of the 2nd Battalion Gordon Highlanders:[5]

> *"The old smoke helmet is of little value, for if saved from the gas, one is compelled to breathe expired air."*

Many men struggled to breathe, succumbing tragically to the effects of British poisonous gas after ripping off their hoods. The rest pressed on with the attack, spurred on by the distinctive sound of Piper Munro's pipes. The Gordons were cut down in large numbers by both machine gun and artillery fire. Even having lost most of their officers the Gordons reached most of their objectives on that first day. At about

8.30am, a party of a hundred Gordons managed to reach Estaminet Corner and began digging in. Later that night the 20th Brigade came under fire. The Gordons were attacked in the dark from their flanks and from the rear and were forced to retreat. During the day's action James Halliday (below) was gassed and wounded, dying in a military hospital two days later.

Lance Corporal James Halliday, aged 30 years
2nd Battalion Gordon Highlanders
Died 27 September 1915

James was the son of Mr J Halliday of Market Street. Before enlisting at the outbreak of war, James was employed as a baker in Hexham. He was also a member of the Church Lads Brigade and attended the Coronation Review of the Church Lads in London, 1902.

James enlisted in Aberdeen and was sent to the Front in April of that year. The Courant reported in May that James had been wounded in the knee, probably during the Battle of Festubert (15 – 25 May). However, within weeks he was back with his battalion. During the fighting around Loos he was once again wounded and evacuated to an army hospital where he later died of his wounds.

James is buried in Boulogne Eastern Cemetery. Boulogne was the site of a number of Allied hospitals.

Many deaths were not the result of full scale attacks on or by the Germans, but were caused by a constant attrition from snipers and artillery fire. The lives of over 20,000 officers and men were lost at the Battle of Loos.

Along The Western Front

On 31 July all three brigades of the 50th Division were transferred to the Armentières Sector. Armentières is a town famed for its weaving, spinning and brewing industries and is situated on the River Lys, 13 miles southeast of Ypres. On the night of 3 August the 149th Brigade (1/4th Northumberland Fusiliers) went to the Front Line.

The History of the 50th Division reports that in this sector:[6]

> *"The enemy was quiescent and was inclined to adopt an attitude of 'live and let live'. But that was not war, and it was necessary to remind him very frequently of this fact."*

So, it was arranged that a field gun should be brought up to destroy the opposing German trench system on the following day. At 8pm the gun fired lyddite and shrapnel whilst the infantry opened up with rifle and machine gun fire. In retaliation the Germans replied with field and maxim gun, grenades and sniper fire.

Private Francis Riley, aged 36 years
'A' Company 1/4th Northumberland Fusiliers
Died 4 August 1915

Francis 'Frank' Riley was the son of James and Esther Riley and was the husband of Ethel Riley of Bells Court, Hexham. He was the father of four children, the eldest being only eleven when his father died. He had been a Territorial and he rejoined at the outset of hostilities. He was a bricklayer by

trade. His brother Matt, of the Duke of Wellington Regiment, was the first wounded soldier to arrive home from the Front. The war office notified Mrs Riley that her husband had been killed in action.

Company Sergeant-Major Smith wrote:

> *"Frank was seriously wounded in the head at about 8.30 am on the 4th and died about half an hour later."*

Captain Arkwright wrote to Mrs. Riley:

> *"He gave his life for his country, and I am very sorry indeed to have lost him."*

Frank is buried in Ration Farm Military Cemetery La Chapelle D'Armentières.

The 1/6th Durham Light Infantry were part of 151st Brigade (50th Division) and from the middle of July 1915 they were stationed in the Armentières sector. At this stage of the war, infantry battalions served between twelve and sixteen days in the Front Line at a time. The History of the 50th Division records an incident from this period:

> *On 7th November Lance-Corporal Carr was out in front of the wire. Fog covered the ground, but lifted suddenly and he was shot. At once Lieutenant Palmer and Private Bell ran out and brought the wounded man in.*

Was this brave man the Edward Bell described below? It is certainly possible, but one cannot know for certain.

The tour of this sector for the 50th Division finished on 12 November and they were sent to Merris La Crèche for training. By late December they had gone back in the Line near Ypres.[6]

Private Edward Shotton Bell, aged 27
1/6th Battalion Durham Light Infantry
Died 5 December 1915

Edward was born in Blackhill, County Durham and was a married man living at Tyne Green, Hexham, when war broke out. Before this he worked at Acomb Colliery. It is reported that he died of wounds received in action.

Edward is buried at Bailleul Communal Cemetery.

The 11th Battalion Durham Light Infantry, part of the 20th Division, took their turn in the Front Line trenches near Laventie, southeast of Estaires, and continued their pioneer work when out of the Line.

Extracts from the battalion diary report that 'casualties were light during this turn of duty, but the weather was wet and the trenches, into which all the ditches seemed to drain, were in an awful state.' [7, 8]

Private William Henry Hill, aged 31 years
11th (Service) Battalion Durham Light Infantry
Died 16 November 1915

William was born in Hexham in 1884 and was the middle son of Thomas and Elizabeth Hill of Orchard Terrace, Hexham. He was the husband of Mrs F C Hill of Mansfield Street, Gateshead and the father of five children. He was employed in the coalmines at Gateshead. A few years previously he had won the Gold Medal and Race Cup for winning a

walking race from Low Fell to Durham, which he accomplished in three hours and fifty-six minutes. William enlisted only a few days after hostilities began.

Mr and Mrs Hill had another son, Thomas, who was with the local battalion of the Northumberland Fusiliers and was wounded at Ypres in April 1915. Their daughter's husband, Private S Newman, was also at the Front, where he was awarded the Military Medal.

It is reported that William died of his wounds and is buried in Merville Community Cemetery. Until April 1918, the town of Merville was in Allied hands and was the site of a number of casualty clearing stations.

References

1. Rawson, A. *Loos- Hollenzollern.*
    Pub: Pen and Sword Books 2003.

2. Rawson, A. *Loos- Hill 70.*
    Pub: Pen and Sword Books 2002.

3. WO 95/1219 War Diary, *1ˢᵗ Battalion Scots Guards.*

4. Greagh, Sir O' Moore. *Distinguished Service Order, 6th September 1886 to the 31st December 1915.*
    Naval & Military Press republished 2001.

5. WO 95/1656 War Diary, *2ⁿᵈ Battalion Gordon Highlanders.*

6. Wyrell, E. *The Fiftieth Division, 1914-1919.*
    Pub: 1939, reprinted Naval and Military Press 2002.

7. WO 95/2108 War Diary, *11ᵗʰ Battalion Durham Light Infantry (Pioneers)*.

8. Miles, Captain Wilfred. *The Durham forces in the Field 1914-1918*
    Pub: 1920 reprinted Naval and Military Press, 2004.

CHAPTER SEVEN

1916: THE EARLY MONTHS

… and nations great in reputation of the arts
that bind the world with hopes of Heaven
sink to the state of brute barbarians …

Robert Palmer, *How Long, O Lord*
Killed in action, 1916

Overview

In February 1916, the third year of the war, the Germans attacked the French at Verdun with the aim of bleeding them dry – the battle raged on for over ten months. In the end, Verdun and the gateway to Paris remained defended, but the campaign had caused great losses on both sides: French fatalities were roughly 275,000 and German 220,000. Both sides gained no tactical or strategic advantage for their efforts. The war in Italy against Austria-Hungary continued, with Italy finally declaring war on Germany in August. During the summer, the Russians inflicted significant defeats on both the Turkish and the Austro-Hungarian armies.

Elsewhere, British forces advanced against the Turks in Mesopotamia in their quest to occupy Baghdad, and in the Arab regions T E Lawrence (of Arabia) fomented rebellion against the Turks. At home, the Easter Rising against British rule in Ireland added to the Government's difficulties. As W B Yeats observed in his poem *Easter 1916*, it was 'all changed, changed utterly'.

At sea, the Navy fought history's biggest sea battle, *Jutland*, which resulted in no clear victor although the British could justify their claim of a strategic victory. However, of greater significance, the German submarine fleet was inflicting significant losses on all of the world's merchant fleets, leading to America's declaration of war on Germany.

On 1 July the British began a titanic struggle along the Somme Front in an attempt to break through the German defences. This monumental effort over five months resulted in heavy losses on both sides, with the British suffering over 23,000 deaths on the first day.

At home, David Lloyd George replaced Asquith as Prime Minister.

The gigantic struggles of 1916 cost the participating countries shocking numbers of dead and wounded.

1916: The Early Months

Following the Battle of Hooge (9 – 10 August 1915), the 2nd Battalion Durham Light Infantry (DLI) remained in the Ypres Salient until July 1916. They held to a routine of spending several days at the Front, followed by days in support, in reserve or in rest billets.

During the night of 14 January the DLI relieved a battalion of the West Yorkshire Regiment in the Front Line near Potijze Wood and on 15 January were shelled heavily by the Germans. This resulted in a powerful retaliatory British bombardment. On 19 January the Germans shelled the trenches in the Potijze-St Jean area, resulting in considerable damage but with only a small number of casualties.[1] That night, the Durham Battalion was relieved by other forces. Only five soldiers were killed during this tour of duty.

Private John Keen Bell, aged 29
2nd Battalion, Durham Light Infantry
Died 19 January 1916

John was born at Chollerton, Northumberland, and was the husband of Mrs A Watson (formerly Bell). They lived at Ridley Terrace, Tyne Green. He was the father of one child. Before mobilisation with the Northumberland Fusiliers he worked at Tynedale Colliery, Acomb. He went with the local Battalion to France in April 1915. Later he was transferred to the Durham Light Infantry.

John is buried in Potijze Burial Ground Cemetery, Ypres.

During the early months of 1916 the 1/4th Northumberland Fusiliers (149th Brigade, 50th Division) were stationed in the southern sector of the Ypres salient, and in their turn manned Front Line trenches near Hill 60, Sanctuary Wood, and the Village of Wyschaete.

As mentioned above in Chapter 4, Hill 60, an important military position southwest of Ypres, was merely a low ridge formed from the spoils when a cutting for the Ypres to Comines railway was made. In the flat landscape of this battlefield, troops that commanded its summit had the advantage of uninterrupted views of this sector of the battlefield, allowing them to direct accurate artillery fire on enemy movements.

The Germans captured Hill 60 in December 1914, but it was wrested back with great courage and loss of life in the middle of April 1915 by the British. It was lost again in early May following a gas attack. After this it would remain in German hands until the summer of 1917.

On 31 January the 1/4th relieved their colleagues, the 1/6th Northumberland Fusiliers, in the Front Line facing Hill 60. The Battalion Diary[2] for 2 February records that the Germans were very active that day with rifle grenades; that evening Private William Watt was killed during one of many attacks made by the enemy.

Private William Watt, aged 46
1/4th Battalion Northumberland Fusiliers
Died 2 February 1916

William was born in Hexham and was the son of William and Catherine Watt. He was unmarried and lived with his sisters in Kingsgate Terrace, Hexham. Some time before enlisting in January 1915 he had lived in Warden and had worked at the South Tyne Paper Mill. Latterly he had worked on the Border Counties Branch of the North British Railways. In his younger days he was a local sprinter of some repute. William went out to France in September 1915.

William is buried in Railway Dugouts Burial Ground, Ypres.

His headstone carries the following inscription:

ON WHOSE SOUL
SWEET JESUS HAVE MERCY
R.I.P.

On 4 February, the Front Line came under intense artillery bombardment and it is recorded that during a period of ninety minutes 130 shells cascaded down on the battalion, although amazingly it suffered no casualties. However, on 5 February they were not as lucky – a number of men were wounded, two of whom died shortly afterwards: Private Forster and Lieutenant Sharp. The battalion was relieved on the evening of 6 February and spent the next six days resting and on work duties. On 12 February they were back on the Front Line at Sanctuary Wood, southeast of Ypres.[2]

Private Adolphus Forster aged 22
'A' Company, 1/4th Battalion Northumberland Fusiliers
Died 5 February 1916

Adolphus was the husband of Emily Forster of Excelsior Buildings, Hexham, and he left one child. Before the war he was an engineer working with his brother Mr T W Forster in his cycle business in Hencotes. A keen football player, he had played for both Northern Star (Hexham) and Hexham Argyle in the West Tyne League. He was playing for Hexham Argyle when they won the Second Division of the West Tyne League.

A letter sent to his brother explained that both 'Dolf' and Second Lieutenant C G Sharp were killed by a shell and that Robson Smith of Corbridge had been wounded. The writer goes on to say that he had been one of the burial party.

Aldophus is buried in Railway Dugouts Burial Ground, Ypres.

His headstone is inscribed with the words:

UNTIL THE DAY BREAKS

The 23rd Battalion, 3rd Tyneside Scottish Northumberland Fusiliers was formed in Newcastle on 5 November 1914. First of all the men trained at Alnwick and then they moved on to Salisbury Plain in August 1915. They embarked for France on 23 January and from 5 February were attached to two battalions already at the Front near Armentières. Companies 'A' and 'B' were attached to the 9th Battalion Yorkshire Light Infantry and companies 'C' and 'D' were with the 11th Sherwood Foresters. The idea was to integrate the new men with those who had experience of the rigours of trench warfare. They were to be trained by the old hands, including how to perform sentry duty. During their time at the Front they were subjected to enemy shelling. The Battalion Diary states that Privates Young and Thompson were wounded on 6 February, with Young dying the next day. Furthermore, a man from the 11th Sherwood Foresters accidentally killed a Tyneside soldier (Private John Watts Harrison).[3, 4] By 8 February the period of training and familiarisation was complete and the Battalion left for Estaires.

Private Frank Young, aged 29
23rd (Service) Battalion (Tyneside Scottish)
Northumberland Fusiliers
Died 7 February 1916

Frank was born in Hexham and was the eldest son of William and Elizabeth Young, of Skinners Arms Cottage, Hexham. He had enlisted in November 1914, but did not go to the Front until early January 1916. It appears that he had already served with the Coldstream Guards before the outbreak of war. It is reported that Frank was shot in the head by a sniper whilst on sentry duty. This took place at a part of the Front where the enemy trenches were only 200 yards apart.

96

Frank was the first of many casualties that this Tyneside battalion would suffer during the war. He was buried in Sailly-sur-la-Lys Canadian Cemetery.

On 14 February the Germans attacked the sector of the Bluff defended by the 1/9th Durham Light Infantry (151st Brigade); the German attackers were able to dislodge the defenders from their Front Line trenches. On 20 February the Battalion War Diary,[5] states that the brigade was in reserve and notes the death of Lieutenant R E Atkinson, Brigade Bombing Officer, killed in action:

Lieutenant Rollo Edwards Atkinson, aged 26
1/9th Durham Light Infantry
Died 20 February 1916

Rollo Atkinson was a son of Mr T H Atkinson of Eilan's Gate, Hexham. He was born in 1890 and was educated at Sedbergh School and Emmanuel College Cambridge where he took his BA. At school he was an accomplished runner; in 1910, the year he went up to college, he won the Ten Miles, the Mile and the Half-Mile Cross Country. In 1912 he won the Mile and the Three Miles at the Freshmen's sports. He represented his university against Oxford in 1911, 1912, and 1913. In 1914 he won the Half-Mile against Oxford in 1 minute 56 seconds, defeating an American Rhodes Scholar called N S Taber. This Dark Blue had previously beaten W G

George's World Record for the mile, 4 minutes 12.75 seconds, in a race in America. He was a prolific runner with over thirty cups to his name including a Gold Medal won in Budapest. He was Honorary Secretary for Cambridge University Athletics Club for the 1913-14 season.

Rollo enlisted just after the outbreak of war and was gazetted 2nd Lieutenant to the 9th Battalion Durham Light Infantry in late September 1914, rising to full Lieutenant in the middle of May 1915. He was posted to the Front in April 1915 and was involved in the desperate fighting around Ypres as part of the 50th Northumbrian Division. During the early part of 1916 he was wounded, receiving severe facial injuries. After a period of convalescence he returned to the Front on February 13, 1916 and was killed a week later.

Rollo is buried in Railway Dugouts Burial Ground, Ypres.

On 1 March, the 1/4th Northumberland Fusiliers moved up to Bedford House (southeast of Ypres) whilst an artillery barrage was being directed upon a position called The Bluff, (another artificial mound built from debris from the Ypres to Comines railway). On 2 March the battalion went over the top at 4.30am at the same time as another bombardment, and were successful in regaining a number of trenches and taking some German prisoners.

On 3 March the Fusiliers sent stretcher-bearers to help their fellows near Hill 60 where the British trenches were under an intense artillery bombardment. A number of these courageous men were killed.[2]

Lance Corporal Joshua Benjamin Robson, aged 26 years
1/4ᵗʰ Battalion Northumberland Fusiliers
Died 3 March 1916

Joshua was the second son of Joshua Robson, a grocer of Market Street. At the time of his enlistment shortly after the outbreak of war he was employed by Messrs W M Robb – he had worked in the upholstery department for several years. He was a keen supporter of Association Football and was on the Committee of Hexham Athletic FC. He was also a member of Hexham's Unionist Club who had members fighting in many parts of the world.

Reports state that as he was going up through the trenches as a stretcher-bearer to bring out the wounded, a shell burst, killing Private Robson. He was with a party of eight men when the shell burst near them, slightly wounding four members of the party and severely wounding Joshua, who died within minutes. He left a wife.

Joshua is buried in Railway Dugouts Burial Ground, Ypres.

Between 3 – 8 April, the 1/4ᵗʰ Northumberland Fusiliers were manning trenches near the village of Locre in what was known as the Wyschaete (Wijtshate) Sector to the south of Ypres. The Battalion Diary[2] records that this turn of duty was relatively peaceful, apart from one unfortunate incident on 8 April: a dugout received a direct hit from a heavy artillery shell, killing two men. These were Privates Cathrae and Hedley (of West Woodburn). Four others were wounded. That night the 1/5ᵗʰ Northumberland Fusiliers relieved the 1/4ᵗʰ.

Drummer Thomas William Cathrae, aged 22
1/4th Battalion, Northumberland Fusiliers
Died 8 April 1916

Thomas was born in Hexham, the son of John and Jane Cathrae of Prior Terrace. Before the war he was employed on the permanent staff at Hexham Railway Station. Captain Plummer wrote to Mrs Cathrae explaining that the dugout in which her son and others had been sitting received a direct hit by a shell. When in action, drummers and all other musicians acted as stretcher-bearers.

Captain Plummer wrote:

"...Your son acted as stretcher-bearer to B Company and was ever ready to give a helping hand and in several cases he has done very excellent work..."

Thomas is buried in La Laiterie Military Cemetery, Ypres. The following inscription is to be found on his headstone:

A SILENT THOUGHT
A SECRET TEAR
KEEPS OUR LOVED ONE EVER NEAR
LOVING MOTHER

After some rest time and a spell doing the inevitable work duties, the 1/4th Northumberland Fusiliers went back up to the Front Line in the Wyschaete sector on 14 April. It was generally quiet during the first three days of this duty, but on 19 April they were subjected to heavy shelling, resulting in the death of David Salkeld. The Battalion Diary[2] states that on that night the 1/5th Northumberland Fusiliers relieved them.

Private David Salkeld, aged 24
'A' Company, 1/4th Battalion, Northumberland Fusiliers
Died 19 April 1916

David was born in Hexham and was the son of Mrs Salkeld of Haugh Lane. He was married and his widow Mrs E Salkeld lived at Chareway Cottage, Hexham with their only child. Before enlisting he was employed at Tynedale Colliery.

Captain D T Turner, commander of 'A' Company wrote to his mother in a letter dated 21 April:

> *"I am very sorry to inform you that your son was seriously wounded while out on a working party the night before last and died two hours later in the dressing station. He never regained consciousness after being hit and suffered no pain. He will be greatly missed by all of us. He was a good soldier always doing his work well and cheerfully.....""*

David was buried in La Laiterie Military Cemetery, Ypres. At his interment the mourners sang the hymn *Now the Labourer's Task is Over*. The following words were published in the Hexham Herald, to commemorate Private Salkeld's death:

In Memorium of my husband, Private David Salkeld

Abroad he rests in peace a soldier true and brave,
And there with honour now he sleeps in a noble soldier's grave;
The sorrow in my soul, no human eye can trace,
For many a broken heart lies behind a smiling face.

Ever remembered by his sorrowing wife and daughter,
also his loving mother, brother (in France) and sister.

On 13 June, the 1/4th Battalion Northumberland Fusiliers relieved the 1/5th in trenches near Petite Wood, which was in

101

German hands. Their Front Line positions were subjected to heavy shelling by the Germans using trench mortars.[2] During this duty the 24th Division to their right was subjected to a gas attack, but no casualties were confirmed for the Northumbrians.

On 17 June the battalion was subjected to vicious artillery and trench mortar activity, and during the night the battalion was relieved from Front Line duties.

Second Lieutenant Frank Priestman Lees, aged 26
1/4th Battalion Northumberland Fusiliers
Died 17 June 1916

Frank was the eldest son of Councillor Herbert and Annie Lees of Elvaston Road, Hexham. Frank was born in Workington in Cumbria, coming to Hexham very early in his life when his father took charge of Hexham Gas Works. He was educated at Battle Hill School and subsequently at the Friends' School at Ackworth, where it is reported that he was academically bright. He returned to Hexham to qualify as a gas engineer under his father at Hexham Gas Works, after which he went to work at Preston Gas Works as a chemist, followed by two years at Leeds University. After university he worked at Barnard Castle and Wolverhampton before coming back to Hexham to join his father as his assistant. After this he joined the West's Gas Improvement Company Limited in Manchester. At the outbreak of war his job was to supervise the installation of vertical retorts at Darlington. He immediately joined the 16th Northumberland Fusiliers (1st Commercials) at Newcastle. In April 1915 he was

gazetted Second Lieutenant with the 1/4th Battalion and went out to France in July. He was killed by shrapnel whilst on duty in the trenches near Ypres.

Captain Robb wrote to Frank's father:

> *"Whilst on duty in the trenches this morning Frank was hit by shrapnel and severely wounded on the left side. I was talking to him at the time it happened and no time was wasted in getting him to the dressing station, but the doctor could give us little hope and within two hours he passed away......"*

Frank was buried just behind the trenches at La Laiterie Military Cemetery. A Nonconformist minister read the service with a large number of men and officers in attendance, including Colonel Gibson, Major Robinson, Captains Arkwright, Robb, Plummer and Turner, Lieutenants Pickering (the doctor), Carrick and Cranage, and Second Lieutenants Charley-Wood, Bagnall and Walton.

The following inscription is found at the base of his headstone:

*THAT THOSE THINGS WHICH ARE NOT SHAKEN
MAY REMAIN*

The Battle for Mount Sorrel was fought between 2 – 13 June and took place along the Front between Hill 60 (southeast of Ypres) and Hooge (east of Ypres). The eastern edges of Armagh Wood and Sanctuary Wood lay on a slight rise topped by the promontories of Mount Sorrell and Tor Top (Hill 62). If the Germans could occupy this ridge, then they would have a panoramic view into the Ypres salient, Ypres town and its approaches. At this point three Canadian Divisions held the Front. The attack on the 2 June was made by the XIII

(Wurttemberg) Corps whose objective was to occupy the last observation point in front of Ypres.

From 8am to 12.30pm the Germans bombarded the Front Line and destroyed all of the defences, followed at 1pm by the detonation of mines just short of the Allied Front Line on Mount Sorrel. Apart from localised places the Germans easily overran the defensive line and progressed down the back slope. On 2 June the 10th Battalion Canadian Infantry was holding the line in Armagh Wood, Square Wood and Leicester Square, in the southern sector of the German attack. During the action on 2 – 3 June, the Battalion Diary[6] reports that forty men, including Joseph Bell, were killed, and well over a hundred men were wounded.

Private Joseph Bell, aged 30
10th Battalion Canadian Infantry (Alberta Regiment)
Died 3 June 1916

Joseph was the son of Jonathan and Jane Bell of Cecil Terrace, Hexham. He was born in July 1886 and worked as a cabinet-maker before emigrating to Canada. In Canada he settled in Calgary and was employed as a teamster. His attestation papers show that he was unmarried, giving his next of kin as C Patterson of Calgary. It was recorded that he was 5 feet 6 inches tall, with a dark complexion, brown eyes and black hair.

Joseph is commemorated on the Menin Gate Memorial, Ypres.

References

1. WO 95/1617. War Diary, *2ⁿᵈ Battalion Durham light Infantry.*

2. WO 95/2826. *War Diary, 1/4ᵗʰ Battalion Northumberland Fusiliers.*

3. Stewart, G. and Sheen, J. *A History of the Tyneside Scottish*
    Pub: Pen and Sword Books, 1999.

4. Shakespear, Lt Col. J. *Thirty Fourth Division, 1915-1919,*
    Pub: 1921 reprinted Naval & Military Press 1998.

5. WO 95/2840. *War Diary 1/9ᵗʰ Durham Light Infantry.*

6. *War Diary 10ᵗʰ Battalion Canadian Infantry.*
    http://data2.collectionscanada.ca

Memorial to 50th Northumbrian Division
(1/4th Northumberland Fusiliers)
near Ypres

CHAPTER EIGHT

THE BATTLE OF THE SOMME, 1916

"Know that we fools, now with the foolish dead,
Died not for flag, nor King, nor Emperor,
But for a dream …
And for the secret Scripture of the poor"

T. M. Kettle, *To My Daughter Betty**

Overview

The Battle of the Somme was the main Allied attack of 1916. Initial planning for this infamous offensive began in late 1915. It was to be launched over a nineteen mile Front running from Arras to the River Somme; French forces were to attack south of the river. At the planning stage the bulk of the offensive was to be carried out by French forces, but the earlier attack by the Germans at Verdun effectively prevented widespread use of French troops on the Western Front. As a consequence, the French demanded that Britain should bear the brunt of the attack on the Somme, and also that the planned date of 1 August be brought forward to 1 July.

The 9th Inniskilling Fusiliers as part of 109 Brigade (36 Division) spent 22 – 23 June taking up their assault positions in the right-hand sector of Thiepval wood. The Divisional history records:[1]

> *"These troops had a purgatory to endure. For the most part in the narrow slit assembly trenches with the rain pouring steadily down on them, they were under furious German*

*Written four days before he died on the Somme, September 1916

107

bombardments that wreathed the wood in smoke and flame, and made the crashing of the great trees the accompaniment to the roar of the bursting shells."

❧   ❧   ❧

Private Michael Irwin, aged 28
9th (Service) Battalion Royal Inniskilling Fusiliers
Died 23 June 1916

Michael was born in Benburb, County Tyrone. He was the husband of Mrs Irwin of Haugh Lane, Hexham and was the father of two young children, Tommy and Annie. He was the son of Mr and Mrs William Irwin of Gilesgate Bank. He was a well-known footballer as his photograph here suggests. Michael enlisted in March 1915 with the Tyneside Irish and was transferred to the Inniskilling Fusiliers; he had been in France for seven months when he died. The day before his wife heard about his death she received a field card from Michael making a heartfelt plea for food, to which she responded immediately. Of course he did not live to receive his parcel.

Mrs Irwin received a letter (part of which is quoted in Chapter 1) from the Chaplain, the Reverend F M Clifford, which informed her of Michael's death:

"Dear Madam, God knows that I feel it intensely having to write this letter to you with the news it contains, namely that your husband, Pte M Irwin of the 9th R.I.F. was killed last night during heavy shelling by the enemy. I know that intense grief must come to you by this news, but after the first shock has passed – the thought that your husband offered and gave his life in this holy cause – dying on the field of honour, it will, I feel sure, be some consolation to you. Do not think of your husband as dead, but just passed over into – and entered upon – a higher, a happier more perfect life. I feel sure that our heavenly Father is looking down with infinite mercy and regard upon all these noble sacrifices, nobly made, and that the way of sacrifice (the way His own dear Son followed) is a way that meets his fullest approval. May God grant that we and the world turn unto him and seek His grace to do His will with greater courage and perseverance."

It was recorded that Michael was buried in Authuille Military Cemetery. Although the exact site of his burial is unknown, there is a headstone that bears his name (see photograph).

The attack on the Somme was preceded by a preliminary bombardment of the German lines, beginning on Saturday 24 June.

The aim of the bombardment was the destruction of all forward German defences, enabling British Troops easily to take possession of them. Over 3000 British and French guns were used in this bombardment. Unfortunately, the bombardment destroyed neither the barbed wire that formed the German Front Line nor the immensely strong concrete bunkers that the Germans had constructed. Further, a disturbing amount of the munitions used by the British proved to be defective as a result of bad workmanship. Thus, the German troops sheltering in these bunkers were not affected by the bombardment and emerged unscathed to use their machine guns – weapons which provided a deadly and accurate stream of fire.

The fighting on the Somme in 1916 lasted from 1 July to 18 November. This being the case, the fighting over this period has been divided into a number of distinct phases.

The First Battle of Albert
1 – 13 July 1916

The attack was scheduled for 7.30am with the detonation of a series of seventeen mines along the Front. The first, at Hawthorn Crater, detonated ten minutes earlier than was intended; it is not known why this happened.

At the northern extremity of the battlefield two Territorial divisions, the 46th (North Midlands) and the 56th (London) attacked around Gommecourt to create a diversion whilst also trying to straighten a German-held bulge in the line. After initial success by the Londoners, the attack ground to a halt with no gains and can only be classified as a disaster: 56th Division suffered 4,300 casualties.

Further south, the 31st Division – primarily made up of *Pals* Battalions from cities of Northern England: Bradford, Leeds, Barnsley and Hull – were detailed to capture the village of Serre. The Division suffered heavy losses for minimal gains. In an epitaph to the *Pals* Battalion the following was written:

"Two years in the making. Ten minutes in the destroying."

A little way to the south, the 4th Division, made up of Regular troops, captured the Quadrilateral Redoubt (Heidenkoft to the Germans). However, due to the failure of the Divisions to the north (31st) and to the south (29th), to capture their objectives, this Division came under fire from both the front and the sides making their position untenable. By the morning of 2 July the position was abandoned, with a wasteful loss of 4700 men.[2]

Involved in this attack by the 4th Division was the 2nd Battalion Duke of Wellington's, who formed part of 10th Brigade.

Lance Serjeant Alfred Addison, aged 32
2nd Battalion Duke of Wellington's (West Riding Regiment)
Died 4 July 1916

Alfred was the eldest son of John Edward Addison of Front Street, East Stanley, Co Durham, who had lived for a number of years in Hexham. Whilst living in Hexham, Alfred worked at Davidson's Foundry and enlisted in the army in 1904. He went with his regiment to India in October 1905 where he saw seven years of service. He took part in the Nutra Fete in Calcutta and in the Delhi Durbar, when George V was crowned in India. As a result he possessed the Coronation Medal. The 2nd Battalion Duke of Wellington's were part of the first British troops to land in France in 1914 and fought in the desperate actions of 1914. Alfred was one of the 'Old Contemptibles', a name coined by troops in recognition of a slur made on the British Army by the Kaiser. Alfred was gassed and wounded on Hill 60 in May 1915. During the attack on 1 July 1916 he was wounded and died of these wounds on 4 July.

Alfred is buried in Doullens Communal Cemetery, Extension No 1. The following inscription is found at the bottom of his headstone:

HE DIED FOR HIS COUNTRY'S SAKE
GONE BUT NOT FORGOTTEN

Further south, the 29th Division attacked around Beaumont Hamel. This formation was mainly made up of Regular battalions, many of whose men had seen active service in Gallipoli. They were to find that fighting the Germans was significantly more difficult a task. The German defences were particularly strong on this part of the Front, with the Redan Ridge dominating the battlefield with its defensive position called the Hawthorn Redoubt. A mine under this position packed with 40,000 lb of high explosive was blown at 7.20am, ten minutes before zero hour. The idea was that the crater thus formed could be occupied before the main assault. However, it merely alerted the Germans and the attacking troops were unable to secure the crater; those men attacking from 86th and 87th Brigades were killed in No Man's Land before reaching the enemy Front Line. As a result of bad communications, the Reserve 88th Brigade was committed to the battle and suffered enormous losses. The 1st Newfoundland Battalion suffered 684 casualties, 91% of its original strength.

Over the top

Yards to the south, the 36th (Ulster) Division made spectacular gains from its initial attack. Effective artillery fire allowed the men to crawl out into No Man's Land before zero hour, after which these men won the race to the German Front Line where they captured the key positions of Schwaben and Stuff Redoubts. This success could not be built upon, as both the Divisions to the north (29th) and to the south (32nd) were unable to gain any significant ground, leaving the 36th Division isolated and being fired upon from both the front and the sides. As a result the Ulsters were pushed back from their spectacular initial gains.

Southwards, the 32nd Division was given the task of capturing the Thiepval plateau, which eventually fell on 27 September. A new army battalion from Glasgow initially captured the Leipzig Salient, but no other gains could be achieved.

The 16th Battalion Northumberland Fusiliers as part of the 96th Brigade were also involved in this action. The Battalion History recounts that even on the approach to their battle position, many casualties occurred. As the fusiliers of 'A' and 'B' companies went over the top at 7.30am, the Germans poured fire into the advancing line of soldiers. As darkness covered the battlefield the 16th Battalion was withdrawn. On this day six officers and three hundred and fifty NCOs and men died.[3]

Private William Lynch, aged 22
16th (Service) Battalion Northumberland Fusiliers
Died 1 July 1916

William was the eldest son of the late John Joseph and Annie Lynch of St Hilda's Road, Hexham. He enlisted in June 1915 and went to France in the November of that year. Before the onset of hostilities he was employed for a time as a printer with the Hexham Courant, but due to ill health he eventually worked as a gardener. He was employed at the Leazes and subsequently in Wylam. One

of his other brothers was in France with the Northumberland Fusiliers, whilst the other was serving with the merchant navy.

William is buried at Lonsdale Cemetery, Authuille.

Private John N Rowell, aged 38
16th (Service) Battalion Northumberland Fusiliers
Died 1 July 1916

John was born in Warden and was the son of William and Sarah Ann Rowell of Newburn. Before enlisting, he had been employed by the Newcastle and Gateshead Water Company.

John is buried in Lonsdale Cemetery, Authuille.

At the part of the battlefield which straddled the Albert to Bapaume road, the 8th Division, made up of Regular Army battalions, was ordered to capture the Ovilliers spur. At this point, No Man's Land was particularly wide – 750 yards in some places. The attack's only approach was through Mash Valley, which was a lethal killing ground for the Germans. All three of the Division's brigades attacked at the same time and, at great cost, managed to penetrate the German lines. However, the Germans were very adept at cutting off assault troops from the follow up forces by laying down near impenetrable barrages in No Man's Land and so any successes were short lived and retreat was difficult but inevitable.

Next in line was the 34th Division whose 102nd and 103rd Brigades were made up of a *Pals* battalion of Northumberland Fusiliers, primarily from Tyneside. The 102nd Brigade was based on four battalions known as the Tyneside Scottish, whilst the 103rd Brigade was made up of four battalions known as the Tyneside Irish. Other *Pals* Battalions made up 101st Brigade. These two brigades were to attack north and south of the village of La Boisselle. The Tyneside Scottish battalions were delegated to begin the attack, and were arranged with the 20th and 23rd Battalions to the north and the 21st Battalion to the south. The 22nd followed behind the 21st. As the village was not to be attacked, the gap was held by 'C' Company of 18th Northumberland Fusiliers. The four Tyneside Irish battalions were held in reserve: the 25th behind the 23rd Scottish, with the 24th 26th and 27th Battalions arranged on the right hand side of the Albert-Bapaume road.

The attack began with the detonation of two mines, one to the north of La Boisselle and the other to the south, at 7.28 am. Two minutes later the attack began. The Tyneside Scottish battalions had between 200 – 500 yards to traverse before reaching the German lines. The Irish in reserve had 1000 to 1500 yards to travel over exposed terrain even to cross the British Front. After the explosion the German defenders, who had been safe in their deep bunkers, emerged. Their deadly machine gun fire was directed against the slowly advancing British soldiers. The British, who had been ordered to advance in rows at walking pace, were mown down indiscriminately. The Irish took up to twenty minutes to reach the British Front Line – in full view and range of the German guns. The Division sustained 6,380 casualties, the highest of any division on that day.[4, 5, 6, 7]

Private George Smith, aged 29 years
22nd (Service) Battalion (Tyneside Scottish)
Northumberland Fusiliers
Died 1 July 1916

George was born in Hexham and was the second son of Mrs Smith of Whorlton, Westerhope and formerly of Hexham. He was the son of the late John Smith who had been employed as a coachman by Doctor Stewart of Hexham. Before joining up George had been employed for six years as a coachman and groom at Chipchase Castle. Before this, he was employed by John Dodd, a Hexham butcher. George's only brother was serving with the Canadians.

George is commemorated on the Thiepval Memorial to the missing.

Thiepval Memorial
Unveiled 1932

The Thiepval Memorial was erected to commemorate men who died in the War between July 1915 and March 1918 and who have no known grave. The names of nearly 73,000 soldiers and sailors are inscribed on this majestic edifice and for them it 'stands for grave and headstone', as it says in the introduction to the register. Most of the soldiers remembered at Thiepval died on just one day – the first day of the Somme, 1 July 1916. As that day was huge in terror, so this immense structure is the largest of all the monuments on the Western Front. Men of every rank are mentioned here, listed by regiment on huge panels in order of rank, then name, although in the monument register the names appear in simple alphabetical order. The name of the youngest soldier to die on the Somme is on Thiepval: Private Reginald Giles was a boy of fourteen when he was killed.

The monument was designed by Sir Edwin Lutyens, a leading architect of the late 19th and early 20th Century. His work will be known to those familiar with Lindisfarne Castle or the Manor House at Whalton, near Morpeth. The Northumberland Fusiliers has more names on Thiepval than does any other regiment with the exception of The London Regiment, which was made up entirely of Territorials.

Thiepval

Private Thomas Pencott, aged 30
22nd (Service) Battalion (Tyneside Scottish)
Northumberland Fusiliers
Died 1 July 1916

Thomas was born in Ashington, Northumberland, and enlisted in that town into the Northumberland Fusiliers. His mother lived in Glover's Place, Hexham. The Hexham Courant reports that on 26 August 1915 Thomas was in hospital suffering from trench fever.

Thomas was killed in action on the first day of the Somme and is buried in Ovilliers Military Cemetery.

Sergeant Francis Forster (Foster), aged 24
27th (Service) Battalion (Tyneside Irish)
Northumberland Fusiliers
Died 1 July 1916

Frank (Francis) was born in Hexham and was the third son of Mrs Elizabeth Forster and the late Robert Forster of Jubilee Buildings, Hexham. He was a single man who before the war had served a four-year apprenticeship as a draper with Mr Edward Riddle. He joined the Tyneside Irish shortly after its formation in Newcastle and was quickly promoted because he had experience as a former Territorial in Hexham.

Frank is commemorated on the Thiepval memorial to the missing.

Three of Frank's brothers had been in France with the 1/4th Northumberland Fusiliers. Private B Forster had been wounded and discharged, Company Sergeant-Major R Forster was on munitions and Joe Forster was a Drum-Major. His late father had also served 25 years with the old volunteers and the Territorials.

Databases record Francis' name as *Forster*, which is the name used on the Abbey Memorial, but the Hexham Herald uses the name *Foster*. Frank's rank is also recorded as Lance Corporal, but the Herald reports it as Sergeant.

In the southern section of the battlefield on this the first day of the battle, the British forces made significant gains. The 50th Brigade (21st Division) captured the village strongpoint of Fricourt, albeit a day late. The 7th Division captured the heavily defended village of Mametz. Furthermore, both the 18th and 30th Divisions, who captured the village of

118

Montauban, made gains.

On 2 July the 8th Battalion Border Regiment as part of the 25th Division moved up to the Front, for an attack on Thiepval village from Authville, beginning at 6am the next day. In this attack, 180 yards of German line were taken with very heavy British casualties. Later in the day the battalion was forced to withdraw as it suffered from flanking machine gun fire. Casualties included four officers killed and ten wounded, casualties to other ranks being over four hundred and thirty. After a number of days away from the Front, the 8th Battalion was ordered back for an attack on the south side of Ovilliers on the 14 July. The German Front Line was taken with heavy casualties.[8]

Private Henry (Harry) Abbott, aged 29
8th (Service) Battalion Border Regiment
Died 24 July 1916

Harry was born in Richmond, Yorkshire and was a married man with three children. Before enlisting he worked in the lead mines near Alston. He is a member of the Abbott family who lived in Hexham and from which no fewer than five brothers were serving in the forces. It is reported that he died of his wounds.

Harry was buried in St Sever Cemetery, Rouen. Rouen was the site of a number of large military hospitals.

On capturing Mametz Wood the battle inched forward with the intention of shifting the Germans from High Wood. But the length of time required to capture Mametz Wood by the 38th (Welsh) Division allowed the Germans ample time to prepare elaborate and deadly defences in High Wood. This delay was to cost the British dearly – attack after attack over the next two months foundered with many men injured or killed.

The 9th Battalion Highland Light Infantry, known as the Glasgow Highlanders, undertook the first attack on High Wood on the evening of 14 July. At the same time, the Germans mounted a counter-attack and the Highlanders took very heavy casualties. The supporting battalions of 1st South Staffs and 1st Queens managed to enter the wood and at this time a cavalry charge was mounted which was successful at first. However, eventually the Germans got the upper hand and they were forced to withdraw.

On 20 July another attack on the defences of High Wood was undertaken by the 1st Battalion Cameronians, (north-west half), the 5/6th Scottish Rifles (north-east half) and the 20th Royal Fusiliers. At 3.35am both battalions rushed the wood – which was burning – and took many prisoners without too much difficulty. In the centre of the wood they met only light opposition. However, the Cameronians came up against machine gun fire which wrought havoc in the western corner. The Battalion War Diary reports the following casualties:
Officers: 5 killed, 4 wounded and 4 missing
Rank and File: 52 killed, 160 wounded and 157 missing.[9, 10]

The author Robert Graves is perhaps best known for his book *Good-bye To All That*, a finely detailed and intensely moving account of his experiences in the First World War. He was seriously injured at High Wood on 20 July, the day that John Gilhespy (below) died. Graves describes this action in Chapter 20, remarking that 'the Germans put down a barrage along the ridge where we were lying, and we lost about a third of the battalion before our show started'. Graves was hit by pieces of shell as his battalion was trying to move back fifty yards to avoid the barrage. So serious were his wounds that Graves' colonel wrote to his mother telling her that her 'son had died of wounds'. Graves goes on to say:

120

*"Later he made out an official casualty list and reported me
died of wounds. It was a long casualty list, because only
eighty men were left of the battalion."*

Second Lieutenant John William Gilhespy, aged 39
Attached 1ˢᵗ Battalion Cameronians (Scottish Rifles)
Died 20 July 1917

John was born in Hexham in 1876.
He was the second son of John and
Jane Gilhespy of East Land Banks,
Hexham. After leaving school he
served his apprenticeship as an
ironmonger with the firm of John
S Moffatt of Hexham. Following
this, he spent time in Birmingham,
London and Newcastle and finally
made his way to South Africa. He
lived in Johannesburg for a
number of years and managed a
firm called Stanford and Company, based in Middleburg
in the Transvaal.

In early 1914, John returned to England and joined the
Cheshire Yeomanry; he was quickly promoted to
Corporal. In May 1915 he accepted a commission in the
12ᵗʰ Battalion Queen's Own Cameron Highlanders and
was attached to the 1ˢᵗ Battalion Scottish Rifles. He
went to France in March 1916. His younger brother,
Robert, was also serving in France with the Army
Service Corps.

Second Lieutenant Craig wrote to John's elder brother
George at the Albert Hotel in Dunbar saying:

"In going over, leading his men, he was hit about the knee

and after it was bandaged he went on again and in the face of intense machine gun and rifle fire he was shot ... Eight other officers were killed the same day, six wounded and five others returned unwounded of whom I am one ...."

Another officer who was with John in the same attack and was in hospital in London wrote:

"Gilhe and I were great friends in B Company. I felt drawn by his brightness and sincerity. During those long days of bombardment, it was quite refreshing to be in his company. Before the attack we wished each other good luck, but it was God's will he should give himself, as so many thousands of noble souls are giving themselves in this war. Like the brave fellow he was, he continued to lead his men after being wounded and got right up to the enemy's position before he fell."

John is commemorated on the Thiepval Memorial to the missing.

On 1 August, the 9th Battalion Northumberland Fusiliers relieved the 15th Battalion Royal Warwickshire in the Pear Street sector near Fricourt. 'A' Company took up position in the Front Line. This movement to the Front Line was in preparation for an attack to be undertaken on 4 August.

During 2 August, the trenches were subjected to intermittent bombardment, which increased in intensity on the 3 August, particularly in the evening, when it appeared that the Germans were preparing to counter-attack in force.[11, 12]

**Private George Moss aged nearly 19 years
'A' Company, 9th (Service) Battalion
Northumberland Fusiliers
Died 3 August 1916**

 George was the second son of Mr and Mrs Moss of Burswell Terrace, Hexham. He was born in Blyth and enlisted in North Shields. Although the official date for his death is given as 3 August, the Courant notes that he died on the 5 August, which was his 19th birthday. However, the Battalion War Diary confirms the date of 3 August.[15]

His platoon Sergeant stated that:

> *"Private Moss was a brave and true soldier... many of the wounded had blessed him for his quickness in getting to them."*

George was killed in action and is commemorated on the Thiepval Memorial for men who have no known grave.

Following severe casualties in both the 8th and 10th Battalions of the Gordon Highlanders, the battalions were merged to form a composite battalion, part of 44th Brigade 15th (Scottish) Division. The division moved onto the Somme at the end of July and on 14 August moved into the Front Line near Peake Wood. Other elements of this division had been in action two days earlier and had captured part of the Switch Line trenches. These trenches offered extensive observation over this part of the battlefield, allowing observers to direct artillery and machine gun fire on enemy troops advancing from Martinpuich. All along this newly acquired Front Line, elements of the Scottish Division carried out local bombing attacks.[13]

Serjeant Harry Meins, aged 27 years
8th/10th (Service) Battalion Gordon Highlanders
Died 15 August 1916

Harry Meins was the adopted son of the Reverend

Napier-Clavering of Oxford. He was born in Berwickshire and arrived in Hexham in 1910 to manage the Fore Street branch of the Maypole Dairy. He enlisted with the Gordon Highlanders in Edinburgh at the outbreak of war. He saw action at the Battle of Loos in 1915 and was present at the capture of Hill 70. Harry was mentioned in dispatches on 15 June 1916 for bravery whilst serving at the Front near the Hollenzollern Redoubt in the Loos Sector.

The Hexham Courant described Harry as a man with a singularly cheery, open nature, full of high spirits. He was an active member of Hexham Rowing Club and was often spotted swimming in the Tyne.

Lieutenant A F Sprott wrote:
"Serjeant H. Meins was killed outright ... I have not the slightest hesitation in telling you that Meins was the bravest man I ever met. And his men had perfect confidence in him..."

One of the men in Serjeant Meins' Mess Company also paid tribute:

"It is given to few men to win the respect and esteem of his comrades as did Harry Meins."

Another Officer wrote:

"To those under him Sergeant Meins was a friend, sometimes too kind, but his men loved him and would follow him and he won the esteem and respect of all his comrades by his coolness and bravery, for he feared nothing. And now he lies below the soil of France, one more hero who made the supreme sacrifice for his King and country. But the memory of Harry Meins still lives and will never fade in Hexham."

Harry is commemorated on the Thiepval Memorial, which bears the names of 72,000 soldiers who have no known grave.

The 1/1st Durham Field Company, Royal Engineers, was a Territorial Unit formed in mid 1915 from the Durham (Fortress) Engineers, which had headquarters at North Shields and Jarrow. They recruited men who worked along the banks of the Tyne. Upon arrival in France in September 1915 these engineers were attached to the 4th Division, which saw action in the initial phases of the Somme offensive in early July. It appears that at the time of Thomas's death this unit was not involved in any of the major actions, but was probably involved in servicing the lines of communication.[14]

Sapper Thomas William Edwards, aged 31 years
1/1st Durham Field Company Royal Engineers
Died 7 September 1916

Thomas was born in Newcastle. He was the husband of Mrs J Edwards of Cockshaw Terrace, Hexham and was the father of five children. He was employed on the boat of Messrs Ridley and Sons and Tully of Newcastle.

Whilst returning from the Front Line with his section he was hit by an exploding shell, which resulted in his death. In a letter to Mrs Edwards, Lieutenant J B Philipson wrote that Thomas was:

> *"a good reliable soldier and right bravely did his duty. He was buried in a cemetery.".*

It seems that notwithstanding this burial 'in a cemetery', his grave was not marked and therefore was not traced

after the war.

The Hexham Herald printed the following tribute to Thomas from his wife:

Only a private soldier,
Just one of Britain's sons.
Buried on the field of Battle;
We know your duty's done.
You served your King and Country,
God knows you did your best;
Now asleep in Jesus,
A British soldier rests.

Thomas is commemorated on the Thiepval Memorial to the missing.

Flers-Courcelette

This major Allied attack was launched on 15 September 1916 across an eight-mile Front using twelve infantry divisions along with a small number of tanks and artillery. The Front stretched from south of the village of Courcellette, west of the Albert-Baupame road, eastwards to the south of Combles.

The date of 15 September is famous for the introduction of the **tank** to warfare, although of course the primitive tanks of 1916 were totally different from those of today. By September 1916 Britain had built forty-nine tanks which displayed varying degrees of unreliability. On that day only fifteen tanks managed to roll into battle at a speed of 1 mph. Apart from the dangers of the raging conflict, the tank crews had to deal with extreme heat and with breathing carbon monoxide from engine fumes. Although the tanks' armour plating was impervious to small arms fire and to a lesser extent machine gun fire, (metal chips would fly inside the tank), it was susceptible to the impact of artillery shells. However, the tanks were effective in crushing barbed wire and could bring up fire support for infantry. Furthermore, their sinister appearance and size made them an effective *psychological* weapon.

Corporal Gerald Edmond Pattinson, aged 31
Tank Corps
Died 15 September 1916

Gerald was born in Sunderland, the second son of Charles Reginald and Helene Pattinson of Portland Lodge, Hexham. He initially enlisted into the Machine Gun Corps (Heavy Branch), but later transferred into the newly formed Tank Corps. As stated above, tanks were used for the first time on the 15 September on the Somme.
Gerald is buried in Combles Communal Cemetery Extension.

In preparation for the Battle of Fleurs-Courcelette, the Artillery fired over 800,000 shells, a greater intensity than that fired on 1 July but less than some of the other battles during the Somme campaign.

Along this eight-mile Front the 50th Division were to be found to the west of High Wood. Until September 1916 the 50th (Northumbrian) Division had not been involved in the struggles on the Somme. This was all to change; by September 9 the 1/4th Battalion Northumberland Fusiliers (149th Brigade) were deployed on the Front Line between the village of Martinpuich and High Wood.

On 12 September the preliminary bombardment for the

forthcoming attack on 15 September began. On Thursday 14 the battle positions for the attack were established (see map below).

For the attack made by the 149th Brigade, the 1/7th Northumberland assembled on the left with the 1/4th Battalion on the right. The companies of the 1/4th Battalion were in order from left to right 'D', 'B', 'A' and 'C'. There were three objectives for the attack by the 50th Division. First was the capture of Hook Trench which ran westward from High Wood. Second was a further advance of 500 yards and the capture of Martin Trench, the Bow and part of the Starfish Line.   Third was the capture of Prue Trench and the subsequent capture of a further section of the Starfish Line. In its early stages the attacking Front was 1100 yards wide widening to 1800 yards as the objectives were overcome.

The position of the 1/4th Battalion was a difficult one. Earlier fighting had left a dogleg in the Front Line.   The 1/4th Battalion's position was 300 yards ahead of the 47th Division. If for any reason the 47th Division were delayed in their advance then the Northumberland Fusiliers would be exposed to enfilade fire from German strong points on the northwest corner of High Wood (Bois de Foureaux). These strong points allowed the Germans to rake the ground between the wood and Martinpuich with heavy fire. Repeated attacks on this section of High Wood had been carried out in the proceeding weeks without any success.

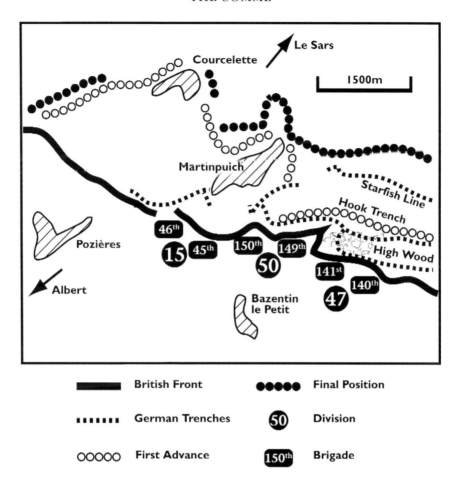

Battle Flers Courcellette (part) 1916

The assault started on time at 6.20am with some support from tanks; two with the 150th Brigade and three with the 47th Division. At 7am it was recorded that 'B' Company (Captain L D Plummer was to die this day, see below) had taken Hook Trench with little opposition and had established contact with 'D' Company (Captain H H Bell would also die this day, see below) on their left flank. Later, wounded 'D' Company men returned to the starting trenches. Shortly afterwards

129

they came under heavy machine gun and rifle fire from High Wood.

At 7.27am the 1/4th Northumberland Fusiliers began an advance towards their second objective; as they started out they received the news that the 47th Division attack on High Wood had been unsuccessful. In spite of this, they went on to capture the second objective and to enter the Starfish Line. The failure of 47th Division's attack left the 1/4th Battalion's right flank very exposed. Enemy fire inflicted heavy casualties and so they were forced to retreat back to Hook Trench, which because of the difficulties in High Wood was also exposed to German attack and was swept continually by machine gun fire.

During the morning, companies from the 1/5th and 1/6th Battalions were moved forward to support the attack. By noon, the 1/4th Northumberland Fusiliers had recaptured Martin Trench. The 47th Division had also finally captured High Wood, but this was of little consolation as the damage to the Fusiliers had already been done. Mid afternoon saw the 1/4th Battalion being forced to retreat back to Hook Trench.

Fighting continued the next day with men from the 50th Division being heavily involved. The 1/4th Battalion captured both the second and third objectives.

0n 15 September the 1/4th Battalion Northumberland fusiliers attacked with 22 officers and 695 men. A roll call three days later recorded that 10 officers and 110 men had been killed, 7 officers and 229 men were wounded and 143 men were classed as missing. Later records show that 180 fusiliers were killed during this engagement. [10, 15, 16, 17, 18, 19]

Scene of Attacks by 50th Division. Sept. 15–Nov. 14, 1916.

Captain Lionel Davey Plummer, aged 25
1/4th Battalion Northumberland Fusiliers
Died 15 September 1916

Lionel Plummer was born in India, returning to England when he was a young child. He was the eldest son of George Henry and Lizzie Plummer of Glengarth, Hexham. He was also the grandson of Joseph Catherall, who launched the Hexham Courant in August 1864.

Lionel was educated at Balliol House, Harrogate and St Bees, Cumbria. His school reports state that he did well academically and was very keen on athletics and rugby; he gained his Colours for cricket. A badly broken leg whilst at school had caused him to give up playing rugby. He was also a member of the St Bees Officers' Training Corps.

After leaving school he worked for his father in the

management of the Hexham Courant and its printing works. He played for Tynedale Cricket Club and appeared with the Northumberland County squad. He also played hockey for Tynedale; before the war this was one of the strongest sides in the North of England.

As a consequence of his training at St Bees, in 1909 he became an officer in the local Territorial Battalion of the Northumberland Fusiliers. At the outbreak of war he was promoted to Captain. He went out to France in April 1915 and was thrust into the fighting around Ypres, where the battalion received a very torrid baptism of fire. During this action he was wounded and spent several weeks in hospital in London. After convalescence in Hexham followed by light duties, he went back to the Front in March 1916.

On 20 September 1915 Lionel married Isabella Little at the Abbey. Isabella was the youngest daughter of Mrs Little of Oakwood and the sister of Captain Andrew Little who died at Ypres in April of that year. As they left the Abbey, the Officers of the Fusiliers provided an arch of swords for the bride and groom.

Reports show that Captain Plummer was killed instantaneously as he encouraged his men whilst attacking the enemy's second line of trenches.

The Colonel of his regiment wrote:

> *"Lionel fell gallantly leading his men in one of the greatest battles of the war and you have the consolation that his life was not sacrificed in vain, as the Battalion and his company did splendidly. I am sure he could not have done better here or died more gloriously. Your sorrow is shared by us all, especially by those who have known and loved him."*

A brother officer wrote to Lionel's father:

"....His leadership and example to the Battalion will always be a source of pride to us, and if he has paid the extreme penalty we who knew him will rejoice that he paid it as only the very bravest and most courageous can pay it ..."

Further correspondence from the Front reported statements from survivors of the engagement:

"They say he was leading his men on to the second German line when he was killed. It was instantaneous. All they can say is that he was perfect. He led them and talked to them as if they were on parade..."

"He died nobly as Lionel would. He was cheering on his company to the final assault when he was hit and his men cannot say enough about the bravery and coolness with which he led them. He died a hero's death and set such an example to us all that in reality he has left the battalion with one aim: to live up to and keep up the standard he set it. Needless to say the battalion mourn him one and all. He was one of the oldest hands, if I might put it like that, and he played an essential part of it. The battalion has made a name for itself during this last attack, which will never die. They held the place of honour, the strongest place in the line and they hung on all day against fearful enfilade fire, they were marvels. It was men like Plummer who enabled the battalion to do so well."

Lionel is buried at Adanac Military Cemetery, Miraumont.

Captain (Tp) Henry Hogarth Bell, aged 20
1/4th Battalion, Northumberland Fusiliers
Died 15 September 1916

Henry was the eldest son of Major G H Hogarth, and Mrs Katherine Daubeney (formerly Bell). He was educated at Seabank, Alnmouth and Charterhouse, Godalming. On

leaving school in 1913 he obtained a commission in the Northumberland Fusiliers (Territorials). In March 1914 he was promoted to full lieutenant. He was connected to the firm of Henry Bell and Sons Limited who had extensive interests in the Hexham area. He was a keen horseman who hunted with both the Tynedale and Haydon Hounds. As did many of the local officers who died, he played for Tynedale Hockey Club.

At the outbreak of hostilities he was mobilized and went out with his battalion to France in April 1915. He was wounded at Ypres in that same April – his battalion suffered terrible losses. As a result of his efforts at Ypres, General French mentioned Henry in dispatches. The Hexham Herald (Saturday 8 January 1916) reported that Lieutenant Bell was responsible for a very gallant deed which it was quite expected would have won the Victoria Cross, although this was not to be.

It appears that his troop ran short of ammunition and was likely to be cut off. Lieutenant Bell rode to an ammunition store over a road that was being showered with shells and returned with enough ammunition to save the situation. On both the outward and return journey the shells were bursting all around him; that he accomplished his mission seemed little short of a miracle.

Returning to duties he was further injured in December 1915 when his horse fell when it lost its footing in a shell hole. He recovered in a London hospital. Early in 1916 he was gazetted to Captain.

Henry is buried in Caterpillar Valley Cemetery, Longueval.

2nd Lieutenant Henry Archibald Long, aged 31
1/4th Battalion Northumberland Fusiliers
Died 15 September 1916

Henry was the eldest son of George Frederick and Blanche Katherine Long of Tynedale Terrace, Hexham. Before the war, when he lived in London, Henry served with the Middlesex Yeomanry. When war was declared Henry was in West Africa where he was employed by the Niger Company Limited. He immediately returned to Hexham to join up. He was given a Commission in August 1915 and went up to the Front in January 1916.

Lieutenant Colonel Gibson wrote to his father:

> " ...*Your son was killed while leading his men in an attack on the 15th September ...*"

Henry is commemorated on the Thiepval Memorial.

Serjeant Alfred Holbrook, aged 32
1/4th Battalion Northumberland Fusiliers
Died 15 September 1916

Alfred was born in London, the son of Mr and Mrs James Frederick Holbrook. He was married to Nora Holbrook, and lived at Eilansgate Terrace, Hexham.

Alfred is commemorated on the Thiepval Memorial.

Alfred's name appears on the Hexham War Memorial as Alfred *Hallbrook*, but two database sources refer to him as Alfred *Holbrook*.

Lance Serjeant Richard Brooks, aged 29
1/4th Battalion Northumberland Fusiliers
Died 15 September 1916

Richard was the eldest son of William and M J Brooks of Prior Terrace, Hexham. He was married to Elizabeth Brooks of Cockshaw Terrace and was the father of two children. A peace-serving member of the Territorials with the rank of Corporal, he was promoted to Serjeant during active service. In July 1916 his parents were informed that he was in hospital suffering from trench fever. Before the war, Richard worked for Mr J Burn of Dipton House, Riding Mill, as a gardener.

Writing to Mrs Brooks, Captain Foster said:

> *"The death of your husband is a great loss to his company. One of the best N.C.O.'s (sic) and one of the finest of my men. …. It was the N.C.O.'s on that memorable day that enabled the men to do their task, for when the officers fell early in the battle the N.C.O.'s carried on magnificently and ultimately gained their objectives. …"*

Richard was buried in Delville Wood Cemetery.

Private Thomas Potts, aged 20
1/4th Battalion Northumberland Fusiliers
Died 15 September 1916

Thomas was born in Carlisle and lived in Kingsgate Terrace, Hexham. He went out to France with the second batch of the Fusiliers.

Thomas is commemorated on the Thiepval Memorial to the missing.

Private William Cooper, aged 42
1/4th Battalion Northumberland Fusiliers
Died 15 September 1916

William was married to Jane Anne Cooper of Hallgate, Hexham and was the father of two children. Before mobilization he was employed as a hewer at Tynedale Colliery, Acomb. He enlisted in April 1915 and had been at the Front for only three months before his death.

The Reverend J. O. Aglionby wrote to his widow to console her, saying:

"His death was instantaneous."

William is commemorated on the Thiepval Monument.

Private Ralph Newton, aged 19
1/4th Battalion Northumberland Fusiliers
Died 15 September 1916

 Ralph who was born in Hexham and was one of four sons of Ralph and Rachel Newton of Prior Terrace, Hexham. All of these sons were serving in the Forces. Before enlisting he was employed as a labourer by Messrs H Bell and Sons of Hexham. Ralph's brother James had just left for France when his bother died.

Ralph is commemorated on the Thiepval Memorial.

Private John Edward Newton, aged 21
1/4th Battalion Northumberland Fusiliers
Died 15 September 1916

John was born in Hexham and was another of the four sons of Ralph and Rachel Newton of Prior Terrace, Hexham. Before the War, John was a Teritorial. He enlisted with his brother Ralph and they went out to France in April 1915. John was originally reported as being wounded, but was later confirmed as being killed on the same day as his brother. In April 1918 the Hexham Herald reported that a further brother, Private Thomas Newton, was ill in hospital.

John is also commemorated on the Thiepval Memorial.

Private John Oliver, aged 28
1/4th Northumberland Fusiliers
Died 15 September 1915

John Oliver of Garden Terrace was the son of George Oliver of Hexham. John enlisted shortly after war broke out and had been in France since April 1915. Early in 1916 it was reported that he had suffered from the effects of gas. Before the war John was employed at Tynedale Colliery as a hewer. He left a wife and two children.

John is commemorated on the Thiepval Memorial.

Private Robert Blackburn, aged 22
1/4th Battalion Northumberland Fusiliers
Died 15 September 1915

Robert was the husband of Mrs Blackburn of Garland Buildings, Gilesgate.

He is buried in Adanac Military Cemetery, Miraumont.

Private Ernest Armstrong, aged 19
1/4ᵗʰ Battalion Northumberland Fusiliers
Died 15 September 1915

Ernest was the third son of Mr and Mrs A Armstrong of Burswell Avenue, Hexham. When war was declared, he was serving an apprenticeship with H Wallace, a Hexham joiner. He went out with the original draft and saw action in April 1915 at the *Second Battle of Ypres* where he was wounded in the shoulder. Three of his brothers were serving with the forces. A month after Ernest's death, his parents were informed that his brother Harry had been severely wounded in the right arm and was in hospital in Birmingham.

Earnest is commemorated on the Thiepval Memorial to the missing.

Private Robert Young, aged 20
1/4ᵗʰ Battalion Northumberland Fusiliers
Died 15 September 1916

Robert was the fifth of six sons of Elizabeth Young of the Police Buildings, Hexham and Jas Young, a cab proprietor. At the time of Robert's death, three other sons, Frank, John and Gilbert were already serving in the Forces for their country. Mrs Young expected that her two other sons would be called up in the following few weeks.

Robert enlisted in September 1914 and was sent to France in April of 1915 and was involved in the fighting around Ypres. In June 1915 he was wounded and, after convalescence, he reported back for duty in September, being killed shortly afterwards.

Robert is commemorated on the Thiepval Memorial.

Private John William Thompson, aged 19
1/4th Battalion Northumberland Fusiliers
Died 15 September 1916

John was the eldest son of Mr and Mrs Thompson of Garden Terrace, Hexham. He enlisted in November 1914 leaving an apprenticeship with Mr Thomas Ellis, Painter and Glazier of Beaumont Street. John also fought at the *Second Battle of Ypres*.

He is commemorated on the Thiepval Memorial.

Private Tom Abbot, aged 20
1/4th Battalion Northumberland Fusiliers
Died 15 September 1916

Tom was the youngest of five sons of Mr and Mrs Abbot of Foundry Lane. His brother Harry had been killed earlier in the year. Before the war, Tom worked as a gardener for Mr J E Tully of West Quarter.

Tom is commemorated on the Thiepval Memorial.

Bandsman James Bell, aged 30
1/4ᵗʰ Battalion Northumberland Fusiliers
Died 15 September 1916

James was born in Byker, Newcastle and was the husband of Mrs Bell of East Gate, Hexham. Before enlisting in November 1915 he was employed by Messrs Graham and Ainsley as a painter, but latterly he had also been employed as a postman. He had been in France for little more than a month before he was killed.

James is commemorated on the Thiepval Memorial to the missing.

Private William Dodd, aged 19
1/4ᵗʰ Battalion Northumberland Fusiliers
Died 15 September 1916

William was the second son of Isaac and Margaret Dodd of Kingsgate, Hexham. He enlisted at the beginning of the war but had remained in England until June 1916. Before the war he was a cart man for Messrs Hogarth of Fore Street, Hexham. At the time of William's death, his father was in Egypt with the Motor Transport Section, Army Service Corps. His elder brother was also serving with the Northumberland Fusiliers in a machine gun section.

William is commemorated on the Thiepval Memorial.

In 1914, every battalion was equipped with two Maxim machine guns. This was increased to four in early 1915. In September 1915 the four battalions which made up a brigade released their weapons to form a single Machine Gun Brigade; the obsolete Maxim gun was replaced by one manufactured by Vickers. The 149th Company Machine Gun Corps was formed from the four Northumberland Fusilier Battalions which made up 149th Brigade and the intention was to support infantry operations undertaken by this brigade.

Serjeant Frederick Nevison, aged 25
149th Company, Machine Gun Corps (Infantry)
Died 15 September 1916

Frederick was the youngest son of Joseph and Elizabeth Nevison of Hexham. He was a married man with one child and lived at Tyne Green, Hexham. Before the war he was employed as a hewer at Tynedale Colliery. He was a very accomplished halfback playing for Tynedale Rugby Football Club. He was an important member of the team which beat Percy Park to win the Northumberland Senior Cup in 1914. He was also selected for County Honours against a side from Bordeaux. The Courant speculated that if he had survived he would have gone on to play rugby at a higher level. He was also a member of the Hexham Rowing Club. At the time of his death, his brother John was also at the Front in France.

In a letter to Mrs Nevison, Dan Clarence (Mickley) wrote:

> *"… During an attack on the German trenches on the 15th inst. Fred when quite close to the enemy's line, was struck by a bullet, which after going through the right arm entered his right breast causing him to bleed heavily. First aid failed to stop the bleeding and he must have died soon after…. I hope it may be of some consolation to you that he died splendidly in the great battle for liberty….."*

Frederick's body was lost with so many others, and he is commemorated on the Thiepval Memorial to men with no known grave.

Serjeant Frederick Harvey, aged 24
1/4th Battalion Northumberland Fusiliers
Died 16 September 1916

Frederick was born in Berwick upon Tweed, the son of Mr and Mrs Harvey who lived in Stocksfield when the War began. He was a married man and lived in Holy Island, Hexham before the hostilities. He was wounded during the attack of the 15 September and died of his wounds the following day.

Frederick was buried in Heilly Station Cemetery, Méricourt-L'Abbé.

During the Battle for the Somme, which raged from the first day of July to mid November, the 15th Company Machine Gun Corps was attached to the 15th Brigade, part of the 5th Division.

Private Harry (Henry) Griffin, aged 21 years
15th Company Machine Gun Corps
Died 23 September 1916

Harry was born in Newburn, and was the husband of Mrs B Griffin of Haugh Lane, Hexham. He had originally enlisted with the Northumberland Fusiliers, but was later transferred to the Machine Gun Corps.

Harry was buried in Bernafay Wood British Cemetery.

A memorial to the Machine Gun Corps is found in Hyde Park, London and bears the following harrowing inscription:

"Saul has slain his thousands; But David his tens of thousands"

The 1/8ᵗʰ Durham Light Infantry were part of 151ˢᵗ Brigade (50 Division). On the first day of the Battle of Flers-Courcellette this brigade was held in reserve. However, late on the evening of 15 Sept, elements of the brigade saw action when they replaced the depleted 149ᵗʰ in the Front Line. On 17 September the 1/8ᵗʰ Durham Light Infantry attacked the German trench system and were repulsed savagely. Further attacks in pouring rain on 18 September also failed to overcome German forces in a position known as the Crescent. On the evening of 20 September the 151ˢᵗ Brigade was relieved, moving back to Mametz Wood. The number of soldiers who died in this battalion during the period 15 – 24 September was two officers and thirty-seven men.[16]

Private Thomas Henry Marsh, aged 18
1/8ᵗʰ Battalion Durham Light Infantry
Died 24 September 1916

Thomas was the second son of Thomas and Mary Marsh of Barrasford. Thomas, however, lived in Gilesgate, Hexham. Before the war Mr Martin of Oakwood employed him as a groom. Thomas enlisted in the Durham Light Infantry at the outbreak of war but because of his young age he had only been at the Front for three months.

Thomas died of his wounds and is buried in Derancourt Communal Cemetery Extension.

Battle of Morval
25 – 28 September 1916

The Battle of Morval, which began on 25 September, was designed only to capture those objectives that had not been captured on 15 September, a total advance of 1200 –1500 yards. The plans were the fore-runner of the 'bite and hold' objectives favoured by General Plummer and were used by him at Messines and during Third Ypres in 1917, (Passchendaele).

The short depth of the potential gain and the limited front of 10,000 yards allowed the British Artillery to concentrate their firepower within this narrow strip and to wreak a devastating attack on the defenders, who since 15 September had been allowed very little chance to produce effective frontline defences. Tanks were used to follow the attack so that they could be directed against any points ahead proving difficult for the advancing infantry.

The infantry attacked at 12.35pm following closely behind a creeping artillery barrage. The time of attack was chosen in order to accommodate a simultaneous attack by the French Army. [21]

The 10th Northumberland Fusiliers, (68th Brigade 23rd Division) attacked north from the village of Martinpuich in order to capture a German trench system known to the Allies as 26th Avenue. The 10th Northumberland Fusiliers were involved in the initial attack and had been allotted two tanks in support; unfortunately only that on the right flank was operational during the attack. At Zero Hour the first lines of fusiliers advanced in the face of very heavy artillery and machine gun fire – they were unable to achieve their aim and many soldiers were killed or injured. The battalion was relieved at 5.15pm by the 12th Durham Light Infantry. During the first day of the attack the 10th Battalion reported that four officers and fifty-seven other ranks were killed in action. [20]

Along the length of the Front the fortified villages of Lesboeufs, Morval and Combles fell to the Allies and during the next morning Gueudecourt was added to these prizes.

Lance Corporal Thomas William Burn, aged 23
10th (Service) Battalion Northumberland Fusiliers
Died 25 September 1915

Thomas was born in Hexham, the third son of Mr J Burn of Crescent Terrace, Hexham. He enlisted soon after the outbreak of hostilities and at the time was working in the offices of Messrs L C and H K Lockhart. Thomas was a keen footballer and had played for Hexham Athletic, Hexham Argyle, Hexham Albion and Tyneside Rovers. He was Captain of Tyneside Rovers when they won the Cup. He also played cricket for Hexham Leazes. Thomas was killed during an attack on an enemy trench whilst leading a team of bombers; he was hit in the head by a bullet.

Thomas is commemorated on the Thiepval Memorial.

Corporal Frederick Robson, aged 21
C Company, 10th (Service) Battalion
Northumberland Fusiliers
Died 28 September 1915

Frederick Robson was the son of William and Annie Robson of North Terrace, Hexham. Before the war he was employed as a clerk in Mr J H Nicholson's office. He also played football for Hexham Albion. He was a cousin of Thomas Burn (see above) and was wounded in the thigh during the same attack that killed his cousin on 25 September; unlike Thomas he was able to get back to his own trenches. However, three days later he died of his wounds.

146

Frederick is buried in St Sever Cemetery, Rouen, which was a centre for Allied hospitals. He was evacuated from the trenches through dressing stations and divisional medical facilities to the army hospital in Rouen where he died of his wounds.

On 27 September, the 8th Battalion Suffolk Regiment (18th Division 53rd Brigade) was detailed to attack the defences of Thiepval, which were defended by the 180th Regiment of Wurtemburgers – defences regarded as impregnable. An intensive artillery bombardment began the offensive three days earlier, including a heavy gas attack of over five hundred 'lachrymatory shells' fired into Thiepval village.

The initial attack went in at 12.35pm using the 8th Suffolk on the right and the 10th Essex on the left (53rd Brigade) with the 54th Brigade to the left and 11th Division on the right. The Zollern Trench was captured late in the afternoon.

At 1pm the next day (28 September) the attack was renewed by the 8th Suffolk using 'B' and 'C' companies; remaining troops were left to hold the Zollern Trench, captured the day before. The Bulgar Trench was taken with relative ease, however during the capture of Schwaben Redoubt the fighting became very intense and it was not until 2.30pm that this position was completely taken and the new Front stabilised. On 29 September the Battalion was relieved and the men travelled by bus to Forceville.

During the fighting, the 8th Suffolk captured a large quantity of trench mortars, machine guns and automatic rifles at an expense of over 200 casualties including Second Lieutenant G S Long. [21, 22]

The Regimental History concludes that this action was the 'battalion's finest'.

Second Lieutenant Guy Steer Long, aged 26
8th (Service) Battalion Suffolk Regiment
Died 28 September 1916

Guy was born in London and was the third and youngest son of George Frederick and Blanche Katherine Long of Hexham. Since leaving school he had been employed by Cox's Bank in London and had been living with his sister in Coulsdon, Surrey. He enlisted in September 1915 and was given a commission in one of the Suffolk Battalions raised as part of Kitchener's Army. He transferred to another battalion of the Suffolk Regiment and went to the Front in June 1916.

Guy is buried in Villers-Bretonneux Military Cemetery.

The 1/7th Battalion West Yorkshire Regiment, a Territorial unit known as the Leeds Rifles, was part of the 146th Brigade that had been withdrawn from the Front and was based at Mailly-Maillet, approximately a mile and a half from the Front. Research shows that eleven soldiers from this battalion died on 27 September 1916. Nine of these are commemorated on the Thiepval Memorial. A possible explanation for this is that these men were part of a working party, wiped out by a direct hit from a shell. As explained earlier in this book, many such deaths occurred behind the Front Line in an area bombarded incessantly by shells. A few bodies were collected and buried, many were lost for ever in the mire of battle.

Rifleman George Mole, aged 29
1/7th Battalion West Yorkshire
(Prince of Wales's Own) Regiment
Died 27 September 1916

George was the second son of Mary Ann Mole of Brockalea Farm, Bardon Mill and was the husband of Hannah Bella Mole. Before enlisting with the Northumberland Fusiliers in Hexham in November 1915 he worked at Home Farm, Whitfield. He was subsequently transferred to the West Yorkshire Regiment.

George was killed in action and is commemorated on the Thiepval Memorial to the missing.

Private Thomas William Robson, aged 22
1/7th Battalion West Yorkshire Regiment
(Prince of Wales's Own)
Died 27 September 1916

William was the youngest son of Joseph and Elizabeth Robson of Ridley Terrace and was a single man. Before enlisting in June 1915 with the local Battalion of the Northumberland Fusiliers, he was employed in the market gardens of W Robinson of Tyne Green. For some time before that he had been employed at Woodley Field as a gardener. He was also a member of Hexham Unionist Club. Subsequently he was transferred to West Yorkshire Regiment.

Thomas is commemorated on the Thiepval Memorial to the missing.

On 24 September the 149th Brigade, including the 1/4th Northumberland Fusiliers, became the Divisional Reserve based at Mametz Wood. During this time the battalion supplied working parties, by day and night, working on the roads and the trench systems. On the afternoon of 29 September the Battalion moved back towards the Front near Bazentin Le Petit.[15] Sad to say, no details about the death of Private Mitchison are available.

Private William Mitchison, aged 26
1/4th Battalion Northumberland Fusiliers
Died 30 September 1916

William was born in Corbridge, the third son of Thomas and Margaret Mitchison of Eilans Gate, Hexham. William appears in the casualty records published in the Hexham Courant on 29 May as being wounded on 26 April at the Second Battle of Ypres. The Mitchisons' second son, Matthew, had already been killed serving with the Australian forces in the Dardanelles on 2 May 1915 and is commemorated on the Lone Pine Memorial to the missing. William's younger brother Nicholas was serving with the 4th/5th Battalion Black Watch nearby on the Somme.

William is commemorated on the Thiepval Memorial to the missing.

The Battle of Ancre Heights

To the north of Courcelette lay one of the most formidable German defensive systems on the Somme battlefield – the Regina Trench. This was two miles long running from south of Grandcourt to near Le Sars. It ran on the back side of a ridge for most of its length, making it difficult for artillery to get its range. At its rear lay Boom Ravine, a quarry, which could shelter several battalions of infantry in reserve. The trench itself was manned by hand-picked troops and defended by thick belts of wire. Not surprisingly, the Germans saw this as a very important defensive position.

The first attempt to take Regina Trench was made on 1 October by the Canadians. In this attack small numbers of men actually got into the trench system but were too few to stand any chance against the ensuing counter-attacks.

The 49th Battalion Canadian Infantry were involved in the second attempt to take Regina Trench and were placed on the extreme left of the attack involving eight Canadian Battalions. The War Diary records the battalion strength as 463 all ranks, a long way below the theoretical level of just over 1000 men. The attack involved elements of the North Lancashire Regiment on the left and Royal Canadian Rifles on the right. Three companies of the 49th Battalion were involved in the initial attack. The attack began in pelting rain on 8 October at 4.58 am, after a short artillery bombardment of the German lines. The advancing troops were met with fierce machine gun and rifle fire from the front and flanks and were very severely handled by the enemy. Men from the battalion reached Regina Trench and were seen no more. What was left of the battalion held Kenora Trench, part of the Zollern Graben, and a number of shell holes in front of the enemy's wire until they were relieved that night by the 42nd Battalion Canadian Infantry.

The Battalion Diary recorded casualties for this attack as thirty nine killed, sixty one missing and a hundred and three wounded.[23, 24]

Private Melvin Wallace Pearson Dent, aged 18
49th Battalion Canadian Infantry (Alberta Regiment)
Died 9 October 1916

Melvin was born in Corbridge in 1899 and was the son of Amos and Elizabeth Dent of Calgary, Alberta. His death was reported in Hexham by his grandparents, Mr and Mrs Pearson of Tyne Green. Amos Dent and his family emigrated to Canada and lived at 120, 13th Avenue West, Calgary. On attestation for the Canadian Military, Melvin lied about his age, as did so many young men. He claimed to have been born in 1896 so as to be of an age to join the services. He appears to have worked as a warehouse man. His medical papers show that he was 5ft 7inches tall with a dark complexion, blue eyes and dark brown hair. At the time of his death his father Amos was also serving in the Canadian Military and was stationed at Shorncliffe, Kent.

Melvin is buried in Regina Trench Cemetery, Grandcourt.

Many attempts were made to capture and hold the Regina Trench. Slowly, and at great cost, small sections were taken. On 25 October, the Canadian 44th Battalion attempted to take a further section of the trench near Farmer's Road but they were caught by enfilade machine gun fire on the right flank which inflicted heavy casualties. The War Diary states that the operation failed due to insufficient artillery barrage. Recorded casualties were: three officers killed, nine wounded and thirty seven other ranks killed, one hundred and twenty five wounded and twenty six missing, believed killed.[25]

It required another full attack on 11 November to capture the final length of Regina Trench.

Corporal Wilfred Jefferson, aged 25 years
44th Battalion Canadian Infantry
(New Brunswick Regiment)
Died 25 October 1916

Wilfred was the son of F W Jefferson who lived at the Woodlands, Hexham, before emigrating with his son to Canada. Both were plumbers while they lived in Hexham and followed the same trade in Canada. Wilfred joined the Canadian force in April 1915 and was trained as a bomber. In August he went to the Front. During a week's leave at Christmas, on 30 December, he married Daisy Mary Elizabeth Davidson of Delegate Hall, in Hexham Abbey.

A keen footballer, he had played for Northern Star Football Club and often gave demonstrations of Indian Club Swinging at St Wilfred's Institute in Hexham. Reports state that Wilfred was killed in action.

Wilfred is buried in Adanac Military Cemetery, Miraumont

During the Battle of Festubert in early 1916, both the 4th and 5th Battalions of the Black Watch lost huge numbers of men, dead and wounded; as a result, these two battalions were merged to form the 4th/5th Battalion and transferred to the 38th Division.

This amalgamated force entered the Battle of the Somme in late August and saw action during an attack on Hamel between 9 – 12 September where they suffered two hundred and eighteen deaths.

On 14 October they attacked the south face of the Schwaben Redoubt. In the early afternoon, 'B', 'C' and 'D' Companies advanced with 'A' Company in close support. Although the British barrage killed many of their men (that is to say they were lost to 'friendly fire'), they were able to take and hold their objective, holding on until they were relieved the next day. During this time they had suffered over 290 casualties. [22]

Private Nicholas Mitchison, aged 23
4th/5th Battalion Back Watch (Royal Highlanders)
Died 14 October 1916

Nicholas, who was born in Corbridge, was the youngest son of Thomas and Margaret Mitchison of Eilans Gate, Hexham. It is tragic to relate that before Nicholas died the family had already lost two sons: Matthew was killed in the Dardanelles in 1915, and is commemorated on the Corbridge Memorial and William died two weeks previously.

Nicholas is buried in Mill Road Cemetery, Thiepval.

The 2nd Battalion Royal Berkshire Regiment as part of the 25th Brigade, 8th Division were ordered to attack Zenith Trench which lay south of the village of Le Transloy between it and the village of Lesboeufs, running in a northwest to southeast direction. The attack began on the afternoon of 23 October. The advancing troops failed to achieve their first objective and a follow up attack began very early on 24 October. Again this failed, this time because of heavy machine gun and rifle fire coming from Zenith Trench. Later that morning the battalion was ordered to withdraw to its original starting position and was provided with troops to support a further attempt at taking the trench. By 25 October the 2nd Battalion was ordered to return to a support trench where they stayed until relieved by the 2nd Devonshire Regiment on the night of 27 October 1916. [26, 27]

Serjeant William Richard Thew, aged 21 years
Northumberland Hussars
Attached 2nd Battalion Royal Berkshire Regiment
Died 25 October 1916

William was the only child of Philip and Dorothy Thew of Shaftoe Leazes, Hexham. He joined the Northumberland Hussars, a territorial cavalry regiment, in 1913. Before the war Thomas was employed at Lloyds Bank, Collingwood Street, Newcastle and previously at the National Savings Bank. He was active in the Boy Scout Movement and was a founder member of St Wilfred's Debating Society.

The regiment was sent to the war zone shortly after war was declared. He saw action at the 1st Battle of Ypres in October 1914.

Late in 1915 he was attached to the 8th Division and was the confidential clerk to Lieutenant Colonel Roland Haig of the Royal Berkshire Regiment who wrote to his family:

> *"…I am most terribly sorry that I have lost a personal friend and I can sympathize with you in your great loss … He and I were both coming out for a few hours rest from the battle and he was hit by a shell and killed. I can say he did invaluable work in the firing line at Battalion Headquarters…"*

Roland Haig also made the following tribute, which was published in Hexham Parish Magazine December 1916:

> *"To these and to all others who have been called to pay the sorest price of victory we tender our heartfelt sympathy. The Mother of Him who bore the worlds sorrows, through whose own soul also the sword pierced at the Sacrifice of*

her Son, knows the thoughts and anguish of all mothers' hearts today."

William is commemorated on the Thiepval Memorial.

During late October the 149th Brigade (including the 1/5th Northumberland Fusiliers) were based in the Front Line waiting to take part in further attacks on the German positions. These attacks were postponed twice, eventually going in on 3 November. The Battalion War Diary reports that a further attack was postponed because of the bad state of the roads and the ground. During those two weeks there appears to have been torrential rainfall, turning the terrain into a quagmire. The War Diary does not mention the circumstances of Robert's death[16, 28] although the War Diary for the sister battalion, 1/4 Northumberland Fusiliers, reports that the German artillery was very active during this time.[15]

Private Robert Matthew Welch, aged 19 years
1/5th Battalion Northumberland Fusiliers
Died 28 October 1916

Robert was born in North Terrace, Hexham on 28 October 1898. He was the eldest son of Robert and Leah Mary Welch of Priestpopple, Hexham. Mr Welch ran a local hairdressing and tobacconist business based in Priestpopple. Robert attended Hexham Grammar School. After leaving, he was employed at Lloyds Bank in Gateshead. He joined the Colours in May 1915. He was a member at Hexham Golf Club and attended Hexham Congregational Church.

In July 1916 the Hexham Herald reported that Robert was in King George's Hospital London, suffering from shellshock. It appears that in the terrible months of 1916 Robert suffered on a number of occasions from this dreadful condition.

Robert is commemorated on the Thiepval Memorial to the missing.

The 149th Brigade attack on Grid Trench and Hook Sap
13 – 19 November 1916

During the middle of November, the 149th Brigade (1/4, 1/5, 1/6, and 1/7 Northumberland Fusiliers) made attacks both on Grid Trench and Hook Sap, which had been the scene of great activity by the Germans in the attempt to increase the overall strength of these positions; they were strongly defended.

The initial attack on 14 November took place using the 1/5th Battalion Northumberland Fusiliers on the right and the 1/7th on the left. The 1/4th was to be in support, whist the 1/6th was ordered to hold the Front Line to the left of the 1/7th and to support the attack using Lewis gun and rifle fire.

The initial objective for the 1/5th Northumberland Fusiliers was Grid Trench, and for the 1/7th the capture of Hook Sap and Grid Trench and also Blind Trench. It was a period of appallingly wet weather on the Somme at this time, and all of the trenches were waterlogged.

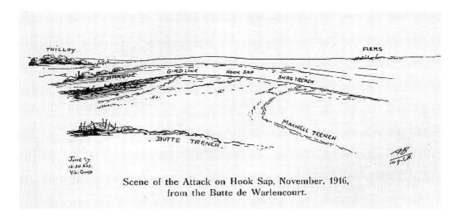

Scene of the Attack on Hook Sap, November, 1916,
from the Butte de Warlencourt.

Captain Buckley wrote:

"Mud was everywhere, in parts up to the waist, and what was worse, the thicker, more tenacious kind that just covered the boots and clung in heavy masses. The exertion of forcing our way step by step in an already heavily burdened state during our various moves about this line remains in my mind as some of most strenuous and exhausting times of the whole War." [17]

By 3pm the 1/5th Northumberland Fusiliers had occupied 150 yards of Grid Trench; the 1/7th had also taken their objectives and repulsed a number of counter-attacks. Later that night part of the 1/4th Northumberland Fusiliers were brought into the attack and formed part of the defence line in Snag Trench. After a number of enemy counter-attacks on 6 November the Brigade was forced back to the original jumping-off trenches; the British were left without any portion of the Grid Line.

During the night of 17 November the 149th Brigade was relieved by troops of the 1st Division.

During these attacks and desperate defences, the 149th Brigade made up of territorial regiments from Northumberland lost 10 officers and 297 men killed. The greatest number of casualties was from the 1/5th and 1/7th Battalions, who were involved in the initial attack.

Private Ernest Cairns Riley, aged 23 years
1/5th Battalion Northumberland Fusiliers
Died 14 November 1916

Ernest was the eldest son of Mrs Riley of Haugh Lane, Hexham. When war broke out he was a newly married man, living in Hallstile Bank. Before the war he worked for Messrs Lobley of Hallstile Bank. He was well known for his interest in football and billiards and was secretary of the 'Pats'. He went out to France with the first consignment of 1/4th Northumberland Fusiliers in April 1915. Ernest was gassed in the initial days of the *Second Battle of Ypres* and returned to England to recover. On returning to France he was transferred to the 1/5th and was part of the Bombing Company. It appears that Ernest was killed during a charge against the enemy lines.

His company commanding officer Lieutenant H Armstrong, wrote to his wife:

"Your husband was a gallant soldier and a credit to his company."

At the time of Ernest's death, his brother Justin (Tyneside Scottish) was lying wounded in hospital in Glasgow.

Ernest's body lies in Warlencourt British Cemetery.

Private Samuel Robert Hutton, aged 26 years
1/7th Battalion Northumberland Fusiliers
Died 14 November 1916

Samuel was the son of Wallace and Hannah Hutton and was born in Birtley, Co Durham. He was a married man with one child and lived in Eilan's Gate Hexham. He was an experienced Territorial, having served four years with the Durham Light Infantry. Before the war he was employed as a stoker at Hexham Gas Works. He was drafted through the Derby Scheme into the Northumberland Fusiliers and went to France in September 1916.

Samuel was killed in action and is commemorated on the Thiepval Memorial to the missing.

Captain John Wilfred Robinson, aged 22 years
1/4th Battalion Northumberland Fusiliers
Died 15 November 1916

John Robinson was the second son of Mr and Mrs John Robinson of South Park, Hexham. He was educated at Battle Hill School under Mr Rogerson and then at St Bees in Cumbria. After leaving school he became a law student with Messrs Baty and Fisher, to whom he was articled. He had attained his intermediate examinations and was studying for his finals when war broke out. He was a playing member of Tynedale Rugby Club and enjoyed motor sports. John, known as Wilfie to his friends, joined the Northumberland Fusiliers in early

August and was gazetted 2nd Lieutenant in September 1914. He travelled to France in April 1915 and was involved in the Second Battle of Ypres. He was wounded at St Julien on 25 April 1915 but was able to return to the Battalion in November 1915, spending the winter months in the trenches around the Ypres Salient. He was not with the Battalion during their attacks on the Somme during September 1916 as he was at an instruction course for company commanders. He was recalled to the Battalion to take command of 'B' Company following the great loss of life the Northumberland Fusiliers suffered on 15 September near High Wood.

Wilfie was killed by a bullet to the head and died instantaneously whilst leading 'B' Company in its attack on German trenches.

Wilfie is commemorated on the Thiepval Monument.

Private George William Boustead, aged 21 years
'A' Company, 1/4th Battalion Northumberland Fusiliers
Died 15 November 1916

George was the eldest son of George and Annie Boustead of Orchard Terrace; before the war he worked as miner. He joined up shortly after the outbreak of war and saw action at the *Second Battle of Ypres* in April 1915. His bother Jack was serving with the Navy.

George was killed by a bullet in his head and is commemorated on the Thiepval Memorial to the missing.

Serjeant William Anthony Charlton, aged 37 years
1/6th Battalion Northumberland Fusiliers
Died 16 November 1916

William was the second son of Mr and Mrs G Charlton of Jobbler's Stile, Hallstile Bank and before the war was employed with his father in the family joinery business. He was a single man. He had seen service in the Boer War in South Africa with the old 1st V.B.N.F. For this service William had been presented with the King Edward Medal and four bars. On his return from the Boer War, with the other surviving heroes he was presented with a silver watch from the tradesmen of the town. In 1908 he was presented with the Territorial Force Efficiency Medal and a certificate commemorating service of 10 years and 56 days from 4 February 1898 until 31 March 1908. As a Private, William won the Robinson Trophy for general efficiency in 1909. After mobilization in 1914 he remained at the Ponteland ranges as a musketry instructor until he went to the Front in September 1916.

William is commemorated on the Thiepval Memorial, having no known grave.

From 5 November the 1/9th Durham Light Infantry (DLI) was in action during the attack on Grid Trench and Hook Sap, with 'A' and 'C' companies going over the top at 9am. By mid morning they had captured Grid Trench. However, the Germans mounted fierce counter-attacks and the remnants of 1/9th were forced to withdraw. On the evening of 6 November they were relieved by the 1/5th DLI and spent the time until 16 November in a camp near Mametz Wood. The Battalion War Diary records 406 casualties of which 2 officers and 79 other ranks were killed.

On 16 November the majority of what remained of the

battalion moved to Millencourt (about two miles east of Albert). The diary also records that a hundred men were sent to Meault (just over a mile south of Albert) to help in the unloading of ammunition in a railway siding.[29]

Captain Harry John Spencer, aged 42 years
1/9ᵗʰ Battalion Durham Light Infantry,
Died 17 November 1916

Harry Spencer was the third son of George Edward Spencer of Newcastle (who died before the war) and Mrs Spencer of Hazelhurst, Hexham. He was educated at the Royal Grammar School Newcastle and served his apprenticeship with Messrs Hawthorn, Leslie and Company. Subsequently he worked in the drawing office and latterly in the Elswick Works. After this he joined his father in the family tea and coffee business. At his father's death he ran this business with the help of his brother, who during the war served in the King Edward's Horse. He was an accomplished and eclectic sportsman. A keen rower, he stroked several winning crews for the Tyne Rowing Club. He played football and captained Summerhill F.C. He also played rugby and captained Percy Park R.F.C. and played occasionally for Tynedale. Harry served as Vice President of the Northumberland Rugby Union. He was a member of Hexham and Corbridge Golf Club and in the summer played cricket with Hexham Cricket Club.

Having joined the Citizens' Training Corps at the onset of war, he took a commission with the Durham Light Infantry in April 1915, going to the Front in June. In December he was promoted to Lieutenant and was

attached to the Machine Gun Corps in the spring of 1916. He was wounded by a sniper's bullet in June, returning to the Front in September. Soon afterwards he was promoted to Captain and placed in charge of a trench mortar battery.

The Hexham Courant reported that Captain Spencer died of wounds accidentally received. It is likely that some munitions exploded as Harry and his fellow soldiers were unloading a train as was often the case.

Harry is buried in Dernancourt Communal Cemetery Extension, near Albert.

Even though the Battle of the Somme officially ended on 18 November, the Front Line continued to demand manning and repairing. Unlike medieval campaigns, modern armies did not allow the troops to go home when the battle was over. The winter of 1916 – 17 was particularly severe for the troops in the field.

The Battalions (1/4th, 1/5th, 1/6th and 1/7th Northumberland Fusiliers) moved to Front Line trenches near the Butte of Warlencourt on the evening of 30 December relieving four battalions of the 1st and 3rd Divisions.

During this tour of duty, which lasted throughout January, the Headquarters Diary for the 50th Division stated: "casualties (killed and wounded) suffered by the Division averaged 12 per diem".
On the last day of the year the 1/5th lost two men: Lance Corporal James Pearson from Newcastle and Private Robert Henderson from Hexham.

Private Robert Henderson, aged 22
1/5ᵗʰ Battalion, Northumberland Fusiliers
Died 31 December 1916

Robert was born in Gosforth, and was the son of John T Henderson. He was married to Mary Alice Henderson of Gilesgate, Hexham and was the father of one child. Before enlisting he was employed as a barman at the Broom Hill.

Early on in the war he was wounded and spent time in convalescence at Hexham, returning to the Front in November 1916.

Robert is buried in A.I.F. Burial Ground, Fleurs.

References

1. Falls, C. *History of the 36ᵗʰ (Ulster) Division,*
    Pub: 1922, reprinted Naval and Military Press 2003.

2. Middlebrook, M. *The First Day of the Somme.*
    Pub: Penguin Books 1971.

3. Cooke, Captain C.H. *Historical records of the 16ᵗʰ (Service) Battalion Northumberland Fusiliers.*
    Pub: Council of Newcastle and Gateshead Incorporated Chamber of Commerce 1923.

4. Stewart, G. and Sheen, J. *A History of the Tyneside Scottish,*
    Pub: Pen and Sword Books, 1999.

5. Shakespear, Lt Col. J. *Thirty Fourth Division, 1915-1919,*
    Pub: 1921, reprinted Naval & Military Press 1998.

6. Terman, Brig-Gen T. *History of Tyneside Scottish,*
    Pub: 1919, reprinted Naval & Military Press 2003.

7. Sheen, J. A. *History of the Tyneside Irish,*
    Pub: Pen and Sword, 1998.

8. Wylly, Col H. C. *The Border Regiment in the Great War,*
    Pub: Gale and Polden Ltd, 1924.

9. WO 95/2422. War Diary, *1st Battalion Cameronians (Scottish Rifles).*

10. Norman, T. *The Hell they called High Wood,*
    Pub: Pen and Sword, 2003.

11. WO 95/2013. War Diary, 9th Battalion *Northumberland Fusiliers.*

12. Cooke, Captain C. H. *Historical Records of the 9th (Service) Battalion Northumberland Fusiliers.*
    Pub: Council of Newcastle and Gateshead Incorporated Chamber of Commerce 1928.

13. Stewart, Lt Col. J. *Fifteenth (Scottish) Division 1914-1919,*
    Pub: 1926, reprinted Naval and Military Press 2003.

14. Private Communication.

15. WO 95/2826. *War Diary, 1/4th Battalion Northumberland Fusiliers.*

16. Wyrell, E. *The Fiftieth Division, 1914-1919,*
    Pub: 1939, reprinted Naval and Military Press 2002.

17. Buckley, Captain F. *War History of the Seventh Northumberland Fusiliers,*
Pub: T. M. Grierson.

18. Sheffield, G. *The Somme,*
Pub: Cassell, 2003.

19. Hart, P. *The Somme,*
Pub: Weidenfield & Nicholson, 2005.

20. WO 95/2182. War Diary, *10th Battalion Northumberland Fusiliers.*

21. Murphy, Lieut-Col C.C.R. *History of the Suffolk Regiment, 1914-1927,*
Pub: 1928, reprinted naval & Military Press 2002.

22. Stedman, M. *Thiepval,*
Pub: Pen and Sword, 1995.

23. War Diary, *49th Battalion Canadian Infantry.*
http://data2.collectionscanada.ca

24. Reed, P. *Courcelette,*
Pub; Pen and Sword, 1998.

25. War Diary, *44th Battalion Canadian Infantry,*
http://data2.collectionscanada.ca

26. WO 95/1729. *War Diary, 2nd Battalion Royal Berkshire Regiment.*

27. War Diary, *2nd Battalion Royal Berkshire Regiment,*
www.thewardrobe.org.uk

28. WO 95/2828. *War Diary, 1/5th Battalion Northumberland Fusiliers.*

29. WO 95/2840. *War Diary, 1/9th Durham Light Infantry.*

CHAPTER NINE

THE WESTERN FRONT, 1916

"...they endure
Sad, smoking, flat horizons, reeking woods,
And foundered trench-lines volleying doom for doom ...
The legions who have suffered and are dust."

Siegried Sassoon, *Prelude, The Troops*

The Howe Battalion, (188th Brigade), as part of the 63rd Royal Naval Division arrived at the Front on the 30 July 1916, with the 189th and 190th Brigades arriving slightly later to relieve the 47th Division. The sector held by the division was between Lens and Vimy Ridge, through the ruins of the two mining towns of Calonne and Angres and south to the Souchez River. They held this sector until 16 September when the 37th Division relieved them.

The soldiers of Howe Battalion were in trenches south of Bully Grenay. Although this sector was regarded as a quiet posting, this did not mean that there were no casualties. It is reported in Frederick Cornelius's book that in one incident four men of the Howe Battalion were killed and twenty-two wounded.[1]

**Able Seaman Louis Charlton, aged 29
Howe Battalion, Royal Naval Division
Died 29 August 1916**

Louis was born in Haydon Bridge and was the youngest son of Anthony and Anne Charlton of Allendale and latterly of Kitty Fisk, Hexham. His brother, Mr J J Charlton lived at Glenside, Hexham. He enlisted in the

Royal Naval Division within days of the onset of hostilities. In February 1915 he went with the Howe Battalion to Gallipoli and was wounded in action. Subsequently he was sent to Egypt to recover from enteric fever. After the withdrawal of troops from the Dardanelles the Howe Battalion was transferred to the Western Front and was involved in heavy fighting. Louis died a hero's death, in action.

Louis' commanding officer wrote to his relatives:

> *" I am very sorry to have to write to you ...There was a very fierce bombardment of our trenches and the enemy were dropping very large shells when a sentry was struck and your brother without any regard for his own danger, rushed from his shelter and he was killed tending the wounded man. No man could have a nobler death. He was in the same Company with me on the landing (Dardanelles) and I have known and trusted him ever since... I told him how I relied on his cheerfulness and kindness to my wounded."*

Louis is buried in Tranchée de Mecknes Cemetery, Aix-Noulette.

Flanders 1916

The 10th Battalion South Wales Borders (38th Division) left the Somme Battlefield at the end of July 1916. During their time on the Somme this unit had been used during the assault on the Mametz Wood and had lost many of its men. It was unable to return to major action until one year later at

Passchendaele. After a period of rest near Bollezelle the 38th replaced the 4th Division in the St Julien sector in the Ypres salient.

On 6 October a patrol from the 10th South Wales Borders rushed a sap under the command of Captain G F H Charlton. A sap was a trench system running into No Man's Land at 90 degrees to the main trench, which could be used as a listening point or a point for localised action. They killed the six Germans in residence, but had to retire when strong enemy reinforcements arrived. As the raiding party retired it was noticed that Captain Charlton and Private Daniel Spanswick were missing. Second Lieutenant Taylor and Sergeant P F Evans returned to look for them, despite heavy machine gun fire. No trace of Private Spanswick was found, but Captain Charlton was seen being carried away on a stretcher by the Germans. Later he was reported by the Germans as having been killed. Taylor and Evans received the MC and MM respectively for their gallantry.[2]

Captain George Fenwick Hedley Charlton, aged 24
10th (Service) Battalion South Wales Borderers
Died 6 October 1916

George was the eldest son of John Charlton JP and Ann Fenwick Charlton of School House, Seaton Delaval, Northumberland. He was the grandson of Mr G F Hedley of Hexham. He was educated at Morpeth Grammar School, where he held a Governors' Scholarship. He graduated from Armstrong College (Newcastle), Durham University, with a BSc in Mining Engineering in 1913. Whilst at Armstrong College he obtained his Colours for cricket and athletics. At University he was also a member of the Officers Training Corps. At the beginning of hostilities George was employed by Ebbw Vale Steel, Coal and Iron Company in South Wales and initially joined the South Wales Borderers as a Private.

In January 1915 he was given a commission and in April was gazetted Captain. Just before he left for France he was given the command of a company and rode at its head when the battalion was reviewed by Queen Anne at Winchester. He was killed whilst leading his men in a night raid on German trenches.

George is buried in Bedford House Cemetery, Ypres.

The following is found on his headstone:

SLEEP LIGHTLY LAD
THOU ART KING'S GUARD
AT DAYBREAK

Two years later, on 26 August 1918, his only brother, Lieutenant William Godfrey Charlton (15th Battalion Durham Light Infantry), was killed and is buried in Warlencourt British Cemetery on the Somme.

References

1.   Cornelius, F. *Path of Duty,*

2.   Atkinson C T. *History of the South Wales Borders,*
     Pub: 1931, reprinted Ray Westlake, Newport 1999.

CHAPTER TEN

WAGNERIAN OVERTURES

"What passing-bells for these who die as cattle?"
Wilfred Owen, *Anthem for Doomed Youth*

Overview

The Battle of the Somme was officially recognised as being over after the capture of Beaumont Hamel in November 1916. Fighting to capture the other surrounding heights continued through the winter of 1916-1917. The winter was unusually severe with long periods of sub-zero temperatures.

During an icy January the Royal Naval Division (63rd Division) was involved in holding the Front Line near Grandcourt, which was still occupied by the Germans; on the nights of 18 and 19 January 1917 both the 188th and 189th Brigades (Drake Battalion, see Percy Robson, below) occupied the trenches opposite Grandcourt running south of the River Ancre. The War Diary states that on the night of 19 January they were escorted by guides from the Duke of Wellington's Regiment and 'C' and 'D' Companies took over the Front Line, with the Nelson Battalion on the left and the Royal Marine Light Infantry on the right. Throughout this time the Front was under dangerous artillery fire from both sides. [1, 2]

The ground was too hard for digging, so frozen-over shell holes were used as forward outposts. Any movement during the day or night brought on continuous shelling.

Able Seaman Percy Robson, aged 19
Drake Battalion, Royal Naval Division
Died 19 January 1917

Percy was the son of Mr and Mrs R Robson of Richmond Place, Hexham. Before enlisting in March 1915, he was employed by the North-Eastern Railways as a fireman. After his basic training at Crystal Palace and at Blandford he served in the Dardanelles. Following the evacuation of all forces from the Dardanelles the battalion was transferred to France in May 1916. Percy was wounded in November 1916 returning to his battalion later that year.

Percy is commemorated on the Thiepval Memorial.

Action of Miraumont, 17 – 18 February 1917

The 23rd Royal Fusiliers, stationed near Courcelette, were also suffering from the cold conditions. A few days before the attack it was recorded that a sentry froze to death at his post. It was also recorded that water carried up to the Front Line arrived as blocks of ice.

On the day before the attack the weather became milder and a thaw set in. The attack on 17 February was made in the dark at 5.45am across No Man's Land, which by now was knee deep in mud and slush. The assaulting troops were met immediately by heavy machine-gun fire, although they were able to secure a small section of the German Front Line trench. The War Diary reports that by 7.50am the battalion had suffered heavy casualties and after another counter attack they were forced to withdraw and consolidate. Later in the day the remnants of the battalion were reorganised under the orders of the 1st Kings Royal Rifle Corps.[3]

During the attack, the Battalion lost eight officers and thirty other ranks killed, with four officers and one hundred and sixty five other ranks wounded and one officer and thirty two other ranks missing.

Lance Corporal Nevison Charles Barnfather, aged 31
23rd (Service) Battalion Royal Fusiliers
Died 17 February 1917

Nevison was the youngest son of Mr and Mrs Barnfather of Brookside, Hexham. After gaining a County Scholarship at the Hexham Board School, he completed his education at Rutherford College, Newcastle. From August 1901, he was employed by the Hexham Courant, initially in the commercial department and latterly as a reporter.

However, it was in the field of flat green bowling that he will be remembered. He won numerous competitions at the Hexham Bowling Club, winning the club championship and Overstone Cup in 1912. He was a member of the side that won the Heart of England championship and was also a member of the Hexham side which played the Australian Team when they visited in 1912. In 1913 Nevison represented North Eastern Counties with Mr R B Charlton, reaching the finals when they were beaten by a pair from Bristol. He joined the Royal Fusiliers under the Derby Scheme in early 1916 and completed his training at Portobello near Edinburgh.
In July 1916 he went out to France

and was promoted to Lance Corporal. He was killed by a sniper's bullet as his battalion went over the top on 17 February.

Nevison is buried at Regina Trench Cemetery, Grandcourt.

Towards the end of February, along the entire length of the war-torn Somme battleground, there were indications that the Germans were retreating eastwards. As the Allies began advancing into No Man's Land they nonetheless met tough rearguard troops whose role was to resist any large-scale penetration.

Australian forces were detailed to capture the town of Bapaume during the early part of March. Both the 1st and 5th Divisions (56th Battalion) faced the Germans in front of the town and on 3 March the bombardment of the German defences began, even though it was known that the Germans were preparing to leave the town. The main attack went in on 10 March when a significant part of the German Front Line was taken by Australian forces with the minimum of opposition.[4]

Lieutenant Arthur Davison, aged 32
56th Battalion Australian Infantry
Died 8 March 1917

Arthur was born in Newcastle, the son of Grace Davison who was, by the time of his death, a widow living in Woodside, Hexham. His father was John Davison, a shipbroker of Blyth. He was educated at Darlington Grammar School, after which he was employed as a clerk with the London

Joint Stock Bank in Newcastle. He was also a member of the local Territorials.

Arthur emigrated to Australia in 1912 to become a farmer. Shortly after the start of hostilities he enlisted in the Australian Infantry as a Private and set sail from Sydney in November 1914 as part of the 43rd Battalion Australian Infantry. He fought with the Anzac forces in Gallipoli and during 1915 was promoted to Company Sergeant-Major. In early 1916 he was posted to France and recommended for a commission, which he received at the beginning of 1917. He was killed whilst in action with the 56th Battalion near Bapaume.

Arthur is buried in the Guards' Cemetery, Lesboeufs.

Arthur is not commemorated on the memorial in the Abbey Grounds, but his name is on the memorial in St Aidan's United Reformed Church, Hencotes. His headstone at Lesboeufs bears the following inscription:

THE DEARLY LOVED SON OF THE
LATE JOHN AND GRACE DAVISON
BLYTH

While the Battle of the Somme was still raging in 1916, the German High Command ordered the development of a trench fortress system at a significant distance behind the existing Front. The Germans knew this system as Siegfriedstellung but to the Allies it was known as the Hindenburg Line.

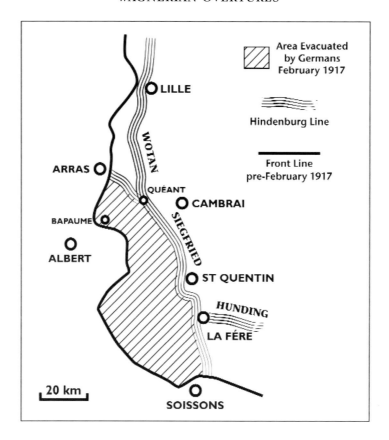

The concept was to build a fortified defensive zone from the Belgian coast to the Moselle River. The most important part of this defensive line was known as the Seigfriedstellung which ran between Arras and St Quentin, continuing past Laon to the Ainse near Soisson. This cut off a large salient held by the Germans which was to be made redundant. Further sectors of this line also were named after Wagnerian gods: the Wotanstellung ran north from Quéant up to Lille from where it ran to the coast at Ostend and was known as the Flandernstellung; the Hundingstellung ran from La Fére to the Champagne battlefield.

Thus, the Hindenburg Line was a system of successive *stellung* systems in the area between Arras and St Quentin. They were made up of between two and five trenches with

178

communication trenches between, artillery observation posts and batteries, machine gun emplacements, shellproof infantry accommodation, command posts and aid stations. This defensive zone could be up to five miles deep. Each trench was fronted by thick belts of barbed wire in spiralled bands up to twenty yards thick and positioned to funnel attacking troops into the deadly killing zone of the concrete machine gun nests.

The *stellungs* were built on the reverse slopes of hills, denying observation to the attackers. Groups of soldiers crossing over the crests of the slope could be slaughtered by unseen artillery.

The earlier German practice of packing their Front Line trenches with defenders, who would suffer from artillery bombardment, was dropped. Instead, outposts and machine-gun positions would thinly defend the new Front Line, which was about six hundred yards wide. If this zone were breached then attackers would face a second zone of defence made up of inter-connecting strongpoints, supported by a third line consisting of deep ditches and ferro-concrete blockhouses.

The main date for the retreat by the German forces was set for 16 March and was code-named Operation Alberich, after the malicious dwarf of the Wagnerian Nibelung Saga. This German retreat involved following the order:

> *"Der Gegner muss ein vollig ausgesogenes land vorfinden."*

The import of this was that the entire zone between the old fighting line and the new was to be made into a desert. To meet this aim the Germans razed villages to the ground, poisoned wells, cut down all trees and where possible laid all manner of booby traps and delayed-action explosives. The malicious booby-traps included trip-wires in trenches, dugouts and cellars, connected to a wide range of articles likely to be moved – souvenirs, doorways, woodpiles etc. Many explosives were found in chimneys and stoves, designed to explode when a fire was lit. Bombs with time-delayed fuses set off by acid corrosion, clockwork or friction were used to cause maximum disruption and to slow down the Allied advance into the zone vacated by the Germans.[5]

The author Ernst Junger, a lieutenant in the Hanoverian Fusilier Regiment, describes the retreat as 'an orgy of destruction' in his book *Storm of Steel*: [6]

> *"The country over which the enemy were to advance had been turned into an utter desolation. The moral justification of this has been much discussed. However, it seems to me that the gratified approval of armchair warriors and journalists is incomprehensible. When thousands of peaceful persons are robbed of their homes, the self-destruction of power may at least keep silence. As for the necessity, I have of course as a Prussian officer, no doubt whatever. War is the harshest of all trades, and masters of it can only entertain humane feelings so as they do not harm."*

References

1. WO 95/3114. War Diary, *Drake Battalion.*

2. Jerrold, D. *Royal Naval Division,*
    Pub: 1923, republished Naval & Military Press 2002.

3. WO 95/1372. *War Diary, 23rd Battalion Royal Fusiliers.*

4. Australian Official Histories, First World War.
    www.awm.gov.au

5. Oldham, P. *The Hindenburg Line,*
    Pub: Pen and Sword 1997.

6. Junger, E. *Storm of Steel,*
    Pub: Penguin 2003.

CHAPTER ELEVEN

1917 – ATTACK, ATTACK, ATTACK

"But with the best and meanest Englishmen
I am one in crying, God save England …
She is all we know and live by, and we trust
She is good and must endure, loving her so"

Edward Thomas, d. 9 April 1917, *This is no Case of Petty Right and Wrong*

Overview

At sea, Germany declared unrestricted submarine warfare (see Chapter 18), which would eventually bring America into the war on the side of the Allies (April 6) and which very nearly brought the Allies to their knees. The French, under Nivelle, conducted disastrous attacks on the *Aisne*, causing mutinies within the ranks of the French Army from which it was never to recover. As a result the British Army had to shoulder more and more of the fighting on the Western Front. The Canadians fought a highly successful battle at *Vimy Ridge*. The need for attacks by British and forces from the Empire during April and May – to cover up deficiencies in the French Army – led to an extended campaign with ever increasing numbers of casualties.

In Russia, Tsar Nicholas II abdicated as a result of the Russian Revolution which eventually brought Lenin and the Communists to power. After a number of German victories on the Eastern Front the Russians opened separate peace negotiations with Germany – known as Brest-Litovsk – which would take Russia out of the war.

During the summer months the Italians fought the 10th, 11th, and 12th Battles of Isonzo, which ended in failure and which

181

forced the British to deploy much-needed troops from the Western Front to Italy to support their ally.

Fighting against the Turks in the Middle East, British troops entered Baghdad; later in the year T E Lawrence and his Arab Allies captured Aguaba. In December the Turks suffered further reversals as Jerusalem fell to the British.

On the Western Front the British captured the *Messines Ridge* near Ypres in spectacular fashion, but were later dragged through a costly, five-month's campaign east of Ypres, known as *Passchendaele*.

In November the British launched a surprise attack at *Cambrai* using tanks; after initial successes this ground to a halt.

The Battles of Arras and Vimy Ridge

The withdrawal to the Hindenburg line by the Germans began in February 1917. As described above in Chapter Nine, the Hindenburg Line was a meticulously prepared defensive position consisting of deep, well-engineered trenches and dugouts, well-positioned machine-gun post and field-gun emplacements. In some places up to five successive lines of fortification were evident.[1]

The British attack (*Arras*) in April was designed to act as a diversionary action to the forth-coming French attack devised by the French Commander-in-Chief Robert Nivelle, who had promised the French Government that he could swiftly bring about the end of the war. The British forces prepared to attack on a Front to the north and east of Arras on 9 April. In the north the British First Army Canadian Corps under Lieutenant General Sir Julian Byng had Vimy Ridge as its objective. Other British forces attacked eastwards on Fronts to both the north and south of Arras.

However, the French plans for the *Second Battle of the Aisne,* scheduled for 16 April, were readily known by the Germans who took appropriate defensive measures.

The attack by the French army was an unmitigated failure, with the French suffering over 40,000 casualties on the first day, which mounted steadily over the next few days to a staggering 187,000 casualties. As a result Nivelle was dismissed but more of a problem was the occurrence of wide scale mutinies in the French army, which were never detected by the Germans. However, to cover up this dissent in the French Army, British troops were forced to prolong their attack along the Arras Front into June, which resulted in mounting casualties for very little gain.

Vimy Ridge

On Easter Monday, 9 April 1917, all four Canadian divisions attacked together for the first and only time at *Vimy Ridge.* It is generally accepted that this was a defining moment in Canada's history, since the divisions were fighting as a national body. Having said this, Newfoundland was not yet part of Canada, and its troops fought under their own banner as part of the British Empire. *Vimy Ridge* was an important part of the German defences, which protected the mines and factories of the Douai plain, products from which were essential to the Germans for the continuation of the war.

The ridge was over 450 feet high and was riddled with caves. To these had been added strong points, elaborate trench systems and underground tunnels. Previous attempts to capture the ridge had failed and there was a large body of opinion that it was impregnable.

The Canadian infantry attack was preceded by an intense artillery bombardment which lasted three weeks and involved 1000 guns.

The attack began at 5.30am in freezing snow and sleet. The initial forces advanced behind a creeping barrage – a 'curtain' of falling shells which crept forward just ahead of the advancing troops. The ground conditions were very bad, with cloying, slippery mud hampering the heavily-laden Canadians as they crossed No Mans Land which was a lunar landscape of shell holes.

By the middle of the afternoon, three of the four divisions had captured most of Vimy Ridge. On the next day Hill 145 was also taken, and by 12 April the victory was complete.[2]

The poet Edward Thomas, quoted at the head of this chapter, died on 9 July, as did Ernest Walton and many others. Siegfried Sassoon, another great poet of the time was injured by a sniper and returned to England.

The 78th Battalion Canadian Infantry was part of 12th Brigade which had been allocated the task of capturing Hill 145. This was the dominant point on Vimy Ridge giving unrestricted observation of the German held territory to the east and therefore a key feature in the German defence network of trenches. It had been converted into a formidable redoubt. During the attack the troops to the left flank of 12th Brigade broke down and although the summit was taken, the Canadians were forced to withdraw when they came under sustained flanking fire from the right. By the evening the Germans had been removed from the top of Hill 145, but still the 12th Brigade suffered from incoming hostile fire from both its left and right flanks.[3]

Private Ernest Walton, aged 27
78th Battalion (Manitoba Regiment) Canadian Infantry
Died 9 April 1917

Ernest was the husband of Jean Walton (nee Balmer) of Nether Warden. He was the second son of John and Isabella Walton of Portland Terrace, Hexham. He was born in 1889 and emigrated to Canada in 1913. His future wife followed him and they were married in Winnipeg. Ernest made his living as a plumber, having served his apprenticeship with Mr G. Long of Hexham. He was involved in the local militia, the Winnipeg Grenadiers. He joined the Canadian Forces in 1915 and his attestation papers state he was 5 feet 7 inches tall with a ruddy complexion, fair hair and blue eyes.

When he came to England with the Canadian Forces, his wife came back to Hexham. He was killed during the Easter Monday attack on Vimy Ridge.

Major H R Linnells wrote to his wife:

> "... The one consolation that I can give you is that he died nobly doing his duty... He is buried on the ridge with a number of his comrades ... His death occurred very quickly and was quite painless. His last words to me were, 'please write and tell my wife'...."

Ernest is commemorated on the Vimy Memorial for men with no known grave.

The Vimy Memorial

It took twelve years to build this magnificent memorial to the Canadians who died in the Great War. With its two enormous 'pylons' and its twice life-sized figures, the edifice was constructed on Hill 145, the highest point of Vimy Ridge, overlooking the Douai Plain. It was designed by the Canadian sculptor and architect W S Allward, and his two giant pylons and twenty figures were carved *in situ* from limestone brought from Yugoslavia.

North rampant of Vimy Memorial looking down on symbolic tomb of Canadian soldier

After the war, the site for the Vimy battlefield park was 'the free gift in perpetuity of the French nation to the people of Canada', in recognition of the sixty thousand lives lost by that country, then part of the British Empire. It was the King of England, Edward VIII, who unveiled the memorial on 26 July 1936, calling it 'a consecration of love'. Of the men who died, eleven thousand two hundred and forty-nine have no known grave, and the names of these soldiers are inscribed on the memorial.

Vimy Ridge remains a dangerous area. Visitors are strongly recommended never to leave the marked paths because unexploded munitions are lurking still, ready to fulfill their deadly purpose. For a few years Vimy memorial has been effectively closed because extensive restoration is underway to restore the names, eroded by weathering.

View of Vimy Memorial

The Princess Patricia's Light Infantry attacked as part of the Canadian 3ʳᵈ Division on a Front of 250 yards. The initial phase of the attack was relatively straightforward because the preceding artillery bombardment had done its job. After passing the crater area in No Man's Land, the German Front and support lines were easily captured – the Bavarian troops surrendered with little fight. As they progressed into La Folie Wood, opposition increased and capturing Britt Trench proved to be a very difficult objective. It was eventually stormed, but the regiment began to take a lot of casualties from snipers on Hill 145, which units of the 4ᵗʰ Division had been unable to capture. During the afternoon of 10 April, Hill 145 was captured.[4]

Private John Christopher Forster, aged 28
Princess Patricia's Canadian Light Infantry
(Eastern Ontario Regiment)
Died between 9 and 10 April 1917

Christopher was the youngest son of John and Elizabeth Forster of Macleod, Alberta but formerly of Hexham. Mr and Mrs Forster and their two sons emigrated to Canada in 1911. Christopher enlisted in the Canadian Army in

January 1915 arriving in France in August 1916. His medical papers show that he was 5 ft 6 ins tall with fair complexion, hazel eyes and brown hair. Before going to Canada where he worked in farming, he had worked for Messrs William Fell and Company Limited, Nurserymen and Seedsmen of Hexham. His older brother George, also of the Canadian forces, had also been wounded.

Christopher is buried in La Chaudiere, Military Cemetery, Vimy. At the base of his headstone is the following inscription:

I HAVE FOUGHT A GOOD FIGHT
I HAVE KEPT THE FAITH
ASLEEP IN JESUS

Of the 100,000 Canadians that took part in the attack on Vimy Ridge, 3598 were killed and 7,004 were wounded.

In preparation for the *First Battle of the Scarpe*, 20th Northumberland Fusiliers were in the Front Line south of Arras. On 4th April at 6.20am the British bombardment for the forthcoming attack began, during which it is likely that Frederick Newman was killed by retaliatory enemy fire. On this first day the fusiliers had about fifty-five men wounded or killed. The bombardment lasted until Zero Hour on 9th April when the major attack began, in which all of the Tyneside Scottish Battalions were fully involved.

Private Frederick George Newman, aged 36
20ᵗʰ (Service) Battalion (Tyneside Scottish)
Northumberland Fusiliers
Died 4 April 1917

Frederick was born in Bournemouth, Hampshire, the son of George Newman and the late Mrs F. A Newman. He was married to Isabella and was the father of three children. They lived at Westbourne Grove, Hexham.

Before enlisting in late 1916 Frederick was a self-employed plasterer. He had been in France for only five weeks before he was killed. Frederick is buried in St Nicholas British Cemetery, Arras. Frederick had three brothers serving with the forces in France.

The First Battle of Scarpe: 9 – 14 April 1917

Further south, the British Army was also able to make dramatic advances on 9 April. North of the River Scarpe the 4ᵗʰ Division penetrated the German Lines and captured the village of Fampoux. South of the river the advances were less impressive. The objective of 34ᵗʰ Division attack, involving all three of its brigades (101ˢᵗ, 102ⁿᵈ, and 103ʳᵈ), was the capture of a ridge on which was positioned the German strongpoint of le Point du Jour Farm and three German Trench Systems designated Black, Blue and Brown. The 102ⁿᵈ Brigade (20ᵗʰ, 21ˢᵗ, 22ⁿᵈ and 23ʳᵈ Battalions Northumberland Fusiliers, Tyneside Scottish) formed the centre of the attack and to its left was 103rd Brigade, (24ᵗʰ, 25ᵗʰ, 26ᵗʰ and 27ᵗʰ Battalions Northumberland Fusiliers, Tyneside Irish).

The leading waves of the 21ˢᵗ and 22ⁿᵈ Battalions moved quietly into No Man's Land at 4.30am, close to the German wire. When the initial barrage lifted these battalions rushed into the enemy lines. Both these battalions took their initial objective, the Black Line, with ease and with minimal casualties. At about 8.30am 22nd Battalion captured its second objective, the Blue Line. The 20th and 23rd Battalions passed through these leading battalions in order to capture the third objective, the Brown Line. This was achieved, but at some cost. [567]

Private George Potts, aged 38
22nd (Service) Battalion (Tyneside Scottish)
Northumberland Fusiliers
Died 9 April 1917

George was the second son of William and Margaret Potts of Tyne Green, Hexham. Initially he had been rejected by the Forces but he joined up in November 1916 and was sent out to the Front in February 1917. George was employed by Messrs Henry Bell and Sons of Hexham. William was a keen rugby player who had been a member of the Tynedale team which beat Percy Park in the Northumberland Senior Cup at the County Ground, Gosforth, in March 1914. He was described as 'fast strong and untiring' and was regarded as one of Tynedale's best forwards. For a short time he was also associated with Winlaton Vulcans. He had taken part in foot racing at a number of local sports events.

Two of his brothers, Sergeant-Major W Potts (R.A.M.C) and Private Ralph Potts (Northumberland Fusiliers) were serving in France when George was killed.

It is believed that George was killed in his first action. He is commemorated on the Arras Memorial, which contains the names of over 35,000 soldiers who have no known graves.

Private Frederick Harold Gibson, aged 25
20th (Service) Battalion (Tyneside Scottish)
Northumberland Fusiliers
Died 9 April 1917

Fred was born in Willington Quay, the son of James and Ellen Gibson of Station Road, Willington Quay. When he enlisted in the army at the beginning of the war, he lived and worked in Hexham.

He had been employed as a hairdresser by Mr Welch of Priestpopple for a number of years and was a member of Hexham's Primitive Methodist Church where he sang in the choir. He was also a member of the Christian Endeavour Society.

Fred had been in France for over a year when he was killed. He was a trained sniper and was killed in action. Four of his brothers were also serving at the Front. Fred is buried in Bailleul Road East Cemetery, St Laurent-Blangy, northeast of Arras.

Although not commemorated on Hexham's War Memorial, his name is found on a memorial to the men of the Primitive Methodist Church and School, now to be found in Trinity Methodist Church, Beaumont Street.

To the left of the 102nd Brigade (see above), the 103rd Brigade (24th, 25th, 26th and 27th Battalions Northumberland Fusiliers, Tyneside Irish) met with stiffer resistance. Under the cover of darkness and in a similar fashion to their Scottish counterparts, the men of the 24th and 25th Battalions crept out into No Man's Land. As the Allied barrage finished they were able to rush the enemy trenches before the Germans knew what had hit them. Both formations took the Black Line on time although a lot of their officers had been killed. As they moved up to the Blue

Line, they came under extremely heavy and accurate fire from their left flank and suffered a lot of casualties. Through acts of extreme courage, men of the 24th Battalion managed to take their allocated Blue Line objective. [58]

Private George Dodd, aged 34
24th (Service) Battalion (Tyneside Irish)
Northumberland Fusiliers
Died 9 April 1917

George Dodd was the son of George Dodd and Mrs Elspeth Walker (formerly Dodd) of Gilesgate Hexham. He was a married man. He enlisted in August 1915 and was sent to the Front soon afterwards. He survived the action on the first day of the Somme, 1 July 1916.

In a letter to his sister, a serjeant in the battalion wrote:

> *"Just a few lines, to offer you my deepest sympathy in the loss of your brother George in the recent advance. He was killed instantly on Easter Monday, and consequently suffered no pain. You have one consolation and that is he died a glorious death and one that ought never be forgotten at a time when his King and Country needed him the most …. Death claimed a hero in your brother…."*

George is buried in Roclincourt Military Cemetery.

Second Lieutenant Harold Walton, aged 23
27th (Service) Battalion (Tyneside Irish)
Northumberland Fusiliers
Died 11 April 1917

Harold was the only son of Joseph and Ruth Walton of the Station House, Hexham. He was born in Alston but

was educated at the Duke's School Alnwick, when his father was stationmaster at Alnmouth. After school he joined the North-Eastern Railway Company in their accounts office. Together with his father he was a member of the Hexham Abbey Choir and sang in the choir on the Sunday before he left for the Front.

Harold enrolled at the outset of the war and went out with the Hexham Territorial Battalion; he was involved in the fighting around Ypres in April 1915. He returned to the UK in the summer of 1916 for a Commission and returned to the Front with the 25th Battalion Northumberland Fusiliers in March 1917. Harold was wounded on 9 April and died of these wounds two days later on the 11 April.

Harold is buried in Aubigny Communal Cemetery.

Three to four miles south of Telegraph Hill, both the 9th and 10th Battalions King's Own Yorkshire Light Infantry went into action in the afternoon of 9 April. The objectives for the attack were positions in the Hindenberg Line in the area around the Henin to Heninel road. The preceding artillery barrage had been insufficient to cut the wire along the Front allotted to the 9th Yorkshire Light Infantry, although the companies in the first wave of the attack managed to get through some gaps and take the first objective. However the wire in front of the second objective was impenetrable. Many men died as they tried desperately to cut gaps in the barbed wire. At 6pm it was realized that this second objective was not going to fall to the 9th Battalion that day and so they were withdrawn to consolidate their initial success immediately south of Heninel. [9]

Lance Corporal Philip McMahon, aged 30
9th (Service) Battalion King's Own Yorkshire Light Infantry
Died 9 April 1917

Philip was born in Dublin and was a married man who lived at Haugh Lane, Hexham; he was the father to two children. Before the hostilities he worked for Messrs Henry Bell and Sons. He initially enlisted in Hexham with the Northumberland Fusiliers, but was subsequently transferred to the Yorkshire Light Infantry. Philip was klled by a shot to the head (see Lillian McMahon's story, below).

Philip is commemorated on the Arras Memorial for men who have no known grave

Operations around Arras were suspended on 14 April, but renewed on 23 April with an increasing cost in lives.

Lillian McMahon's Story

Lillian McMahon, a future daughter-in-law of Lance Corporal Philip McMahon, was a child of three at the opening ceremony of the Abbey Cross. On the other side of the crowd, as yet unknown to her, sat Philip's two small sons with their mother Mary, each clutching flowers to lay in honour of their father.

In conversation with the author, Lillian related that for years after the war Philip's grieving wife and children (one of whom was her late husband, also named Philip) had great difficulty in believing that he would not return home one day. This was because after the war his body was never found,

194

leaving room for a tiny glimmer of hope. However, conclusive evidence of his death finally emerged: Philip's widow met a soldier called Gibson, a Hexham man who had been in the battle in which Philip was killed. He had noticed during the course of 9 April that Philip was missing, and had shouted over to some men engaged in burying the fallen whether they had come across "Philip McMahon from Hexham", to which they had replied "Yes, we've just buried him", indicating the rough mound. They also said that he had been shot in the head, presumably by a sniper.

Years later, in about 1935, there was a most moving and astonishing event. A parcel arrived, addressed to 'Mrs McMahon, 36 Haugh Lane, Hexham'. In the parcel was her late husband's Catholic bible, given to him by his mother and lost on the field of battle. That bible had been taken home by a medic, also Catholic, who had found it on the battlefield. He had given it to his sister who had used it constantly until the time of its being restored to the family. She explained in a letter that as she used it she had always thought about the 'poor man who had died' and had felt a sense of guilt for many years, hence its eventual return to the address written inside. The bible remains a treasured possession of the McMahons to this day.

The Second Battle of the Scarpe: 23 – 24 April 1917

Nelson and Drake Battalions of 189th Brigade (Royal Naval Division) were designated to capture the heavily defended village of Gavrelle. During 22 April preparations for the assault were severely hindered by a heavy German bombardment in which four Able Seamen were killed and a large number were wounded. All day the British guns bombarded the positions at Oppy and Gavrelle and by late evening the attacking forces were ready for a dawn attack on St George's Day, 23 April 1917.

The British barrage opened up at 4.45pm and crept forward towards the village which was followed closely by Nelson Battalion in four waves, with Drake Battalion on the right. Within fifteen minutes the forward German trenches in front of the village were taken. However the village was a tougher nut to crack, with a myriad of concealed machine guns and snipers. The number of casualties began to rise as the result of hand-to-hand fighting, but soon they managed to capture the centre of Gavrelle and make a defensive line on its eastern edge, giving up any idea of further advances.

As the high ground to the north had not been secured by elements of the 190th Brigade the troops in Gavrelle were subjected to constant, intense artillery barrage which caused many deaths. At dawn the next day the Germans continued to pour rifle fire from the high ground to the north. [10] [11]

The Nelson Battalion's War Diary [12] for 24 April states:

> *Enemy furiously bombarded Gavrelle from 10am to 3pm during which time he massed for attack and about 3.30pm assaulted our line in force. At no point did he gain any success and suffered severely. We held our line intact throughout the night.*

Before dawn on 25 April, after 48 hours of continuous fighting, the remnants of the Nelson Battalion left the Front for some well earned rest.

Able Seaman John Edward Thompson, aged 22
Nelson Battalion, Royal Naval Division
Died 23 April 1917

John was the youngest son of Mr and Mrs Matthew Thompson of Woodbine Terrace, Hexham. He was a chorister at Hexham Abbey. Initially he served his time with Knight and Sons Bakers and Confectioners of Hexham. He then worked for Messrs Tilley of Newcastle and lastly for a Mr Claus of Whitley Bay. He enlisted late in 1915 and had been in France for a year when he was killed. The Hexham Herald reported 3 February 1917 that John had been admitted to hospital in France.

John was killed in action and is commemorated on the Arras Memorial.

In the early stages of this work, the date for John's death was given as 23 *May* 1917. This has now been rectified on the Commonwealth War Graves Commission Database.

A new series of attacks was launched on 3 May, attacks which were eventually called off on 17 May. These included *The Third Battle of the Scarpe* (3 – 4 May) and the capture of the village of Roeux (13 – 14 May). In the extreme south of the battle zone the ruins of the heavily defended village of Bullecourt were eventually taken. Over this time the Allies suffered 158,660 casualties (killed, wounded or missing).

In early 1916, the 2/3rd London Field Ambulance was attached to the 58th (1st London Division) and in May was involved in fighting near Tilloy-Les-Mofflaines, south of Arras. On 2 May the unit moved up from Arras towards the battlefield and on 3 May was subjected to intense and continuous artillery fire.

**Private Charles John Darley Waddilove, aged 35
2/3rd London Field Ambulance
Royal Army Medical Corps
Died 3 May 1917**

Charles was born in Hexham and was the eldest son of Admiral Charles Lodovic Darley and Mary Elizabeth Waddilove who resided for a number of years at Beacon Grange, Hexham.

The Hexham Herald reported that the family was revered

by the people of Hexham for their charitable works and for their unfailing kindness to the poor and needy of the town.

The Waddilove family following the death of their parents decided to reside in the South of England but maintained a connection with Hexham through its estates. Charles often visited his uncle at Brunton. His sister Katherine lived in Tunbridge Wells.

Before enlisting in the forces Charles had travelled widely. He joined the London Field Ambulance part of the Territorial Force in 1915, enlisting in Chelsea.

Private Alec Ellis, C Section, 2/3rd London Field Ambulance, wrote in his diary of 3 May 1917. [13] (reproduced in *History of the 2/3 London FA*):

> "*A day of terrific and continuous shelling. The unit's heaviest losses today, the most important being that of Private C J D Waddilove (son of Admiral), the most perfect gentleman and the bravest man in the British Army.*"

Charles was killed in action and is buried at Tilloy British Cemetery, Tilloy-Les-Moffaines

The 123rd Brigade of the Royal Field Artillery consisted of four batteries: three batteries each of 18-pdrs and one battery of 4.5 inch howitzers. The Brigade's rôle was to support attacks made by 37th Division (110th, 111th and 112th Infantry Brigades). Elements of this Division were involved in the *Battle of Arleux*, 28 – 29 April. Many of the infantry battalions who went into action that day were no more than 200 men strong (their nominal strength would be just over 1000 men). The job of the artillery would be to produce a *creeping barrage* in front of the infantry attack, allowing the infantry enough time to maintain contact with it as it moved forward.

Each 18-pdr gun and limber was hauled into action by a team of three pairs of horses with a driver mounted on the nearside horse. The lead driver would usually be a Lance Bombardier or a Bombardier. The rest of the men who served the gun and who were referred to as the 'gun team' were also mounted, but were Gunners, Lance Bombardiers etc. Drivers were also responsible for driving the GS wagon of supplies (one for each Section of two guns), and the ammunition wagons.

Driver Thomas William Smith, aged 20
'C' Battery, 123rd Brigade, Royal Field Artillery
Died 11 May 1917

Thomas was born in Hexham and was the eldest son of William and Leah Smith of Priestpopple, Hexham. As a youth he was a member of Hexham Church Lad's Brigade. Before the beginning of hostilities he was employed as baker by Messrs James White and Sons, Hexham.

Thomas initially enlisted in January 1915 with the Northumberland Fusiliers, but before proceeding to France in the September he transferred to the Royal Field Artillery. He was involved in the fighting on the Somme in the summer and autumn of 1916. He died of gunshot wounds at a field ambulance station. His brother Private Norman Smith was also serving in France.

At the Primitive Methodist Service on Sunday 20 May the Reverend J T Gallon made sympathetic reference to the death of Thomas Smith. The service closed with the playing of the Death March.

Thomas is buried in Bucquoy Road Cemetery, Ficheux.

References

1. Oldham, P. *The Hindenburg Line*,
   Pub: Pen and Sword 1997.

2. Cave, N. *Vimy Ridge*,
   Pub: Pen and Sword, 1996.

3. War Diary, *78th Battalion Canadian Infantry*
   http://data2.collectionscanada.ca

4. War Diary. *Princess Patricia's Light Infantry*, (Eastern Ontario Regiment).
   http://data2.collectionscanada.ca

5. Shakespear, Lt Col. J. *Thirty Fourth Division, 1915-1919*,
   Pub: 1921, reprinted Naval & Military Press 1998

6. Stewart, G. and Sheen, J A. *History of the Tyneside Scottish*,
   Pub: Pen and Sword, 1999.

7. Terman, Brig-Gen T. *History of Tyneside Scottish*,
   Pub: 1919, reprinted Naval & Military Press 2003.

8. Sheen, J A. *History of the Tyneside Irish*,
   Pub: Pen and Sword, 1998.

9. Bond, R C. *History of the Kings Own Yorkshire Light Infantry in the Great War*,
   Pub: 1929, reprinted Naval & Military Press 2004.

10. Swales, R. *Nelson at War,*
    Pub: Pen and Sword, 2004.

11. Page, C. *Command in the Royal Naval Division*,
    Pub: Spellmount Limited 1999.

12. WO 95/3114. War Diary, *Nelson Battalion*.

13. Atkinson, A. *History of 2/3rd London F A*,
    Pub: 1969.

CHAPTER TWELVE

ACTIONS AGAINST THE HINDENBURG LINE

> "The poignant misery of dawn begins to grow …
> We only know war lasts, rain soaks, and clouds sag stormy.
> Dawn massing in the east her melancholy army
> Attacks once more in ranks on shivering ranks of grey …"
>
> Wilfred Owen, *Exposure*

Overview

From June 5 – 8 1917 the 102nd Brigade consisting of the 20th, 21st, 22nd, and 23rd Battalions Northumberland Fusiliers, Tyneside Scottish, together with the 27th Lowland Brigade of 9th Division, were detailed to attack Greenland Hill and to force the Germans from its crest. The four Tyneside Battalions took up position, with the 20th on the right, 21st in the centre, 22nd on the left and the 23rd taking up position in support. The action was well supported by artillery. Just before the time for the troops to advance the Germans began shelling the British Front Line, killing a number of men in the ranks of the 22nd Battalion.

At 8.00am after a four minute barrage which blasted the defenders of Greenland Hill, the leading waves of soldiers advanced over No Man's Land. On the right the 20th Battalion reached its objectives, whilst in the centre the 21st Battalion met with strong resistance. Men of the 22nd Battalion came under fire as they advanced and many of them were wounded or killed. Eventually a number of German machine gun posts were destroyed and the position of the attackers strengthened when the second objective was secured. All through the night the Germans attempted to recapture their lost positions without much success. In the early hours of 7 June the 22nd Battalion Front was attacked and after severe fighting the enemy regained a short length of their trench system. A determined counter-attack forced the Germans to retreat. In the middle of the night, after further German counter-attacks, the Scots of 101st Brigade relieved the remnants of 102nd. [1, 2, 3]

Private Thomas Christopher Hill, aged 23
20th (Service) Battalion (Tyneside Scottish)
Northumberland Fusiliers
Died 5 June 1917

Thomas (Kit) was the youngest son of Thomas and Elizabeth Hill of Orchard Terrace Hexham. Kit served his apprenticeship to be a butcher at Low Fell, but when he enlisted just after the outbreak of the hostilities he was working at Wall Colliery. He went out to France with the local battalion (1/4th Northumberland Fusiliers) in April 1915 and was wounded in the shoulder during the action around Ypres. In January 1916 he was wounded for a second time, spending ten weeks in hospital in Nottingham and a further period of convalescence at Redcar. On returning to the Front in the summer of 1916 he was transferred to the Tyneside Scottish. Kit was killed by the explosion of a shell whilst attacking a German strongpoint with six other soldiers.

Thomas is commemorated on the Arras Memorial, which contains the names of 35,000 men who have no known grave.

Thomas and Elizabeth Hill lost two sons to the war. It was reported that their eldest son and their daughter also died, as a result of 'anxiety and grief'.

Private Edward Blackburn, aged 25
22nd (Service) Battalion (Tyneside Scottish)
Northumberland Fusiliers
Died 7 June 1917

Edward was a married man with one child; he and his family lived in Hencotes, Hexham, before the war. He was born in Eltringham and before he joined up in 1914 he was employed as a miner at Wall Colliery. He was a keen footballer who played for a number of sides in both Hexham and Prudhoe. He went to the Front with the Hexham Battalion of the Northumberland Fusiliers and was involved in the fighting at Ypres in April 1915. It is reported that he was twice wounded in action. During the course of the war he was transferred to 22nd Battalion.

Edward is buried in the Point-du-Jour Military Cemetery.

The 12th Northumberland Fusiliers were heavily involved in an attack scheduled for 16 June, east of Arras and the Sensée Valley. At 3.10am under the cover of an artillery barrage the battalion attacked with the 13th Northumberland Fusiliers on their left and the 2/2nd London Regiment on their right. The 12th Northumberland Fusiliers attacked on a single company Front across three hundred yards of No Man's Land in order to capture a trench system called Tunnel Trench.

In defence, the Germans used a heavy artillery barrage and considerable fire from rifles and machine-guns. As the attackers approached the trench they were showered with stick grenades.

Despite the opposition some members of 'C' and 'D' Companies managed to penetrate Tunnel Trench but were eventually overwhelmed by the defenders and killed. 'A' and 'B' Companies realised that they were unable to get into the heavily defended trench and consolidated their positions in shell holes just in front of the German Front Line, withdrawing later under the cover of darkness.

Of the ten officers and three hundred and ninety one other ranks involved in the attack, three officers and fifty four other ranks were killed that day, including Edward Fletcher.[4]

Private Edward Allan Fletcher, aged 30
12th (Service) Battalion Northumberland Fusiliers
Died 16 June 1917

 Edward was born in Haltwhistle. He was the youngest son of John and Hannah Fletcher of Windsor Terrace, Hexham. Before the war he served his apprenticeship as a joiner with Mr John Civil and at the beginning of hostilities was working on the Beaufront Estate. He was also a member of the Hexham Unionist Club.

He went to France with the local Territorial Battalion and was severely wounded on 26 April 1915 at the *Second Battle of Ypres*. He returned to Hexham for convalescence. In June 1916 he returned to France with 12th Battalion Northumberland Fusiliers.

Edward is commemorated on the Arras Memorial to the missing.

On 10 September the 25th Northumberland Fusiliers relieved the composite 24/27th Northumberland Fusiliers in the Front Line (Farm Trench) near Hargicourt (about ten miles northwest of St Quentin) and immediately came under heavy enemy shelling. Patrols were sent into No Mans Land, but the Germans were content to use artillery in shelling both the back and forward areas of the sector. The battalion was relieved during 17 September. [1, 2, 3]

Lance Corporal William Allen, aged 39
25th (Service) Battalion (Tyneside Irish)
Northumberland Fusiliers
Died 14 September 1917

William was the husband of Johana Allen of Haugh Lane, Hexham and was the father of three children. He was born in Carlisle and before enlisting at the onset of hostilities William worked for Hexham Urban District Council. He had been a member of the Old Northumberland Militia for twelve years and was therefore drafted into the Hexham Territorial Battalion. William had seen action in April 1915 at the *Second Battle of Ypres.* He was subsequently transferred to 25th Battalion Northumberland Fusiliers. Three months before his death he was home in Hexham on leave. A letter from 2nd Lieutenant Adams to Mrs Allen stated:

> *"Lance Corporal Allen was killed on the night of 14th Sept. He was one of a carrying party taking materials to the front line. It may be some slight consolation to you to know that death was instantaneous and that he was properly buried..."*

William is buried in Hargicourt British Cemetery.

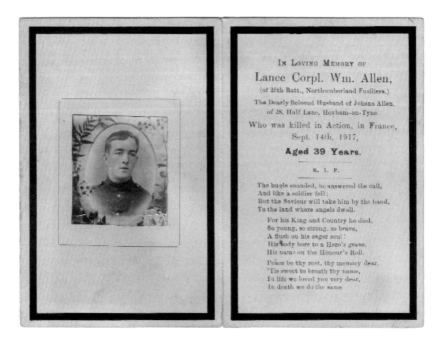

By kind permission of The Fusiliers Museum of Northumberland

References

1. Shakespear, Lt Col. J. *Thirty Fourth Division, 1915-1919*,
    Pub: 1921 reprinted Naval & Military Press 1998.

2. Stewart, G. and Sheen, J A. *History of the Tyneside Scottish*,
    Pub: Pen and Sword Books, 1999.

3. Terman, Brig-Gen T. *History of Tyneside Scottish*,
    Pub: 1919 reprinted Naval & Military Press 2003.

4. WO 95/2155. War Diary, *12th Battalion Northumberland Fusiliers*.

Trefcon British Cemetery, Caulaincourt, in the Aisne region of France. A typical Western Front cemetery.

Preserved trenches at Sanctuary Wood near Ypres.

Helles Memorial to 20,841 men with no known graves
Gallipoli Peninsula, Turkey

Menin Gate, Ypres. Within this huge structure are carved the names of 54,896 men who have no known graves. See Chapter Three.
(Northern Staircase) 'They shall receive a crown of glory that fadeth not away'

CHAPTER THIRTEEN

1917: DEATH ALONG THE WESTERN FRONT

"....what a glorious death a soldier's death is
when he is upholding everything good
and conquering all things that are bad.
So don't worry: I hope none of you at home will do that."

Chaplain's letter to the family of Isaac Reay, died 21 June aged 23

Overview

In January 1917 Sir Douglas Haig sought to explain the reasons behind the movement of British troops, extending their line to south of the River Somme:

> *"To meet the wishes of our Allies in connection with the plan of campaign for the spring of 1917, a gradual extension of the British front southwards as far as a point opposite the town of Roye was decided on in January, and was completed without incident of importance by the 26th of February, 1917."*

Accordingly, the 1/4th Northumberland Fusiliers relieved the French 123rd Regiment at 8pm on 11 February near Belloy-en-Santerre, situated south of the River Somme, four miles south east of Péronne.

The War Diary reports that the French trenches were in unusually good condition, although dirty. The weather was bitterly cold and the ground was hard and frozen. For the first three days a lot of time was spent just cleaning – and dodging occasional barrages by German artillery, including a lot of gas shells.

At 4.00pm on 15 February, as the Germans continued to shell the trenches, a French bomb store exploded causing a number of casualties and a fire which took twelve hours to extinguish. As a result one man was killed and six wounded. [1]

Private John Robson, aged 31
1/4ᵗʰ Battalion Northumberland Fusiliers
Died 15 February 1917

John Robson was the son of Mrs Robson of Priestpopple Hexham. Captain C Stephenson wrote to Mrs Robson telling her that her son had died through the explosion of a bomb store. Private Robson acted as a batman to Captain Stephenson, who wrote:

> *"the deceased was one of my best soldiers ... he was always bright and cheerful and performed his duties however difficult and arduous with the same thoroughness and good spirits that has marked our splendid men throughout the war ....I have lost a true friend as well as a gallant soldier ..."*

John is buried in Fouquescourt British Cemetery.

On 18 June, the 26ᵗʰ Northumberland Fusiliers took over the Front Line near Roeux (5 miles east of Arras and on the north bank of the River Scarpe), and stayed in position until they were relieved by elements of 52 Brigade (56 Division) on 22 June. During this period companies of 3/4ᵗʰ Royal West Kent Regiment were attached to the four Tyneside Irish Battalions. All available manpower was used to improve the Gavrelle Trench Line. New fire steps were added to the trench and where possible shelters were constructed. [2,3]

Private Isaac Reay, aged 23
26th (Service) Battalion (Tyneside Irish)
Northumberland Fusiliers
Died 21 June 1917

Isaac was the eldest son of Mr and Mrs Isaac Reay of Glover Place, Hexham. Before joining the Colours in November 1915 he was employed in Messrs Joseph Robson and Sons, Nurseries of Causey Hill, Hexham, where his father was the foreman. He went to the Front in March 1916, but was invalided home, returning in January after spending Christmas at home. The Hexham Herald made note that those who bade him adieu recalled with sadness the wistful look back he gave when leaving home.

The Chaplain wrote to his family stating that a shell had killed their son instantaneously.

In his letter the chaplain wrote:

"I am very sorry I have this bad news for you, but I am sure you will know what a glorious death a soldier's death is when he is upholding everything good and conquering all things that are bad. So don't worry: I hope none of you at home will do that. Just put it into God's hands and ask for His help in your prayers".

Isaac is buried in Bailleul Road East Cemetery, St Laurent-Blangy.

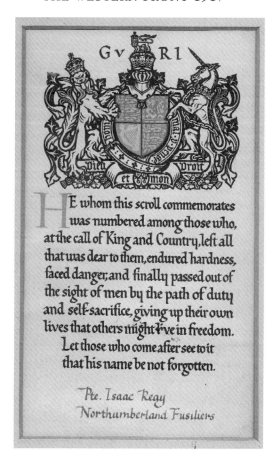

The 10th Battalion Northumberland Fusiliers moved to
Dickebush Camp (about 2 miles southwest of Ypres) on 12
June 1917 to provide working parties for the burying of
cables. During the morning of 20 June the camp was shelled
and both Major W Clifford DSO and the Adjutant Captain G L
Bland were killed. Both were buried that day at Dickebush
Military Cemetery. At the same time Lieutenant Savage was
badly wounded and died later that day at 6.30pm in a casualty
clearing station. More men were killed later in the day. [4]

Lieutenant Cuthbert Farrar Savage, aged 26
'A' Company 10th (Service) Battalion
Northumberland Fusiliers
Died 20 June 1917

Cuthbert Savage was the only son of Canon E Sidney and Mrs Sibyl Savage of the Priory, Hexham. He was born in Barrow in Furness in 1889. He was educated at Aysgarth School, Rugby and New College Oxford where he studied Law. After leaving Oxford he went to Vancouver in British Columbia to further his studies at Messrs Martin, Griffin and Co. At the outbreak of hostilities he enlisted in the Seaforth Highlanders of Canada, arriving in England with the 1st Canadian Contingent. In January 1915 he obtained a commission with the Northumberland Fusiliers arriving in France in August of that year. Cuthbert was wounded at Bulle Grenaille in April 1916 and took part in the *Battle of the Somme*. He was gazetted to Lieutenant on 12 June 1917.

He was wounded by a shell which burst at his feet outside Battalion Headquarters at Dickebusch, near Ypres, and was admitted to a Casualty Clearing Station at Poperinghe with multiple shrapnel wounds and compound fractures of the humorous and the knee. He died that evening.

His Major wrote:

"We shall miss him dreadfully. In the old days before he was wounded he was the best Platoon Commander in my

Company, and I thought, the Battalion, and latterly, during his Staff courses, he turned out to be even more efficient. He was very popular with us all, as he was always cheery and only thought of others and not of himself at all."

Another who knew him well wrote:

"And what a gallant lad – handsome as a young Greek god, courteous, charming, gifted. I have many memories of him, skiing down steep slopes with grace, skill and daring, dancing and laughing and jesting with his friends or discussing serious matters with earnestness and intelligence."

Cuthbert is buried in the Lijssenthoek Military Cemetery.
His gravestone is inscribed with the following:

'So (sic) he passed over the trumpets sounded for him on the other side'

Cuthbert Savage is also commemorated on the Rolls of Honour at the Abbey and at the War Memorial Hospital.

During the summer of 1917 the 50th Division (149th, 150th and 151st Brigades) held a section of the Front Line approximately 3000 yards in length between the villages of Fontaine-lez-Croisilles and Chérisy. As both sets of trenches were on reverse slopes, neither the British nor the Germans were able to observe their respective Front Lines. Both sides lobbed shells at each other incessantly and attempted to gain some advantage by organising small-scale raids on each other's trenches and saps.[5, 6] Although the data-bases report the death of Thomas Chrisp on 22 June, the War Diary reports that Thomas was killed "at 8.00am on June 23":

"CSM Chrisp was killed by a Whizz-bang"

'Whizz-bang' was popular slang for a high velocity German

artillery shell. Obviously, the name describes the sound that it made.

Company Serjeant Major Thomas Chrisp
Military Medal, aged 24
'D' Company, 1/8th Durham Light Infantry
Died 22 June 1917

Thomas was the son of Thomas (Inspector of Police at Wooler) and Annie Chrisp of the Police Buildings, Hexham. He was married to Mary Dickinson Chrisp of Summerleigh, Choppington. Thomas was educated at the Duke's School in Alnwick. Subsequently he taught at Choppington School before entering Bede College, Durham where he had just completed a two-year course when he went to war. He was about to take up a place at St Margaret's School. He was also a keen footballer and played in goal for Hexham Athletic. It was owing to his fine goal keeping that Hexham Athletic beat Haltwhistle United at Dene Park in the Clayton Charity Cup just before the start of the war.

When hostilities began Thomas was in camp with the Bede College Company of the Durham Light Infantry and they proceeded to France in April 1915. At the *Second Battle of Ypres* he was shot in the right arm and thigh and returned to England for medical treatment, after which he was employed in drilling men and was awarded the rank of Serjeant Major. He returned to the Front in June 1916. His older brother William was also serving in France, with the Royal Field Artillery.

37731 Sjt. E. B. Child, R.H.A.
15126 Pte. F. Childs, Shrops. L.I.
86286 Gunner W. H. Childs, R.F.A.
6826 Pte. E. B. Chilvers, W. Rid. R.
1946 Sjt. T. Chrisp, Durh. L.I.
7081 Pte. H. C. Christmas, Lond. R.
5627 Pte. A. E. Clapham, Lond'. R.
2548 Gunner A. Clarke, R.F.A.
32474 Pte. A. Clarke, Notts. & Derby. R.
G/10832 Pte. F. J. Clarke, R.-W. Surr. R.
72718 Bombr. J. J. Clarke, R.F.A.
6674 L./C. J. W. Clarke, Notts. & Derby. R.

Supplement to
London Gazette
9 December 1916

Thomas was awarded the Military Medal in early October 1916 for resourcefully leading his platoon during an advance on the Somme. His award was announced in a supplement to the London Gazette on 9 December 1916.

It was reported that Thomas Chrisp was "killed during a heavy artillery bombardment of the allied trenches".

Thomas is buried in Neuville-Vitasse Road Cemetery, Neuville-Vitasse.

During July, August and September there were no further big attacks along this part of the Front Line, but the rigours of trench warfare remained, as did incessant artillery activity. There was constant patrolling in No Man's Land, with a number of raids designed to confuse the Germans and to keep them busy.

In the early part of July the 1/4th Northumberland Fusiliers were based in the Front Line opposite the village of Chérisy (fifteen miles southeast of Arras). The War Diary reports that: [1]

> *".....the attitude of the enemy was fairly quiet. Curtain Trench was subject to artillery fire enfilade from Vis-en-Artois and was occasionally a very unhealthy spot."*

It also reports that there was not a lot of sniper and machine gun fire. However, William Scott died of gunshot wounds during this period

Private William Scott, aged 20
1/4th Battalion Northumberland Fusiliers
Died 6 July 1917

William was born in Hexham and was the youngest son of J Scott of Fellside, Hexham. Before enlisting at the outbreak of the war he was employed as a gardener at Dukes House, Hexham. William was also a pigeon fancier of some reputation and his loft contained many fine racing and show birds.

Mr Scott received a letter from the Matron of the Casualty Clearing Hospital saying that his son had died from gunshot wounds to the chest. Two further brothers were also serving in France.

William is buried in Achiet-le-Grand Communal Cemetery Extension.

References

1. WO 95/2826. War Diary, *1/4th Battalion Northumberland Fusiliers.*
2. Shakespear, Lt Col. J. *Thirty Fourth Division 1915-1919,* Pub: 1921, reprinted Naval & Military Press 1998.

3. Sheen, J A. *History of the Tyneside Irish,* Pub: Pen and Sword, 1998.

4. WO 95/2182. War Diary, *10th Battalion Northumberland Fusiliers.*

5. Wyrell, E. *The Fiftieth Division, 1914-1919,* Pub: 1939, reprinted, Naval and Military Press 2002.

6. WO 95/2841. War Diary, *1/8th Battalion Durham Light Infantry.*

Compressed cardboard dogtag belonging to
Isaac Reay. Died 21 June 1917.

CHAPTER FOURTEEN

PASSCHENDAELE

"I died in hell – they called it Passchendaele"
Siegfried Sassoon, *Memorial Tablet*

Overview

In 1921, the rather clumsily named B*attles Nomenclature Committee* ruled that the *Third Battle of Ypres*, also commonly called *Passchendaele*, was officially classed to have begun on 31 July and ended on 6 November 1917. For greater clarity, the committee also divided this major engagement into eight phases. It is important to note that in the intervening periods there was no stopping the carnage and death inflicted by both sides as they wallowed in a treacherous sea of mud.

During the six weeks that followed Plumer's successful engagement at *Messines*, a prolonged spell of warm sunny weather allowed the build up of men and munitions for the next battle in Flanders. Field Marshall Sir Douglas Haig was planning to strike into Belgium and besiege the ports (used by the Germans as bases for their U boats) to reduce the destruction that was being wrought at sea. The objectives for this attack were to make a breakthrough and to exploit this using cavalry to range far and wide in the open spaces behind the lines of German trenches. With this in mind Haig chose General Hubert Gough with his flair and panache rather than the meticulous General Herbert Plumer to spearhead this attack.

The Germans observed the Allied build-up from the air and from the relative heights of the Passchendaele Ridge, an objective for the Allied attack. As a counter measure the Germans attacked Nieuport on 10 July, with bitter fighting taking place in the sand dunes. Furthermore the Germans began to shell the British with a new and nasty gas, dichlorodiethyl sulphide, commonly known as *mustard gas* because of its effects. Called by the British soldiers 'HS' (Hun Stuff) it was an odourless gas and was heavier than air so that it accumulated malevolently as an oily, sherry-looking liquid in hollows all over the battlefield from where it evaporated slowly. Contact with this noxious gas resulted in burning and irritation of the skin and if it were inhaled it would cause severe irritation of the lungs and digestive tract. It was first used on 12 July and within three weeks nearly six hundred soldiers had died from its effects. In her autobiography *Testament of Youth*, Vera Brittain gives a vivid account of her time spent nursing gas cases in France:

> *...the poor things burnt and blistered all over, with great mustard coloured suppurating blisters, with blind eyes ... all sticky and stuck together, and always fighting for breath, with voices a mere whisper ...*

The British bombardment opened on 17 June and continued until the opening of the battle at the end of the month. The British fired over 4.25 *million* shells, of which 100,000 contained a deadly chemical called chloropicrin (phosgene). Having been reluctant to use this 'cowardly form of warfare' (Lt Gen Ferguson, commander British II Corps), poisoned gas quickly came to be embraced as an effective weapon, particularly since the prevailing wind was generally in the Allies' favour!

As the start of the battle loomed, the weather changed dramatically. On 31 July, the day of the attack, more than $^3/_4$ inch of rain fell.

Phase 1: Battle of Pilckem
31 July – 2 August 1917

Soldiers of 30th Division were involved in the fighting during the first of day of the Battle of Pilckem on a Front facing Sanctuary Wood. The initial assault went over the top at 3.50am, involving the 2nd Wiltshire Regiment and 18th King's Liverpool. The 20th King's Liverpool (89th Brigade) was allocated a support role for this attack. At 7.00am the position held by the 20th Battalion in Maple Copse was shelled heavily by the enemy which caused considerable injury and death. Together with the 17th King's Liverpool on the left, they advanced at 7.50am and found that troops who had advanced earlier in the morning were pinned down well short of their first objective. These earlier troops were blocking any further advance and by midday they were digging in, in expectation of the inevitable artillery bombardment. Any further thrusts forward were stopped in their tracks by machine gun fire. At nightfall the position was that none of the battalions of the 30th Division had been able to achieve the first objective. [1]

Private Percy Wollaston, aged 32
20th (Service) Battalion The King's
(Liverpool Regiment)
Died 31 July 1917

Percy was born in Ipswich Suffolk and was the son of Mrs H Wollaston of Felix Road, Ipswich. He had lived in Hexham for over twelve years before joining the Colours. He was employed by Mr Rose, tailor and outfitter of Battle Hill and lodged with Mrs Moore of Pearson's Terrace Hexham.

During the advance on 31 July, Percy was hit in the groin by shrapnel. Apparently the wound was dressed and he was left for stretcher-bearers to carry him from the field of battle but sadly there was no further news of him.

Percy is commemorated on the Menin Gate Memorial, for those missing with no known grave.

During the early days of August as the fighting raged to the east of Ypres, the 26th Battalion Royal Fusiliers was in position near Hollebeke (five miles to the south of Ypres) with responsibility for defending the flanks of the main assault. On the evening of 1 August during a heavy rainstorm, the Battalion was sent to relieve the 11th West Kent in the Front Line near Fusilier Wood, which they achieved by the early hours of the next morning. The heavy rain continued into the next day during which their position was constantly under heavy artillery barrage, a miserable state of affairs that continued for the next two days. During the late evening of 5 August and during the next day (see Alexander Pattinson below) the Germans attacked Hollebeke. Eventually the enemy was driven off but the defending battalion had suffered heavy losses. Later that night, the 20th DLI relieved the beleaguered Royal Fusiliers.[2]

Private Alexander John Pattinson, aged 19
26th Battalion Royal Fusiliers
Died 7 August 1917

Alexander was born in Hexham, the only son of Alexander and Elizabeth Pattinson of St Andrew's Road. He was educated at Skerry's College, Newcastle, after which he worked as a clerk for Messrs H Bell and Sons, Hexham. He was an enthusiastic member of the Wesleyan church where he acted as Sunday School Librarian. He enlisted at the age of eighteen in the Royal Fusiliers (Bankers' Battalion) in December 1915. After five months of basic training he went to France in May 1916. He was admitted to London Field Ambulance Operating Centre on 6 August suffering from severe gunshot wounds to the abdomen and died of his wounds the following day.

Private J Mitchell (Hexham) wrote to the family saying that:

> " ... in Private Pattinson's death they lost one of the coolest and bravest boys in the battalion ..."

Alexander is buried in Poperinghe New Military Cemetery. The following is found on his headstone:

> FOR TRIUMPH HE LIVED
> FOR RIGHT HE DIED
> WITH CHRIST HE REIGNS

At his commemoration service at the Wesleyan Church in Hexham the pulpit was draped in black and the organist played the 'Dead March' from Handel's Saul.

At 3.00am on 14 August the 6th Yorkshires withdrew from their outposts to the left bank of the Steenbeck, near St Julien, and formed up in preparation for an advance. 'A' Company attacked on the right using two and a half platoons, with the remainder in support. 'C' Company attacked on the left with a similar formation. At 4.00am the battalion advanced behind a creeping barrage. All through the day the advancing troops came under intense enemy shelling, and at night when the battalion was withdrawn its casualties were twenty men killed, two officers and sixty three other ranks wounded, with twenty six men missing (many of whom would be classified as killed in the following days). [3]

Private George William Smith, aged 19
A Company, 6th (Service) Battalion, Alexandra
Prince of Wales's Own (Yorkshire Regiment)
Died 14 August 1917

George was the only son of George William and Annie Smith. They lived in Ferry Road, Bridge End, Hexham. Before he enlisted in October 1916, he worked for Messrs William Fell and Company, Royal Nurserymen, in their seeds department. He travelled to the Front on New Years Day 1917. George served in the Lewis Gun Section and was killed in action.

George is commemorated on the Menin Gate Memorial, Ypres.

Phase 2: Battle of Langemarck
16 – 18 August 1917

The 7th Battalion Yorkshire Light Infantry were involved on the northern flank of a major attack on 16 August known as the *Battle of Langemarck*. The battalion attacked from positions in front of a stream called the Steembeck and were ordered to help in the capture of the village of Langemarck and to take the ground some short distance beyond the village. The ground to be crossed was very muddy and preparations had been made to allow the men to clean their rifles during the attack.

A German strongpoint known as Au Bon Gîte was captured just after zero hour in a special operation involving the Royal Flying Corps and ground forces. A very through barrage was laid down and Germans from 79th Reserve Division surrendered unhesitatingly. Troops of the 60th Brigade advanced to the south of Langemarck and outflanked the German resistance, which had held up 61st Brigade who had been advancing on the northern side of the village. Eventually the village and the ground beyond was taken.[4]

On the day that Robert Conkleton (below) was killed, Private W Edwards, a colleague from the same battalion won the Victoria Cross for conspicuous bravery: [5]

> *"Private Edwards without hesitation and under heavy machine gun and rifle fire from a strong blockhouse, dashed forward at great risk, bombed through the loopholes, surmounted the blockhouse and waved his company to advance. Three officers and thirty other ranks were taken prisoner by him in the blockhouse. Later he did most valuable work as a runner and eventually guided most of the battalion out through difficult ground. Throughout he set a splendid example and was utterly regardless of danger".*

Private Robert Malcolm Conkleton, aged 25
7th (Service) Battalion King's Own Yorkshire Light Infantry
Died 16 August 1917

Robert was born in Prudhoe and was the third son of Thomas Conkleton of Haugh Lane, Hexham. Before enlisting at the outbreak of war with the Northumberland Fusiliers he was employed by Mr Todd, a carting contractor. He left a widow, Lillian née Peel, and one child. After Robert's death Mrs Conkleton remarried and went to live in High Callerton, near Ponteland. When he was killed he had been out at the Front for only three months.

Robert is commemorated on Tyne Cot Memorial, which like the Menin Gate and Thiepval contains thousands of names of men who have no known grave.

On 25 August Douglas Haig transferred overall responsibility for the Third Battle of Ypres from General Hubert Gough to General Herbert Charles Onslow Plumer. Plumer was a methodical man and set about the task by adopting his established formula of setting limited objectives and basing each operation on detailed and meticulous planning. An important element of this formula was ensuring that his infantry always had artillery support. This formula was termed *bite and hold*. It was another three weeks before he was ready to renew the attack. By then the weather had cleared.

Phase 3: Battle of Menin Road
20 – 25 September 1917

At 5.40 am, Allied forces opened up a new attack, with a Front extending from the point where the canal met the railway south of Klein Zillebeke to Langemarck, in the north of the salient. The troops advanced behind a creeping barrage.

The 11th Northumberland Fusiliers as part of 68th Brigade attacked on the first day of the battle (20 September). Initially its advance was hindered by a single German strongpoint in Dumbarton Wood, which resulted in the Brigade losing a lot of men. It appears that advancing troops had difficulty in maintaining the direction of the attack due to a dense cloud of smoke and dust. The Fusiliers reached their objective beyond the marshy ground of Dumbarton Lake within minutes of the end of the barrage, and consolidated a defensive position along the upper reaches of the Bassevillebeek.

The Battalion Diary reports that, given the intensity of the fighting, casualties were comparatively light: five officers were killed and four wounded, other ranks had forty two killed, one hundred and thirty eight wounded and twenty missing. On 23 September the remnants of the battalion were pulled out of the Line and retired to 'J' camp at Dickebush.[6]

Private Ivatt Wright, aged 30
11th (Service) Battalion Northumberland Fusiliers
Died 20 September 1917

Ivatt was born in Hexham, and was the second son of Charles and Margaret Wright. One of his younger brothers lived in Prior Terrace. Whilst he was living in Hexham, he worked for Mr F G Grant at the Hydropathic as a gardener.

However in 1913 he left Hexham and went to work in the coal mines in Ashington. He enlisted at Bedlington in September 1914 and had been in France for over two years when he died at Passchendaele. His older brother of Low Wood Row, North Seaton Colliery, received notification of his death. His younger brother Arthur was serving with the Royal Engineers.

Ivatt is commemorated on the Tyne Cot Memorial to the missing.

In November, the 11th Northumberland Fusiliers were hastily dispatched as part of a reinforcement of two divisions sent to support the Italians who had suffered a shattering reverse of fortune at Caporetto and were in serious danger of collapse. This force was expanded again at the end of the month.

Phase 4: Battle of Polygon Wood
26 September – 3 October 1917

On 26 September the 17th Battalion Sherwood Foresters (117th Brigade) was called upon to support the 116th Brigade attack on the German strongpoint known as Tower Hamlets and during the following day were involved in the consolidation of the previous day's gains. The battalion came under very heavy shellfire. Late that night the 13th Royal Fusiliers relieved them and the battalion proceeded to Locrehof Farm. On 3 October the War Diary reports that the individual companies were under the orders of Company Commanders and that Sergeant Major Creadie took the companies for physical and bayonet training. Since the database indicates that Arthur Atkinson was 'killed in action', he may have been killed accidentally during bayonet exercises, or possibly he died from wounds sustained during the past month's fighting. [7]

Lance Corporal Arthur Atkinson, aged 26
17th Battalion Sherwood Foresters
(Notts and Derby Regiment)
Died 3 October 1917

Arthur was born in Newcastle upon Tyne and was the second son of Mary Atkinson of Eastgate, Hexham. Before enlisting in November 1916 he was employed by Messrs Gray and Sons, provision merchants, of Hexham. He was a member of the Hexham Congregational Church Choir and served as chairman of St Wilfrid's Debating Society. After spending his initial training with the North Staffordshire Regiment at Wallsend, he was sent to France in January. Subsequently he transferred to the Sherwood Foresters. Two other brothers were serving in France, whilst a third brother was fighting in East Africa.

Arthur is buried at Bedford House Cemetery.

The following inscription is found at the base of his headstone:

LOVINGLY REMEMBERED
BY MOTHER
BROTHERS AND SISTERS.

Phase 5: Battle of Broodseinde
4 October 1917

The main attack was carried out by Anzac Troops who were successful in capturing all of their objectives. However, to the north and south the attacking troops made no gains against the German Front Line. No men from Hexham lost their lives during this phase of the advance on the village of Passchendaele.

Phase 6: Battle of Poelcappelle
9 October 1917

The main attack on 9 October was carried out by the 66th and 49th Divisions of II Anzac Corps, which had assembled east of Ypres. The 1/4th York and Lancaster Battalion was part of the 148th Brigade, 49th Division and was detailed to attack up the Wallemoen spur on which the village of Bellevue stands. After this the men were to move on to the main ridge north of Passchendaele.

The men of the battalion marched for eleven hours to their assembly position on the eve of the attack, arriving exhausted at 5.20am, an hour before 'zero hour'. At the outset of the battle they confronted the Ravenbeek stream, the bed of which was thirty to fifty yards wide, a watery morass, waist deep at its centre. Only small groups of men were able to cross this intimidating marsh. Throughout the day the troops came under heavy machine-gun fire from pillboxes on the higher ground ahead. They also received some very accurate sniper fire, particularly effective against the battalion's stretcher-bearers and runners. In the evening the Germans attempted a counter-attack, which was repulsed by rifle and Lewis gun fire. The failure of the artillery to provide support during this attack was very obvious and came in for heavy criticism. On the evening of 10 October the battalion was relieved by New Zealand troops and with some relief they returned to Ypres. Casualties for this attack were four officers and forty two other ranks killed, five officers and one hundred ninety one other ranks wounded and one officer and forty eight other ranks missing, many of whom would be reported as dead in the following days.[8]

Private Walton Bell aged 33
1/4th Battalion York and Lancaster Regiment
(Hallamshire)
Died 9 October 1917

Walton was born in Hexham in 1885. He was a married man; at the time of his death his wife Annie lived with their three children in Elliott Terrace, Wark. Subsequently Annie remarried and lived at Butt Banks, Fourstones as Mrs A Smith. Walton was the grandson of the late Mr Robert Bell of Lane Dykes. He served his time as a butcher with Councillor John Dodd and was for some years employed as a butcher by Haydon Bridge Co-operative Society. Just before the war Mr J Miller of Wark had employed him as a manager in his butchering business. It was reported that when Walton was called up for service in March 1916, Mr Miller was forced to close his business. Walton was initially assigned to the 1/4th Northumberland Fusiliers, but was subsequently transferred to his final regiment.

He had been in France for only six weeks before he was killed.

Walton is commemorated on the Tyne Cot Memorial to the missing.

The 326th Siege Battery arrived on the Western Front in May 1917 after a tour of duty in the Middle East. It had four 6-inch howitzers, each weighing 26 cwt, and was attached to the 98th Heavy Artillery Group which saw action during the Third Battle of Ypres.

Gunner John Edward Charlton, aged 29
326th Siege Battery Royal Garrison Artillery
Died 11 October 1917

John was born in Corbridge, the son of John Charlton of Tyne Green Nurseries, Hexham. He was wounded in action during the *3rd Battle of Ypres* and died as a result of these wounds.

John is buried in Menin Road South Military Cemetery, Ypres.

His headstone contains the following inscription:

SORROW VANQUISHED
LABOUR ENDED
JORDAN PASSED

Phase 7: First Battle of Passchendaele
12 October 1917

There is some confusion about the death of Robert Moulding; both the date and the battalion of the Northumberland Fusiliers in which he was serving at the time are unclear. The Commonwealth War Graves Commission gives the battalion as the 16th Northumberland Fusiliers and the date of death as 12 October, whilst the *Soldiers who died in the Great War* database gives his battalion as the 25th Northumberland Fusiliers and the date of death as 17 October. The inscription on his headstone in Cement House Cemetery states 'Northumberland Fusiliers died 12 October 1917'.

Using material from the War Diaries of both battalions and bearing in mind where he is buried, there is more evidence to support that he was serving with the 25th Battalion Northumberland Fusiliers.

On 12 October the 25th Northumberland Fusiliers relieved the Household Battalion in the Front Line near Poelcapelle. During their stay in the Line they were subjected to heavy shelling which resulted in many deaths. On the evening of 15 October they were relieved by the 24th/27th Northumberland Fusiliers and by 16 October they were based at Bridge Camp, Elverdinghe (north east of Ypres). [9, 10, 11, 12, 13]

Private Robert Moulding, aged 23
25th (Service) Battalion (Tyneside Irish)
Northumberland Fusiliers
Died between 12 – 17 October 1917

Robert was born in Hexham and was the fourth son of George and Mary Moulding of Glovers' Place, Hexham. Before the war his father employed him as a woodcutter.

Robert was posted to the Front in May 1917. Before he was eventually killed, it was reported in the Courant that he had been twice wounded and shell-shocked during his eventful time in France.

On October 12 1918, a tribute to Robert was published in the Hexham Courant. It is clearly a poem, but it is reproduced here as it appeared in the newspaper:

In loving memory of Pte Robert Moulding, 200705, N.F., killed or died through wounds between the 12th -17th Oct 1917, age 23 years, dearly beloved son of George Henry and Mary Jane Moulding of 13 Glovers' Place, Hexham. Dry your eyes, my weeping father and mother, See the crown your dear son has won, Try and say amid your sorrow, God knows best, Thy will be done. Sleep on, my dear son, and take your rest, They miss you most who loved you best. Our thoughts do oftimes wander to a sad but honoured grave. Your name is oftimes spoken, In the home you died to save. Our hearts are all united in the same true love for you, And loving thoughts treasured for one so brave and true. Not dead to those who loved him. Not lost but gone before, He dwells with us in memory still, And will for evermore. A unit from the Khaki line, Which stands so firm and brave, Has paid the price, given his life, Our lands and home to save.
Deeply mourned and sadly missed by his loving father and mother, brothers, sisters, sister-in-law, and all friends. R.I.P.

His brother William was also serving with the Northumberland Fusiliers in France.

Robert is buried in Cement House Cemetery.

The 12th Battalion Durham Light Infantry took over the Front Line east of Polygon Wood on the night of 13 October. They remained in the Line for three days and were subjected to severe enemy shelling. On one occasion the trenches held by the 12th were attacked by a group of low flying German

231

aircraft that repeatedly machine-gunned their position. By the time they left the trenches on the evening of 16 October over thirty men (including Paxton Dodd) had been killed. [14]

Private Paxton Dodd, aged 28
12th (Service) Battalion Durham Light Infantry
Died 14 October 1917

Paxton was born in Hexham, the son of Paxton and Annie Dodd of Haugh Lane. He was married and lived at Bridge End, Bellingham. As a boy he joined the Post Office in Hexham; following this he worked for two years in Humshaugh as a postman. Subsequently he moved with his job to Bellingham. He had only been in France for a few weeks before he was killed in action.

Paxton is commemorated on the Tyne Cot Memorial to the missing.

Orders came on 13 October for the all four Battalions of the Tyneside Scottish Brigade (102 Brigade) to relieve their fellow Geordies, the Tyneside Irish Brigade (103 Brigade), at the Front. On 14 October the 20th Northumberland Fusiliers moved from Hull and Saragossa Camps to the area around Stray Farm and in doing so were subjected to heavy artillery fire, which resulted in the deaths of twelve Fusiliers. However it was not until 18 October that the 20th Northumberland Fusiliers entered the Line. [9, 15, 16]

Sergeant John William Nevison, aged 36
20th (Service) Battalion (Tyneside Scottish)
Northumberland Fusiliers
Died 16 October 1917

 John was born at Blaydon, County Durham, and was one of the four sons of Joseph and Elizabeth Nevison. He was the husband of Sarah Nevison (née Abbott). Before enlisting he was employed as a tailor by Mr H P Rose of Battle Hill, Hexham. As was the case in many families, John was not the only member of his generation to die for his country. His younger brother, Fred, of the Machine Gun Company attached to the Northumberland Fusiliers was killed in September 1916. Two of his wife's brothers Private H Abbott, Border Regiment and Private T A Abbott, Northumberland Fusiliers, were also killed in action.

John is commemorated on the Tyne Cot Memorial to the missing.

Phase 8: Second Battle of Passchendaele
26 October – 14 November 1917

On the night of 24 October the 149th Brigade (1/4th, 1/5th, 1/6th and 1/7th Northumberland Fusiliers) relieved the 34th Division south of Houthulst Forest which straddles the Ypres to Staden railway. They were ordered to attack the German line on 26 October. Three Battalions were used: [17, 18, 19, 20]

The 7th Northumberland Fusiliers were on the left side:

Initially the attack proceeded as planned and the left-hand company reached its objective, but had no support at its flanks. During late morning the battalion suffered severely from sniper fire, which became so serious that the battalion was unable to consolidate its position. Later the battalion withdrew to its original position.

The 5th Northumberland Fusiliers were in the centre:

233

The attack was made using two companies, but almost immediately the right hand company was held up by machine-gun fire from a series of German blockhouses. The left hand company managed to gain a foothold on Hill 23 but was unable to go forward owing to intense machine-gun fire from the woods to their left. The companies held in reserve also incurred heavy casualties. At approximately 3pm the battalion was forced to withdraw to its original position.

The 4th Northumberland fusiliers were on the right:

Two companies attacked and made steady progress until they were held up about 150 yards from a series of concrete German blockhouses known as 'the huts', which poured a stream of murderous machine-gun fire on to the advancing troops. Due to the swampy nature of the ground on which they stood it was impossible to attempt an outflanking attack on these strong German positions. Any ground gained during the attack was abandoned under the cover of darkness.

Wyrell wrote of this attack, recording that it took place in pouring rain beginning at 5.40am with a creeping barrage. If the troops had been able to maintain the forward momentum behind this protecting curtain there would have been fewer deaths: [21]

> *"The rain had, however, done its deadly work, for all the gallant fellows could do was to drag themselves along through the thick clinging mud and water at a much slower pace than the barrage, which soon got ahead. Then from the "pill box" and shell hole murderous fire was poured upon them. Many fell dead; some of the wounded fell into the gaping holes of water and were drowned; fortunate were those who escaped, but on went the survivors."*

The Allied barrage consisted entirely of shrapnel, which was completely useless against the series of reinforced concrete bunkers faced by the attack. By evening the brigade was withdrawn and by nightfall eighteen officers and three hundred and sixty seven men from the 149th Brigade had died. Countless others would die from their wounds in the following days.

Private Joseph T Stewart, aged 22
1/7th Battalion Northumberland Fusiliers
Died 26 October 1917

Joseph was born in Hexham in 1896. He was the third son of John and Sarah Jane Stewart of Holy Island, Hexham. In July 1916 the Hexham herald reported that he was wounded by shrapnel and was in a base hospital in France. He was reported missing in October 1917, but it was not until August 1918 that his death was officially confirmed.

Joseph is commemorated on the Tyne Cot Memorial to the missing.

Private Robert Hudson, aged 21
1/5th Battalion Northumberland Fusiliers
Died 26 October 1917

 Robert was born in Corbridge, the youngest son of John and Mary Ann Hudson. He was the adopted son of Mr and Mrs T Dunwoodie, who had lived at Garden Terrace, Hexham. At the time of his death his address was Munitions Cottages, Scotswood. Before enlisting Robert was employed by Mr Grant at the Hydropathic in Hexham. At the time of enlisting in late 1915 he was a corporal in the Boys' Brigade. He served in France from late 1916.

Robert is commemorated on the Tyne Cot Memorial to the missing.

Private Robert Lendren, aged 24
1/5th Battalion Northumberland Fusiliers
Died 26 October 1917

Robert was born in Hexham and was the husband of Alice Lendren of Market Place, Hexham. Before enlisting he was employed by Messrs W A Temperley, Seed Merchants of Beaufront Street, Hexham. Early in 1917 it was reported that Robert had been wounded and was suffering from compound fractures of the chest. After recuperation he returned to his battalion, only to die at Passchendaele later in the year.

Robert is commemorated on the Tyne Cot Memorial to the missing.

The Commonwealth War Grave Commission records Robert's name as Lendrem.

In similar fashion, the 188th Brigade took over the Front Line in readiness for their part in the first day of the attack. Two battalions from the 189th Brigade were also included in this operation: Hood as a counter attacking force and Hawke as Brigade Reserve. Rain was falling on the morning of 26 October as the attack began at 5.40am. Late in the evening Hood Battalion moved up to take over positions in the vicinity of Varlet Farm, previously occupied by Anson and Howe Battalions. [22, 23]

Able Seaman James Robson, aged 28
Hood Battalion, Royal Naval Division
Died 26 October 1917

James was the third son of Anthony and Mrs A Robson of Priestpopple, Hexham. He had been employed as a passenger parcels porter at Hexham Station, but was working at the Central Station, Newcastle when he enlisted in December 1914. In 1915 he served with Hood Battalion in the Dardanelles for nine months, from where he was invalided home suffering from typhoid and dysentery. After a lengthy period he was posted back to the Front in September 1916. The family has already lost a son earlier in the war, Private John Robson, (killed in action 15 February 1917 serving with the 1/4th Northumberland Fusiliers, see Chapter Thirteen). His other brothers Alfred (Northumberland Fusiliers) and Selby (Army Service Corps), were also serving at the Front when James died.

James is commemorated on the Tyne Cot Memorial, which records the names of men who have no known grave.

By 1917 the Royal Field Artillery, whose primary job was to give close support to attacking infantry, had developed very accurate tactics using its 18-pdr guns and 4.5-inch field howitzers. These tactics involved the development of accurate moving barrages behind which the infantry could be protected as they moved forward. They also mastered the production of a protective curtain of fire between the enemy and the position captured by the advancing infantry, allowing them time to consolidate their gains. The destruction of the formidable German concrete blockhouses was also a priority for the RFA.

In early 1917 the 23rd Brigade Royal Field Artillery, which had supported 3rd Division operations, was transferred to an Army

Brigade. Teams of horses drew both types of gun. 'C' Battery consisted of six 4.5-inch field howitzers. One of the responsibilities of the battery drivers, after they had manoeuvred their guns in to their firing positions, was to supply each of the guns with ammunition.

Driver James Murray Spedding, aged 28
'C' Battery 23ʳᵈ Brigade Royal Field Artillery
Died 28 October 1917

James was the eldest son of Charles and Hannah Spedding, who lived at the Grammar School, Hexham. Before enlisting in the summer of 1915 he worked as a market gardener with Mrs W Alexander. He was also a member of Corbridge Rowing Club. He went to the Front in April 1916 and was wounded in the early part of 1917. After recuperation he returned to France in September of that year.

Major Walton RFA wrote to Mrs Spedding:

"I deeply regret to inform you that your son, Driver Spedding, of the battery under my command, was instantaneously killed by a shell on the evening of the 28th October 1917 at about 4pm. He was at the time bringing munitions up to the guns in action. His body was taken back to a British Military Cemetery about five miles behind the line, and there buried with full military honours by a chaplain of the forces in the presence of many of his comrades, on the 31st October. He was one of the best drivers that I have had and was selected as likely to receive promotion in the near future. The battery officers and men will feel the loss of one of its popular members very keenly. May we offer you our very sincere sympathy in your great bereavement."

James is buried in Duhallow ADS Cemetery, Ypres.

At the beginning of the war, tasks such as the repair of roads and the building of defences was carried out by the fighting soldier who had been withdrawn from the Front for 'rest'. By 1917 it was realised that ever-increasing numbers of men were needed for such work and that the old system was not allowing fighting soldiers to return rested to the Front. As a response to this, the British Army's Labour Corps was formed.

The men who manned the Labour Corps were either ex-Front Line soldiers who had been wounded or ill, or men who on enlistment were unfit for Front Line service because of ill health or age. By the end of the war the Labour Corps consisted of over 400,000 men, (nearly 11% of the army) and a further 300,000 foreign workers, including Chinese.

The duties of the men of the Labour Corps were to undertake any labouring task required, including building and repairing roads and railways, laying cables etc. Some companies guarded prisoners of war, whilst others were employed at the Divisional Baths.

On the Western Front the men worked, unarmed, in extremely dangerous conditions – often within range of German Artillery. Deaths from enemy shelling were a common occurrence. To support a major attack such as Passchendaele across its landscape of desolation and seas of mud it was imperative that both supplies got to the Front and that the artillery was able to support the attacking infantry. This unenviable work was the responsibility of the Labour Corps.

Private Walter Henry Smith, aged 41
33rd Company, Labour Corps
Died 8 November 1917

Walter was eldest son of John Smith of Hexham. He was a married man and had lived in Market Street. Like his father he was a member of the 1st Volunteer Battalion Northumberland Fusiliers and enlisted with the local Battalion of the Fusiliers at the outbreak of hostilities. Before the hostilities he served his apprenticeship and was a journeyman with the Hexham Herald. He also worked as a compositor with a number of the town's printers. He went to the Front in February 1917 as part of the Labour Corps.

On 8 November the 33rd Company were working in a forward area on the light railway system used to transport munitions and supplies to the Front. In a letter to Walter's wife dated the 9 November, Major Wrigley wrote:

"Madam, I deeply regret having to inform you of the death of your husband, Pte W H Smith, of this company. He was killed by a shell whilst returning with a small party from work yesterday and today was buried near where he fell. He will be much missed by all his friends in the company and I would ask you to accept the deep sympathy of myself and all other ranks of the company with you in your loss."

As well as Walter, Private G W Byram of Sunderland was also killed. A further eight men were wounded.

In 1916, Walter's brother Sergeant Major John William Smith was presented with the Legion of Honour by the President of the French Republic, in recognition of distinguished service in the field. Also his two stepsons received discharges from the Army owing to wounds received in action. A further stepson was still with the Colours when Walter died.

Walter is buried in Perth Cemetery, Ypres.

On 15 November the *Third Battle of Ypres* was officially declared over, but the newly established Front needed to be guarded. Constant maintenance of the Front Line trenches was necessary, as were repairs to the infrastructure which had been destroyed throughout the months of this long battle.

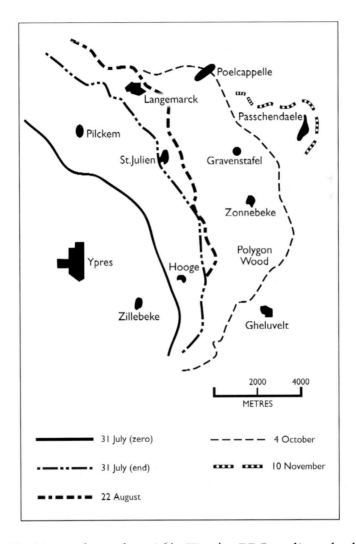

On 29 November the 16th King's RRC relieved the 1st Cameronians in the Passchendale sector to the northeast and southeast of the ruined church in the centre of Passchendaele village. On 1 December the 8th Division on the left carried out

an attack and the King's assisted by offering rifle and machine gun fire. Just after midnight on 2 December, the Germans launched an artillery barrage which lasted for six hours. Later in the day this became more intermittent. As a result of this barrage the King's battalion suffered many casualties, particularly 'A' Company. The battalion stayed in the Line until 5 December and continued to suffer intermittent shelling. [24]

Private Percy Scott Milburn, aged 25
16th (Service) Battalion King's Royal Rifle Corps
Died 2 December 1917

Percy was the youngest son of Mr and Mrs Thomas Milburn of Battle Hill. Before enlisting in late 1915 he was employed by Mr H W Gillies, an ironmonger of Market Place, Hexham.

In the spring of 1917 it was reported that he had been wounded in the shoulder and the leg. After convalescence he returned to France, only five weeks before his death. He was killed in action from a shell bursting in the trench.

Percy is buried at Passchendaele New British Cemetery.

The following inscription is found on his headstone:

THY WILL BE DONE

References

1. Maddocks, G. *Liverpool Pals,*
   Pub: Pen and Sword 1991.

2. WO 95/2644. *War Diary, 26th Battalion Royal Fusiliers.*

3. WO 95/1809. *War Diary, 6th Battalion Yorkshire Regiment.*

4. WO 95/2127. *War Diary, 7th Battalion King's Own Yorkshire Light Infantry.*

5. WO 98/8. *Victoria Cross Register, Private Wilfred Edwards.*

6. WO 95/2182. *War Diary, 11th Battalion Northumberland Fusiliers.*

7. WO 95/2587/2. *War Diary, 17th Battalion Sherwood Foresters.*

8. WO 95/2805. *War Diary, 1/4th Battalion Yorks and Lancaster Regiment.*

9. Shakespear, Lt Col. J. *Thirty Fourth Division, 1915-1919,*
   Pub: 1921, reprinted Naval & Military Press 1998.

10. Sheen, J A. *History of the Tyneside Irish,*
    Pub:Pen and Sword, 1998.

11. WO 95/2398. *War Diary, 16th Battalion Northumberland Fusiliers.*

12. WO/95/2463. *War Diary, 25th Battalion Northumberland Fusiliers.*

13. Cooke, Capt. C H. *Historical Records 16th Battalion Northumberland Fusiliers.*
Pub: Council of Newcastle and Gateshead Incorporated Chamber of Commerce 1923.

14. Miles, Capt. W. *Durham Forces in the Field,*
Pub: 1920, reprinted Naval & Military Press 2004.

15. Stewart, G. and Sheen, J A. *History of the Tyneside Scottish,*
Pub;Pen and Sword Books, 1999.

16. WO 95/2462. *War Diary, 20th Battalion Northumberland Fusiliers.*

17. WO 95/2826. *War Diary, 1/4th Battalion Northumberland Fusiliers.*

18. WO 95/2828. *War Diary, 1/5th Northumberland Fusiliers.*

19. WO/95/2828. *War Diary, 1/7th Northumberland Fusiliers.*

20. Buckley, Capt. F. *War History of the Seventh Northumberland Fusiliers.*

21. Wyrell, E. *The Fiftieth Division, 1914-1919*
Pub: 1939, reprinted, Naval and Military Press 2002.

22. Page, C. *Command in the Royal Naval Division,*
Pub: Spellmount Limited 1999.

23. Sellers, L. *Hood Battalion.*
Pub:Pen And Sword 2004.

24. WO 95/2430. *War Diary, 16th Service Battalion Kings Royal Rifle Corps.*

CHAPTER FIFTEEN

THE SWORD OF DAMOCLES

Shall they return to beatings of great bells
In wild train loads?
A few, a few, too few for drums and yells,
May creep back, silent, to still village wells
Up half-known roads.

Wilfred Owen, *The Send Off*

Overview

In late 1917, exactly a year before the end of the war, the German High Command decided that they must make a decisive attack on the British Army in the Spring of 1918. They saw that the British were clearly taking the lead and that British Forces were continuing to inflict damage on the German Army. Their decision to make a major attack was based on the fair assumption that the British Army was weakened and exhausted after four major campaigns in 1917 (*Arras, Messines, Passchendaele* and *Cambrai*). Another factor weighing on the High Command's mind was that America was about to enter the fray. The Germans envisaged that their proposed offensive – called the *Kaiserschlacht* (Kaiser's Battle) – was going to end their war victoriously.

The winter of 1917 was very severe – in Paris the Seine froze over and at the Front conditions were truly miserable. On 3 March, the Russian allies concluded a separate peace with the signing of the Brest Litovsk Treaty, having sued for peace unilaterally. As a result the Germans were able to transfer large numbers of troops from the Eastern Front to the West.

Thus, more than fifty German Divisions faced the British Front. During the first part of 1918 the Germans launched five major offensives against a tired and under-manned Allied army.

Operation Michael

The first of the German offences was code named *Michael*. The aim of this attack, launched on 21 March, was to punch a hole in the Allied defences on the Somme and then to wheel north-west to cut the British lines of communication behind the Artois Front. This would bottle up the British in Flanders, allowing them no means of escape, and should lead to surrender.

In late 1917 the Allied command in France adopted a two-zone system along its Front:
The *Forward Zone* would contain a number of highly defended redoubts which were not physically connected but which would allow lines of interconnected killing zones between them if the weather were clear.
The Battle Zone would be more stringently defended and would be where the main fighting would occur if the Front were threatened. Many of the troops and Field Commanders did not fully understand this new defensive system.

The majority of the area to be attacked during Operation Michael had only recently been taken over from the French by the British. When it was taken over the Front Line hardly existed and required significant construction to make it defensible. Because of a severe political crisis between Lloyd George (the British Prime Minister) and the Army, hardly any manpower reserves were being allocated to the Army, leaving it severely under-manned. The Divisional system of 12 Battalions was reduced to 9 Battalions. As the battle started, few of the defensive positions were ready and the second and third defensive lines barely existed.

246

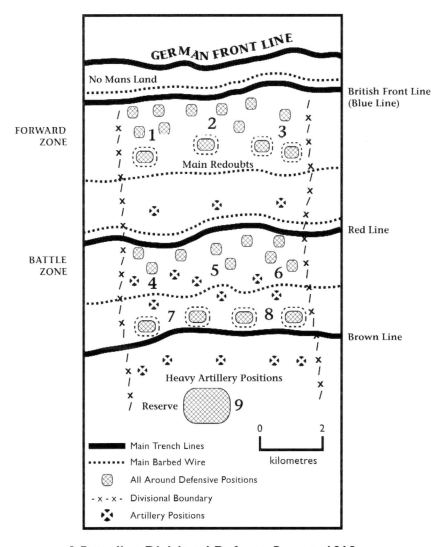

9 Battalion Divisional Defence System 1918

On the foggy morning of 21 March, on a Front from Arras to a few miles south of Saint Quentin, the Germans launched their first offensive. The Germans opened up with their artillery at 4.40am along the whole of the Front. The intense barrage of gas shells and high explosives was concentrated not only on the forward posts but also on British artillery and machine gun positions, headquarters, telephone exchanges, railways and other centres of communication. Its intention was to limit the British ability to respond to the attack. Between 7 – 10am the German infantry moved forward, taking advantage of foggy conditions. Using newly-developed infiltration techniques the first units penetrated gaps in the British defence system whilst stronger points were 'mopped up' later. At many areas of the Front, German soldiers outnumbered the British by four to one.

Both the 22nd and 23rd Battalions Northumberland Fusiliers were in the *Forward Zone* of the defence system on the morning of 21 March, southeast of the village of Croisilles and east of Fontaine les Croisilles, a village that was in German hands. At about 5am the Germans began an intense artillery barrage consisting of gas and high explosive shells, which lasted for five hours. Fortunately, the foggy weather prevented the German artillery observers from correcting their fire, saving the lives of many of the defenders. The 22nd Battalion came under immediate attack while to their right elements of the 59th Division were forced back. According to plan, two platoons from the 25th Northumberland Fusiliers moved up from reserve. It was not until the afternoon that the 23rd Battalion came under pressure from advancing German Storm-Troopers. Soon the headquarters of these battalions had been surrounded and they were forced to surrender. Those who managed to escape fought their way northwards but the enemy, now with the thick fog on their side, were able to outflank their new defensive positions. [1, 2]

The stubborn defence of Bunhill Row and the fighting retreat of the Tyneside Battalions of 102nd Brigade (22nd, 23rd and 25th Northumberland Fusiliers) brought special praise from their Divisional Commander, Major General Nicholson, who wrote: [1, 2]

"On my own behalf I wish to record my high appreciation of the gallantry and the stubborn power of resistance shewn (sic) by all ranks and arms of the Division on the 21ˢᵗ and 22ⁿᵈ of March.

When the full story is known of the gallant fight of the 102ⁿᵈ and part of the 101ˢᵗ Brigade on the 21ˢᵗ March when outflanked and almost surrounded, the stubborn and protracted resistance of the 11ᵗʰ Suffolk on the left of the Division on the 21ˢᵗ and 22ⁿᵈ of March and the steady disciplined gallantry of the 103ʳᵈ Brigade will go down in history among the achievements of the war."

Private John Dodd, aged 23
23ʳᵈ (Service) Battalion, (Tyneside Scottish)
Northumberland Fusiliers
Died 21 March 1918

 John was born in Hexham, the second son of Mr and Mrs Paxton Dodd of Haugh Lane, Hexham. Before joining up in 1915 John was employed by the South Tyne Paper Mill. His older brother Paxton was killed in October 1917, see Chapter 14. His younger brother was also serving in France and in May 1918 Mr and Mrs Dodd received news that their remaining son had been wounded in the left arm and had lost a finger.

John is commemorated on the Arras Memorial to the missing.

Private Thomas Lancaster, aged 38
23rd (Service) Battalion (Tyneside Scottish)
Northumberland Fusiliers
Died 23 March 1918

Thomas was born in Wray in Lancashire and was the husband of Jane, who later remarried and became Jane Campbell. He was the son of Paul and Mary Lancaster of Brisco Road, Carlisle. He joined the forces in early 1916 and was wounded in February 1917, returning to the Front in the summer.

He is commemorated on the Arras Memorial, which names men with no known grave.

In the early hours of 22 March, the 1/5th Northumberland Fusiliers (149th Brigade, 50th Division) were moved to Caulaincourt (about six miles east of St Quentin) and ordered to dig a new line of defence known as the Green Line. At 3pm the Germans attacked this position and broke through the defensive line. In response the battalion mounted a counter-attack and held the enemy on a nearby ridge. Casualties for the day were 1 officer and 70 other ranks killed, 33 other ranks wounded and 2 officers and 35 other ranks missing. The next day the battalion was withdrawn to the east of Monchy - Lagache (a withdrawal of over three miles) and later in the day they were withdrawn to south-east of Athies, where they were outflanked and forced to retire eastwards across the Somme at St Christ. [3]

2nd Lieutenant John McIntosh, aged 32
16th (Service) Battalion Northumberland Fusiliers
Attached 1/5th Battalion Northumberland Fusiliers
Died 22 March 1918

John was one of three sons of Angus and Ellen McIntosh of Kingsgate Terrace, Hexham. In 1900, whilst serving his apprenticeship with J Lee (Blacksmith) of Bridge End, Hexham he enlisted in with the 19th (Queen Alexandria's Own Royal) Hussars, where he rose to the

rank of Company Sergeant Major, going on to serve in South Africa. As a professional soldier he went with the initial British Expeditionary Force to France, *The Old Contemptibles.* He was involved in the drastic fighting during the retreat from Mons and was a proud wearer of the Mons Star. It is reported that his squadron officer, who was killed before the recommendation could be confirmed, recommended him for the Distinguished Conduct Medal. In early 1917 he was granted a Commission with the 16th Battalion Northumberland Fusiliers for services in the field, and was latterly attached to the 1/5th Battalion.

He is commemorated on a special memorial in Trefcon British Cemetery, Caulaincourt:

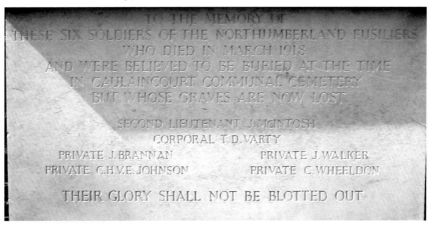

TO THE MEMORY OF
THESE SIX SOLDIERS OF THE NORTHUMBERLAND FUSILIERS
WHO DIED IN MARCH 1918
AND WERE BELIEVED TO BE BURIED AT THE TIME
IN CAULAINCOURT COMMUNAL CEMETERY
BUT WHOSE GRAVES ARE NOW LOST

SECOND LIEUTENANT J. McINTOSH
CORPORAL T.D. VARTY
PRIVATE J. BRANNAN   PRIVATE J. WALKER
PRIVATE C.H.V.E. JOHNSON   PRIVATE C. WHEELDON

THEIR GLORY SHALL NOT BE BLOTTED OUT

While I was researching this book I was sent an account, written by Mr Studleigh Errington of North Shields, relating to information given to him by his late father-in-law, Norman McIntosh, nephew of John. Norman and his brother Stuart both remembered well John's last leave (mentioned in the account), because he gave Stuart a German helmet. Although it seems likely that John was indeed killed on the Somme, there was a family legend about him that is worth inclusion. The following quotes Norman McIntosh's account:

> *"On leaving school John was apprenticed to a blacksmith on the Hexham Bridge End. He disliked the work intensely, but his parents would not allow him to leave. He was subsequently discharged for deliberately applying a hot horse shoe to the rump of a customer's horse. He was then able to pursue his chosen desire to become a regular soldier in the 19th Hussars.*
>
> *The 1914 war duly came, and with his experience he was with the first army units to go to France. About 1916 he was prevailed upon to take a commission much to his dismay as it would appear he had little inclination to be either an officer or a gentleman. In the end he did accept even though it meant his leaving his beloved Hussars and being transferred to the Royal Northumberland Fusiliers.*
>
> *In 1917 he came home on leave, the first time since going to France. It was said that he had formed an attachment to a farmer's daughter in France and had spent most of his free time with her. He bade a last farewell to his crippled mother and said to his brother Angus, "We will never see each other again". This proved to be the case. In March 1918 he was posted as missing in action. After that according to the family nothing else was heard about him. He was never confirmed as being killed and his personal effects and medals were never returned.* [After the war, John's brother Angus, a bank manager in Corbridge, did go to great lengths to try and find any information about the death of his brother.]
>
> *His family had a theory which given the circumstances seemed to fit the situation. It goes like this: he changed his name and his identity, went off with his girlfriend and started a new life. Speaking fluent French as he did, this would have been an easy option at this time".*

It may be that John's family, wishing to shield their 'desperately ailing' crippled mother from the sorrow of her son's death, devised this romantic tale in order to explain his disappearance. As Norman went on to say:

"He had never been close to his family or relations, so just maybe John survived somewhere, we will never know. All that remains of him is this one picture."

One last mystery remains ... If the story *was* an elaborate invention, as suggested, why did they not set the matter straight with their respective children (i.e. John's nephews and nieces) after their mother's death? Whatever the truth of this tale, Studleigh Errington felt a 'great sad relief' when, on visiting Hexham, he noticed by chance John's name inscribed on the west face of the Abbey Memorial:

"His home town had not failed him. He was, and is, remembered with pride"

The 20ᵗʰ Durham Light Infantry, newly arrived from Italy, joined 124ᵗʰ Brigade 41ˢᵗ Division, and were quickly moved to the Somme. On 22 March they took up a position near the village of Vaulx-Vraucourt (about three miles northeast of Bapaume) and by that evening they formed the Front Line, with a battalion of the Queens on their right. After a relatively peaceful night, at 8am the Durhams' trenches were subjected to a fierce bombardment followed by the advance of masses of German infantry. They repulsed this attack using rifle and Lewis gunfire. Even after six attempts by the Germans the Durhams still held their position with wonderful courage. Lance-Corporal E Forman, a Lewis gunner, won the Distinguished Conduct Medal for his efforts that day. At their position astride the Vaulx-Vraucourt road 'B' Company was involved in some of the fiercest fighting; they suffered heavy casualties, including the death of their commander Captain J H Iveson. At 5pm the next evening, after a further day of intense fighting, the order to retire was received and a new defensive line west of Favreuil was established. By 26 March, after a series of withdrawals, the Allied Front Line rested on a position where the German Front line had been before the battle of the Somme in 1916. During this frantic time the 20ᵗʰ

Durham Light Infantry had over fifty men killed.[4]

Captain James Henry Iveson, aged 34
20th (Service) Battalion Durham Light Infantry
Died 23 March 1918

James was the second son of William and Elizabeth Iveson of Tynedale House, Hexham. Before joining the Forces in August 1914 he worked for the family firm of Messrs W and T T Iveson, auctioneers and valuers. Before joining the family business he had worked in Lloyds Bank in Bellingham. James was an enthusiastic golfer and a keen tennis player.

He went out to France at the end of 1914. In January 1916 the Hexham Herald reported that he had been wounded and partially gassed going to the assistance of a fellow officer and was recuperating in base hospital in Boulogne. His younger brother Frank was killed in June 1915 on the Gallipoli Peninsula (see Chapter Five). Another brother, Alfred was also serving at the Front.

James is commemorated on the Arras Memorial to the Missing.

On 22 March the 20th Middlesex Regiment (121st Brigade 20th Battalion) was sent to Mory Abbaye, (about four miles north of Bapaume) and by 5am they had dug new trenches and were installed in their defensive position. Some men were killed by enemy shelling, including Errol Sparke. At 1pm they received orders to reinforce their right flank as the Germans had broken through in the direction of Vaulx-Vraucourt; men were dispatched to occupy trenches north of Beugnatre (on the outskirts of Bapaume) and soon came under heavy shell fire. Although the situation remains extremely obscure, it appears that the Yorkshire and Suffolk regiments on their flanks had been driven in and that they were to fill the gap between these two regiments. This was achieved by late evening. Later scouts reported that the Germans were on the outskirts of the village of Mory. The next day, 23 March, men of the 20th Middlesex were involved in a series of desperate counter-attacks. [56]

Second Lieutenant Errol Sparke, aged 28
20th (Service) Battalion Middlesex Regiment
Died 22 March 1918

Errol was the youngest son of John and Mary Sparke of Elvaston Road, Hexham. In July 1916, whilst serving on the Somme as a corporal with the Bedfordshire Regiment, he was wounded. During his convalescence, he obtained a commission in the Middlesex Regiment.

Errol is commemorated on the Arras Memorial to the missing.

On 24 March the 1st Battalion Coldstream Guards were in trenches west of the village of Hamelincourt, (between Arras and Bapaume). In the evening the Germans took the village of Ervillers to the southeast of Hamelincourt but were later evicted by the 2nd Irish Guards. Later, the Coldstream Guards were ordered to dig a new trench facing southeast as the situation on their right flank was considered critical. During an afternoon with a series of conflicting orders, the battalion retired to a line east of the village of Adinfer (approximately four miles east of their original position near Hamelincourt) into a trench system which existed on the maps but as yet had not been dug. They spent the night digging. Confusing orders had left the neighbouring 31st Division in their original position and so the Guards were left with their right flank exposed. In the afternoon of 26 March, the German artillery was very busy and the villages of Hamelincourt and Moyenville were severely shelled. Shelling continued into the evening.[7]

Private John Alder Ferrol, aged 22
1st Battalion Coldstream Guards
Died 26 March 1918

John was born in Hexham and was the youngest son of Andrew and Elizabeth Ferrol of Prior Terrace. His parents were informed that he had been wounded on the 25 March and had been admitted to a casualty clearing station. He died of his wounds the following day.

John is commemorated on the Arras Memorial to the missing.

On 26 March the 1/4th Northumberland Fusiliers, together with other elements of the 50th Division, formed a defensive Front north of the village of Assevillers on the south side of the River Somme. Early in the morning the Germans attacked in strength from the south. At the same time the 66th Division to the north of the defensive line was attacked and retired under pressure leaving the left flank of the line exposed, which was temporarily restored by counter-attack by two companies of the 1/5th Northumberland Fusiliers. At 10am the 149th Brigade (1/4, 1/5 and 1/6 Northumberland Fusiliers) withdrew to a defensive line between Rosières and Vauvillers. The 1/4th Northumberland Fusiliers occupied posts around the village of Vauvillers and in the afternoon drove the enemy from the village of Framerville, withdrawing back to Vauvillers in the middle of the night.

Early in the morning of 27 March the Germans attacked the Rosières Line held by the 149th Brigade but were unable to make any gains; even so the position was abandoned by noon. The new Line was held by troops from 8th, 39th, 50th (149th Brigade) and 66th Divisions, who during the afternoon counter-attacked and recaptured Vauvilliers inflicting heavy losses on the enemy, whilst men of the 149th Brigade drove the enemy back from Harbonnières, with the 1/4th Northumberland Fusiliers capturing fifty prisoners and two machine guns. Early in the evening the Brigade withdrew to Rosières. At 8pm there was another determined German attack with the enemy advancing in twelve waves, but these were repulsed. [89]

That night the Allied line south of the Somme ran from Mensal-St-George (west of Montdidier) to Hamel via Boussicourt, Arvillers, Warvillers, Rosières and Harbonnières.

Private John Pencott, aged 21
1/4th Battalion Northumberland Fusiliers
Died 27 March 1918

John was born in Hexham and was the second son of Thomas Pencott of Gilesgate Bank, Hexham. Before enlisting under the Derby Scheme, he was employed by H Bell and Sons, Woolstaplers. He was a signaller and was killed by a sniper on Good Friday, 27 March 1918. His brother Thomas was also serving in France and was awarded the Military Medal for outstanding bravery.

John is commemorated on Pozières Memorial, Somme, which commemorates men with no known grave.

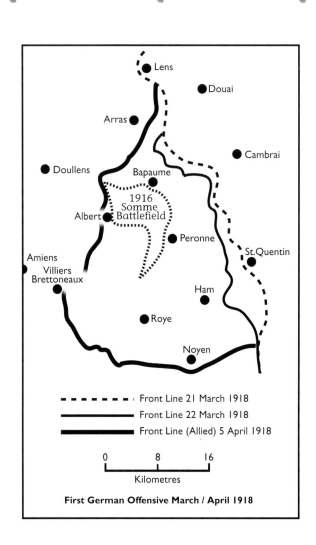

First German Offensive March / April 1918

Officially the battles associated with the German advance (Operation Michael), over the old Somme battlefield ended on 4 April, when the Allies managed to halt the German incursion just east of Villers-Bretonneux (five miles east of Amiens).

Between April and the *Battle of Amiens* (8 –10 August), small-scale actions along the new Front Line were taking place daily, including an Australian led attack to straighten out the Front Line around the village of Le Hamel in July. In early August, the British launched a massive and decisive attack on this Front from which the Germans never recovered. In between these two events men died as they guarded the Front from further German incursion

On 6 April, the day that the Germans captured Albert, the 19th Northumberland Fusiliers moved up to Aveluy Wood, just north of and overlooking Albert. This body of pioneers, whose job it was to prepare defensive positions, were detailed to move towards the village of Senlis and prepare a trench system from a series of rifle pits. They were also detailed to repair the Warloy – Senlis road. During 10 – 11 April the Germans shelled Senlis persistently with high explosive (HE) and gas shells, which warranted an evacuation of the village.

Casualties for the period 10 – 11 April were: other ranks 6 killed and 12 wounded. [10]

The Battalion history makes disparaging comments about the quality of the men that were being received from home: many of them were unable to meet both the physical and mental challenges of digging trenches under enemy fire. A good number of the younger men needed a lot of training at a juncture when time was of the essence and when the Germans were constantly 'breathing down their necks'.[11]

Serjeant Charles Edward Snowball, aged 32
19th (Service) Battalion, (2nd Tyneside Pioneers)
Northumberland Fusiliers
Died 11 April 1918

Charles was born in Hexham and was the fourth son of Mr M Snowball of Prior Terrace. In his formative years he was an active member of the Abbey's Church Brigade and later joined the Territorials. In his year of joining up he won the Recruits' Prize. As a trained joiner he spent some time in Belfast where he was employed on the building of the ill-fated Titanic. A married man with one child, he joined up in Newcastle shortly after the outbreak of the war and saw over two and a half years of service on the Western Front. However, he also spent some time in hospital in Sheffield suffering from trench fever, returning to France on Good Friday, 28 March 1918. An explosion of an artillery shell two weeks later killed him.

Charles is buried in Hédauville Communal Cemetery Extension. Hédauville is about 3 miles north west of Albert.

The 79th Brigade Royal Field Artillery was attached to the 17th Division. The Brigade consisted of both 18-pdr guns and 4.5in howitzers. 'B' Battery was equipped with the standard 18-pdr guns. From 9 May the Brigade was based at Mesnil (approximately four miles north of Albert) and was involved in the shelling of enemy positions using a mixture of shrapnel, high explosive and gas shells. Later in the month the Brigade supported a local action undertaken by the Hawke Battalion of the Royal Naval Division. [12]

Second Lieutenant John Traquair Strang, aged 20
'B' Battery 79th Brigade Royal Field Artillery
Died 18 May 1918

John was the son of J D and D C Strang, formerly of Shanghai, China. At the time of John's death Mrs Strang was living in Hexham. It is reported that he joined up in 1914, although obviously he was under the legal age, and the Hexham Courant reports that he saw a good deal of fighting in France.

He was accepted into officer training college and had obtained his commission only a few months before his death. Reports state that John was killed by splinters from a burst of shrapnel over his gun pit.

John is buried in Varennes Military Cemetery.

On 18 May the Australians prepared to attack the Germans on a Front between the Rivers Ancre and Somme, weakening their position in the Morlancourt basin south of Albert. The attack would involve battalions from the 5th and 6th Australian Brigades. Their objectives were to cut off the village of Ville in the north and advance on Morlancourt in the south. In the early hours of 19 May, two companies of the 18th Battalion (5th Brigade) carried out the main attack. The men from New South Wales made the attack over a Front of 750 yards, with spaces of ten yards between each soldier. They followed a well-laid creeping barrage and had soon captured the first line of trenches. This rapid advance nonetheless left pockets of Germans able to make a lot of mischief until they were mopped up by men of the following 19th Battalion.

The action at Ville and Morlancourt was a complete success, with a low level of casualties: 418 in all. Over 300 Germans were captured together with 45 machine guns. [13]

Private Willie Collins Brown, aged 24
18ᵗʰ Battalion Australian Infantry
Died 19 May 1918

Willie was born in Hexham in the summer of 1894 and after school he initially worked as a labourer before emigrating to Australia.

In Australia he also worked as a labourer and lived in North Yanco, New South Wales. He enlisted in January 1916 and after basic training he arrived in France in January 1917. His military records show that his mother, Jessie Brown of Wingrove Road, Newcastle, was his next of kin.

Willie is buried in Dive Copse British Cemetery.

In early 1918 the 1/9ᵗʰ Durham Light Infantry was transferred from the 151ˢᵗ Brigade 50ᵗʰ Division to become a pioneer battalion in the 62ⁿᵈ Division. At the beginning of June the battalion was working on strengthening the defences of the village of Foncquevillers (about twelve miles north of Albert). On 2 June the area came under heavy gas bombardment which killed two bandsmen (medical orderlies) and a transport soldier in nearby Souastre. It wounded a further two ordinary ranks and on 3 June another man was killed and six men wounded. During the whole of this time the battalion was working on the defences of this strongpoint. The War Diary states that selective platoons were withdrawn from work details in order to have a bath! On 9 June, six men of 'B' Company were wounded or killed, of whom one was a Hexham man:[14]

Private Samuel Bennet Morrison Morris, aged 18
1/9th Durham Light Infantry
Died 9 June 1918

Samuel was born in Aberdeen and was the eldest son of John William and Ann Craig Morris of Prior Terrace, Hexham. Before enlisting in October 1917 he was serving an apprenticeship with Messrs Charlton and Sons as a slater, and was an active member of the Church Lads Brigade.

Samuel was killed in action and is buried in Bienvillers Military Cemetery.

During the morning of 25 July the 1/8th London (174th Brigade 58th Division) was involved in a raid into the German Front Line, from a position near Ebarts Farm, which is near Baizieux, southwest of Albert. The attack began at 10am when about three hundred men went over the top; it was supported by the 58th Battalion Machine Gun Corps who fired 31,000 rounds of ammunition during the operation. Seventeen prisoners were taken during the raid and the history of the Post Office Rifles states that many more were shot when they tried to escape. After the raid the Germans allowed the British to collect their wounded without any interference. The raiders lost one officer and twenty six other ranks. [15] [16]

Lance Corporal John William Archer, aged 27
1/8th Battalion London Regiment (Post Office Rifles)
Died 25 July 1918

William was born in Alston and was the only son of John and Sarah Archer of Rye Terrace, Hexham. Before enlisting he was employed for five years with Robinson and Sons of Hexham and then by the General Post Office in Hexham.

William was killed in action and is buried at Dernancourt Communal Cemetery Extension. His headstone contains the following inscription:

EVER REMEMBERED BY HIS FATHER AND MOTHER AND SISTER

He is also commemorated in the Post Office Sorting Office, Bridge End Industrial Estate. This Plaque was originally situated in the Post Office on Battle Hill.

Georgette Offensive

Following the *Michael* offensive on the Somme, the Germans attacked on 9 April between Armentières and Béthune, on the river Lys west of Lille. This advance was code named Georgette. The Allied line broke at Laventie, about ten miles west of Lille, where a weak Portuguese division was unable to withstand the German attack and forced the Allies to withdraw to Estaires. To the south of the gap, the 55th Division held firm, forcing the main German thrust northwards towards the southern edge of the Ypres salient. The British evacuated Armentières on 11 April. On this day Haig issued an appeal to his army:

" … to fight it out! Every position must be held to the last man: there must be no retirement. With our backs to the wall…. Each one of us must fight on to the end."

By the end of 12 April the Germans had recaptured Ploegsteert Wood, Messines village, Wytschaete and St Eloi. As the Germans approached Hazebrouck the pace of their advance was slowing down and the British were able to hold their ground. The following day at Bailleul the combined 34th and 59th Divisions were able to further frustrate the German advance and on the Messines Ridge (captured spectacularly in June 1917) Australian and New Zealand troops defended their positions with great tenacity and courage.

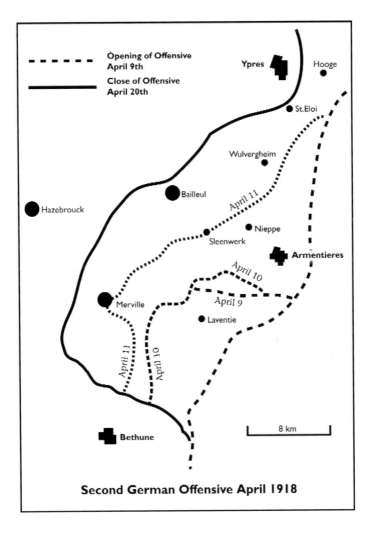

Second German Offensive April 1918

On 15 April the bloodied ground gained during the Passchendaele actions (1917) was evacuated by the Allies and a line around Ypres was defended (similar to their position in 1915). Numerous attempts were made by the Germans to gain the high ground around Ypres and to break the Anglo-French defences around the town. The final German attack on 29 April used thirteen German Divisions and yet was unable to break the Allied defences. This failure brought about the end of the Georgette Offensive.

At 4am on 9 April the Germans opened up their attack with a heavy bombardment of the Front Line. By 10am it was reported that the Portuguese were under attack and only an hour later it was confirmed that the Germans had broken through. The Germans followed this up by attacking the flanks of the 55th Division to the south and the 40th Division to the north. The Portuguese fled the scene, abandoning their guns. During the day the British Line was forced little by little back towards the River Lys. During the late afternoon the 1/4th Battalion Northumberland Fusiliers were ordered to move to the Front.

At the beginning of the offensive, the 102nd Brigade, made up of the Tyneside Scottish Battalion Northumberland Fusiliers, were in the Front Line to the east of Armentières. Until the morning of 10 April they saw very little direct action although they knew that further south the Germans were making progress against the British Front Line. At 2pm the order to withdraw was given and the 22nd Battalion withdrew company by company under withering enemy fire. When they reached the Estaires-Lys line they were ordered to take up defensive positions and soon the battalion was under heavy machine gun fire. The enemy didn't cause any problems during the night but they renewed their advance in the morning of 11 April. Somehow the Germans forced their way around behind the defensive position and were able to fire into the rear of the 22nd Battalion. 'C' Company was detailed to cover the withdrawal of 'A', 'B' and 'D' Companies and in the ensuing fighting nearly every man was injured or killed outright. Later in the day 102nd Brigade was again outflanked and forced into a further withdrawal. Further action was seen on 12 April when the remnants of the battalion were ordered into the Front Line near Steenwerck to stem further German advances.[12]

Private John Evans, aged 32
22nd (Service) Battalion (Tyneside Scottish)
Northumberland Fusiliers
Died 11 April 1918

John was born in Blyth and was the husband of Mrs Evans of St Wilfrid's Road, Hexham.

Before joining the army he was employed by Mrs Charlton of Market Place. Originally reported missing on April 11, it was later confirmed that he had been killed.

John is buried in Cabaret-Rouge British Cemetery, Souchez.

On 8 April the 50th Division had finished its move from the Somme to the Merville area. A draft of over three hundred men arrived to swell the numbers of 1/4th Battalion Northumberland Fusiliers, although according to the Battalion Diary they were all under the age of nineteen and of poor physique. During 9 – 10 April the division was ordered to relieve a Portuguese division in the Front Line east of Merville. Of the brigades making up the 50th Division, the 151st was to take the first turn in the Line. After fighting a number of rear guard actions the 1/4th Battalion was relieved by the Guards Brigade. In the period 13 – 16 April the Battalion was seconded to the 5th Division and the men were set to work as pioneers digging a defence line through the Bois de Vaches. It is reported that these were relatively quiet days, with few casualties, although there was a certain amount of shelling from a gun which was nicknamed 'Silent One'; its heavy calibre shells would arrive before any warning noise could be heard. [8 9 17]

Private Thomas Theodore McAdam, aged 22
1/4th Battalion Northumberland Fusiliers
Died 14 April 1918

Thomas was the son of Alexander and Eliza McAdam of Holy Island, Hexham.

He was killed in action and is buried in Le Grand Hasard Military Cemetery, Morbeccque.

During the early hours of 12 April, the 93rd Brigade (15th/17th West Yorkshire) was asked to extend its defensive line to make a Front of over three thousand yards. As a result the 15th/17th West Yorkshires were ordered up from support to take up a position on the left of the Line. At 9am elements on the right of the line began to retire and as a consequence three of the four companies of the 15th/17th fell back to Rau du Leet. Realizing that the battalion on its left would be exposed, the fourth company kept its position and formed a defensive flank, which became less and less tenable. To ease the situation the company made a successful counter-attack. By noon the position at Rau du Leet was made perilous because of enfilade machine gun fire, so the company made another extremely difficult withdrawal to the railway embankment, where they made contact with soldiers of the DLI and the York and Lancaster Regiment. Throughout, the Germans were able to get around the flank of the 93rd Brigade causing yet another withdrawal towards Merteren which was covered by the West Yorkshire Regiment. Late in the afternoon after further withdrawals, the remnants of the regiment were incorporated into the 33rd Division, taking up positions in a line which extended from the high ground south of Merteren to a point on the road between Merteren and Bailleul.

The fourth company involved in the counter-attack held its position for the rest of the day and late that night those who survived withdrew taking up positions near Bailleul Station. After a quiet time on 13 April the Germans attacked strongly on 14 April; once again the West Yorkshire Regiment were forced to fall back, taking up a position between St Jans Cappel and Mount Noir.[18]

During this action the West Yorkshire's casualties were very heavy: 3 officers killed, (including Lieutenant Colonel Tilley) 6 wounded and 2 missing. In the other ranks: 23 killed, 153 wounded and 143 missing (many missing would be reclassified at a later date as killed).

Private Charles Smith, aged 19
15th/17th Battalion West Yorkshire Regiment
(Prince of Wales's Own)
Died 12 April 1918

Charles was born in Hexham, the son of Mr and Mrs J Smith of Back Street. Before being called up he was a postman in Hexham. He was initially posted as missing but was very quickly confirmed as being killed in action. Charles was the second son that this family had lost to the fighting.

Charles is buried in Cabaret-Rouge British Cemetery, Souchez.

On the evening of 9 April the 1st Northumberland Fusiliers (9th Brigade, 3rd Division) were ordered to Noeux-les-Mines on attachment to the 55th Division who were under great pressure following the German breakthrough in the Portuguese sector. By the afternoon of 10 April the Fusiliers were at the Front, which was no more elaborate than a line of shell holes northeast of Le Hamel. Later the Germans attacked the British stronghold of Loisne Central, but after some little success they were beaten back and the Fusiliers captured a number of prisoners and a machine gun. During the night fresh troops were brought up into the Line. The next morning after a heavy bombardment the Germans attacked in strength against the Front from the River Loisne, west to the Lawe Canal forcing the centre and left portions of the Front back to a line from Mesplaux-le-Casan, leaving a gap in the defences. The Fusiliers filled this gap skilfully but many of them were mown down by machine gun fire.

The morning of 12 April saw all four companies of the 1st Northumberland Fusiliers side by side at the Front Line, which was no more than a trench two feet deep and two feet wide that had been dug hastily during the night. Later that night the Germans attacked the Line again near Mesplaux Farm (near Locon).

Throughout 13 April the Germans shelled the area around Mesplaux Farm and in the afternoon the whole Front was subjected to a heavy bombardment from both light and heavy artillery. At the time this bombardment was assumed by the Allies to be the precursor for a large infantry attack, but fortunately this did not materialise. However, its ferocity inflicted multiple casualties on the troops as they manned the Front in their improvised trenches.[19]

Private Harry Harvey Browne, aged 30
1st Battalion Northumberland Fusiliers
Died between 13 and 14 April 1918

Harry was the son of the late William Robert and Mary Browne of Hall Gate, Hexham. Since leaving school he had been employed by the postal services, initially as telegraph messenger and subsequently as a town postman. He was a committed member of the Salvation Army and was bandmaster for a number of years.

Harry was an unmarried man who lived with brother and sister in Wentworth Place. He enlisted in the army in November 1916 and was initially posted to York as a military bandsman. He went to the Front in August 1917 and had previously been wounded twice before he died in April 1917.

Harry is buried in Chocques Military Cemetery.

On the morning of 16 April the 1/7th Yorkshire held the right hand side of the 62nd Brigade Front from Bogaert Farm to Scott Farm, southwest of Wijtschate. At 4.30am the Germans fired a very heavy barrage, under the cover of which the German infantry advanced. A thick ground fog restricted the firepower of the Yorkshire men. During the morning they fought against overwhelming odds, holding this position until the evening of 17 April when they were ordered to retire to Siege Farm, a mile northeast of Kemmel. The next day they were relieved and rejoined their original brigade (146th). Although no casualty figures are available for the 1/7th during this action, it is believed that there were many.[18]

Rifleman Robert William Smith, aged 33
1/7th Battalion West Yorkshire Regiment
(Prince of Wales's Own)
Died 16 April 1918

 Robert was born in Hexham, the only son of Joseph and Isabella Smith. Before the War he lived in Bells Court, Hexham. After leaving school he trained as a printer. Originally he enlisted in the Northumberland Fusiliers, but was later transferred to the West Yorkshire Regiment.

Robert is commemorated on the Tyne Cot Memorial to the missing.

After their exertions during the earlier part of April, the 1/7th West Yorkshire, which had been reduced to a mere skeleton, spent until 23 April at Siege Farm. On 24 April, organised as a single company, they moved into the Vierstraat line as reserves for the 1/5th and 1/6th Yorkshires.[18]

On 25 April the Germans opened a tremendous bombardment along the entire British Front from Bailleul to Voormezeele. An officer in the 1/6 West Yorkshire described it:

> *"No one in these sectors had ever heard a bombardment which could be compared with it. Gas shells rained down in thousands, and in a few minutes a thick mist of gas covered the whole forward area. Telephone communications were broken instantly and companies were cut off from battalions and battalions from Brigade Headquarters... Under such a bombardment it seemed incredible that any human being in the forward area could survive to check the onrush of the German infantry."*

At 4.30am on a very foggy morning the bombardment lifted, passing over to target the back areas, leaving the front troops waiting for the onrush of German Infantry. This began just after 5.00am; the Germans' objective was the capture of Kemmel Hill.18 The 1/5th, 1/6th and 1/7th West Yorkshire, (146th Brigade) fought with true determination and the Brigade Diary sums up the chaotic position:[18]

> *"No certain news of the front line companies can be obtained as no man from the frontline rejoins his battalion. From evidence at hand, though, it appears that they all fought at their posts and died there."*

On 25 April the Brigade lost seven officers and two hundred and forty three other ranks killed. The 1/7th who had already been reduced to Company level lost a further two officers and sixteen other ranks.

Rifleman John Dunwoodie, aged 24
1/7th Battalion West Yorkshire Regiment
(Prince of Wales's Own)
Died 25 April 1918

John was born in Hexham, the son of John and Rose Anne Dunwoodie of Burn Lane. His parents initially received word that John was posted as 'missing in action', but later it was confirmed that he was dead even though no body could be found.

John is commemorated on the Tyne Cot Memorial to the missing.

The ASC (Army Service Corps), colloquially known as Ally Sloper's Cavalry, was the organisation responsible for the transport of food, equipment and ammunition to soldiers at the Front. The ASC was organised into companies, each one specialising in a mode of transport: horses, motors, canal or rail. In many cases these companies were attached to specific army formations and given the task of delivering specific supplies, such as ammunition.

In late 1918 the Army Service Corps was honoured by the addition of 'Royal' to its title in recognition of the prodigious feats of logistics performed by the Corps and in recognition that the war could not have been won without its considerable efforts.

Private John William Oxley, aged 36
593rd Motor Transport Company, Army Service Corps
Attached to VIII Corps Heavy Artillery
Died 12 April 1918

John was the third son of George Oxley of Hall Stile Bank. John was a married man, the husband of Anna Oxley of St Wilfrid's Lodge, Hexham and was the father of three children. Before enlisting he was employed by his friend J W Robinson. John was a Boer War veteran having served with the local yeomanry; he acted as orderly to Lord Roberts at Bloemfontein and to Lord Kitchener at Paardenburg. During the Boer War he was made captive by the Boers and spent time as a prisoner of war.

In a letter to his widow, an officer explained that John, a lorry driver, was stationed at an advanced tractor park, under direct observation of German guns. He went on to say that:

> *"A shell burst which pierced Oxley's shoulder and finally striking his heart which killed him instantaneously."*

John was buried with due military honours at Ypres Reservoir Cemetery.

Blucher Offensive

On 27 May the Germans launched their third offensive, codenamed *Blucher*, through the Chemin des Dames Ridge in the Champagne Region of France. The subsequent battle is known as the *Third Battle of the Aisne*. At the time of the offensive, four divisions of the British IX Corps, of which the 50th Northumbrian Division was part, were in the Front Line.

Early on 25 May the 1/4th Battalion Northumberland Fusiliers had taken a position in the forward defence zone (nearest to No Man's Land) in the sector allocated to the 149th Brigade. Two companies manned the forward outposts, one company in the first line trenches and one company in the battle line trench system. The 1/6th Battalion was held further back from the Front in reserve.

The death of Lance Corporal James Baty (recorded as Batey on the databases) is recorded for the 24 May 1918; he is recorded as 'died' (as opposed to 'killed') which normally refers to death from *illness*. However his death is commemorated on the Soissons War Memorial, which lists hundreds of his comrades who died during the Blucher Offensive launched by the Germans on 27 May 1918.

Lance Corporal James Baty (Batey), aged 30
1/4th Battalion Northumberland Fusiliers
Died 24 May 1918

James was born in Hexham and was living in Haydon Bridge when he enlisted.

He is commemorated on the Soissons Memorial to the missing.

To muddy the waters still further, the Roll of Honour published by the Hexham Courant in November 1919 records the date of James' death as 27 May 1918.

At 1am on Monday 27 May the forward defence area was subjected to an intense artillery barrage consisting of a mixture of high explosive and gas shells, which resulted in a great deal of injury and death.

The Reverend Callin wrote: [17]

> *"But on the stroke of 1 o'clock the whole front from Soissons to Reims(sic) broke into flame, and we knew that for the third time in ten weeks we were up against the real thing. Within fifteen minutes it was obvious that the Hun had an extraordinary concentration of guns of every calibre, and that his bombardment had been organised beforehand in most thorough and accurate fashion. A big proportion of gas was used, about four varieties being distinguished in the later French and British reports. The whole line was deluged with shells, and the front trenches especially must have been reduced to a pulverised mass."*

At 3.45am the Germans attacked along the whole Front. Survivors from the two companies of Fusiliers which had manned the forward outposts withdrew to a line of trenches, which they defended using Lewis guns and rifles. They managed to break up this initial attack and the enemy fell back. However by 4am the Germans had reformed and this time using four tanks they broke through the Battalion's right flank near Butte de Margrave. The Germans continued towards the Line which was held by one company of the 1/4th and by companies of the 1/6th Northumberland Fusiliers. Although the Fusiliers offered stiff resistance the enemy tanks soon broke the right flank of this defence. Behind this, in the Battle Zone, were four small French-built redoubts. At one of these, Centre Morceau, remnants of the 1/4th and 1/6th Battalions collected under the leadership of Lieutenant-Colonel Gibson and were able to hold it for some time. However, by 5.30 it was under attack – from the front, from the right and from the rear. Survivors finally withdrew to the Butte de l'Edmond, a defensive post which had been badly mauled by the enemy bombardment; all four of its machine guns had been damaged beyond use. Along with men of the Divisional Machine Gun Corps they fought for their lives. At this point, whilst organising the last defences, Lieutenant-Colonel Gibson was killed.[89]

Lieutenant Colonel Bertrand Dees Gibson, DSO, aged 42
Croix de Guerre avec Palms
1/4th Battalion Northumberland Fusiliers
Died 27 May 1918

Bertrand was the only son of Colonel Wilfred and Mrs Gibson of Ruradean, Hexham. He was the grandson of the late Charles Gibson, town clerk of Salford, Lancashire. He was born in January 1876 at Maiden Cross and was educated at Ushaw College, Durham. He was admitted a solicitor in partnership with his father in 1899. He practised in Hexham and Haltwhistle Courts and acted as solicitor to Hexham Farmers' Protection Association. He was married to Margaret Elizabeth Gibson (née Jackson, of Snaiton, Yorkshire).

He was very athletic and was reputed to have ben one of the finest lawn tennis players that Tynedale had produced. A sporting polymath, he also captained Northumberland at hockey. He played cricket and was a playing member of Tynedale Rugby Football Club.

He joined the old 1st VB Northumberland Fusiliers in 1900 and having passed through the school of musketry at Hythe was appointed instructor of musketry to the regiment. At mobilization he was promoted to the rank of Major. He went with the 1/4th Battalion, the local Territorial force, to France in April 1915 and saw action at the *Second Battle of Ypres* within days. During this battle his battalion commander, Lieutenant Colonel Forster, was killed and Bertrand assumed command. In the summer of 1915 he was gazetted to Lieutenant Colonel.

He earned his DSO in January 1917 for his courageous fighting on the Somme in September 1916. In the winter of 1917 he was invalided home with neuritis, but on reporting fit for duty he was not content with a desk job and returned to the Front in April, becoming Senior Officer for the 50th Division. Bertrand was awarded the Croix de Guerre avec Palms posthumously, in recognition of his leadership on the 27 May 1918.

The citation stated:

This officer was in command of his Battalion, which was holding the front line trenches on May 27, 1918 in the Aisne sector. He continued to send information of the enemy's advance until his Headquarters were completely surrounded. He then collected all available men of his Headquarter party, and although attacked on three sides it was due to this officer's personal example and total disregard of danger that the enemy were delayed in their advance for a considerable time. He was shot through the head and killed whilst standing on the parapet to get a better view of the enemy, when at the time they were advancing up a communication trench.

Bertrand is buried in La Ville-aux-Bois British Cemetery (Aisne). He is also commemorated on the Roll of Honour at the Abbey, St Mary's Roman Catholic Church, Tynedale Rugby Football Club, (now at Corbridge) and at the Territorial Drill Hall. He was survived by a wife, a son and a daughter.

His wife had the following inscribed on his French gravestone:

IN GLORIOUSLY PROUD MEMORY
OF MY BELOVED HUSBAND
"UNTIL"
QUO FATA VOCANT

The Hexham Herald reported that a shell had killed Bertrand. This information was received in a letter from Captain Gregory (Adjutant), who was in hospital in England having been wounded at the time that Bertrand was killed. However, the Reverend Callin reports that he was killed by a sniper's bullet.

The Divisional History records that:

> *"Lieutenant-Colonel Gibson was a Territorial Officer of great experience and reputation, a fine soldier and was greatly beloved by his Battalion."*

The Hexham Courant printed the following tribute to 'Lieutenant-Colonel BD Gibson DSO, who fell in action 27 May 1918':

Rest well beloved chief; we do not mourn you dead,
While memory lives o'er battle fields far spread,
And hearts still throb who fought close by thy side,
And speak, amid the hush, their deathless pride.
Sleep well beneath the Cross where thou art laid –
True symbol of the Gift that thou hast made;
While, o'er the mound that marks Life's battle won,
The zephyrs whisper of thy task well done.
Rest well, brave Chief – the Captain of the Guard
Shall mark your sleeping bed till the Award,
When, in the coming dawn, the bugles call
The waking-time to thee and comrades all.
Sleep loved Chief, sleep well,

J A Barton

Callin wrote of Lieutenant-Colonel Gibson:

> *"Thus the Battalion lost its Commanding Officer – a man revered and loved by all. All nerve and will, he died fighting to the last, the very incarnation of courage. A born leader and a superb soldier, he had joined in the early Volunteer days, finally becoming Commanding Officer in the summer of 1915. His name will be ever remembered by those who knew him as one of the straightest, strongest men we have known".*

On the same day, an attempt by two companies of the 1/5th Battalion Northumberland Fusiliers to reinforce the Battle Zone was unsuccessful. Just after 6am the last of their redoubts were taken and from this moment both the 1/4th and 1/6th Battalions Northumberland Fusiliers ceased to exist as fighting units.

Later in the day, remnants of these units formed a defensive position at the canal bridge south of Chaudardes, but by 9am they realised that this position was untenable and they were forced to cross the Aisne where other men from fragmented units gathered together. They held this position until 3.30pm when they were ordered to withdraw and to concentrate on the high ground above Concevreux. They defended this temporary line until 4pm when the enemy drove them out.[89]

Regimental Sergeant Major George Dodd Fewster
aged 42 years
1/4th Northumberland Fusiliers
Died 27 May 1918

George was born in 1876 and was a native of Elswick, Newcastle. He was the husband of

Eliza Jane Fewster who lived at 42 Hencotes, Hexham. George had been a regular soldier with the Northumberland Fusiliers and had 24 years service under his belt. He had soldiered in India, the Sudan and South Africa where he served throughout the entire duration of the Boer War. He was mobilised with the 1/4th Territorial Battalion and accompanied them to France in April 1915, serving in France for the entirety of the war. Initially the Hexham Courant reported simply that he been wounded in battle.

The Reverend R W Callin in his book published in 1919, wrote:

> "A few of us remained in Concevreux during the morning to deal with what wounded we could. Fifty or sixty perhaps passed through our hands and were sent on to hospital at Meurival - on stretchers, on doors, and on barrows. Nicholson (who had been acting as Liaison Officer with the Brigade) came in with a very nasty wound in the thigh, but as cheery and as indomitable as ever. The last we dressed was our Regimental Sergeant Major, Fewster, very badly hit indeed. What happened to poor Fewster after he left us we do not know."

George is commemorated on the Soissons Memorial to the missing.

Falling back to a prepared defensive position running across the Concevreux-Ventelay road, the remaining Fusiliers formed a defence line with the 3rd Worcestershire Regiment to the right and the Lancashire Fusiliers on the left. This position held until late in the evening, when the 1/4th Battalion was forced to withdraw to a new position south of Le Faite Farm. This quickly became untenable and they had to withdraw further, initially to the south of Ventelay. By 5.30am on 28 May the enemy had begun to outflank this position and the defenders were forced to withdraw to some high ground north of Montigny.

For the next two days the remnants of the 149th Brigade spent the time fighting rearguard actions, crossing the Marne on 29 May and finally retiring from the battle zone by the end of the month.

Of this time, Callin wrote:

> *"What happened during the rest of that day and the next must be told in snatches. The long string of transport, making its slow way down the zig zag road to Ventalay and Romaine, was hit with deadly accuracy, and we lost both men and animals. It was a nerve racking time for Pickering, but his coolness and wise leadership never showed to better advantage. They were gassed, shelled, fired on repeatedly by machine gun from aeroplanes, and bombed by the roadside. One thing which imperilled the survivors and the transport was that the Bosche had been able to execute a tremendous flanking movement on the left, and had come round with incredible rapidity. Perhaps the most pathetic thing about it all was that several hospitals in this way fell into his hands before the wounded had all been removed. Many of those we had treated at the Aid Post at Concevreux had to be reported as 'missing' as a result of this".*

Sergeant William Alder, aged 37
1/4th Battalion Northumberland Fusiliers
Died 27 May 1918

William was born in Hexham. He was married and lived in Eilan's Gate Terrace, Hexham. He went out to France in April 1915 with the initial draft of the local Territorial Battalion and was wounded at the *Second Battle of Ypres*. Before the hostilities he was employed by Hexham Urban District Council.

William is commemorated on the Soissons Memorial to the missing.

Private David Sword, aged 36
1/5ᵗʰ Battalion Northumberland Fusiliers
Died 27 May 1918

David was born in Scotland, the son of James and Agnes Sword of South Street, Perth. He was married to Elizabeth Sword of Battle Hill, who (surprisingly enough) worked as a porter at Hexham Railway Station. Before enlisting David was employed at Hexham Dye Works.

David is commemorated on Soissons Memorial to the missing.

For the period 27 – 31 May, the three Northumberland Fusilier Battalions, 1/4ᵗʰ, 1/5ᵗʰ, and 1/6ᵗʰ, which made up the 149ᵗʰ Brigade, reported 8 officers and 167 men killed.

When the Germans attacked on the 27 May, the 1/4ᵗʰ East Yorkshire Regiment as part of the 150ᵗʰ Brigade, 50ᵗʰ Division was on the left of the Divisional position on the Californie Plateau. The 50ᵗʰ Divisional history reports:

> " ...no news was received from the 1/4ᵗʰ East Yorkshires, very few of whose men came back, but it is probable that they were overwhelmed by the enemy".

It was confirmed that one officer and eighty eight men were killed on 27 May.

Private Matthew Thompson, aged 21
1/4ᵗʰ Battalion East Yorkshire Regiment
Died 27 May 1918

Matthew was born in Hexham and was the son of Mr and Mrs Matthew Thomson of Market Street. Before enlisting he worked at Hexham Railway Station and initially served with the Yorkshire Regiment, before transferring to the East Yorkshires. Initially, he was reported as missing, but was later confirmed as killed in action.

Matthew is buried in Vendresse British Cemetery.

The 1ˢᵗ Northumbrian Brigade of the Royal Field Artillery, a pre-war Territorial Force, was in support of the 149ᵗʰ Brigade. As was the case with their infantry counterparts the Artillery were buzzing with rumours that something big was going to take place. At 1.00am all hell did indeed break loose and the Germans took advantage of the mayhem to infiltrate the defensive positions of the infantry along their flanks.

Letters written by Colonel Johnstone describe how the gun batteries received direct hits as soldiers working in respirators because of high levels of gas became increasingly weary as they tried vainly to man their guns. The batteries were soon surrounded by German troops and were forced to surrender.

At 4.30am, 'A' Battery was threatened with encirclement by the German troops and so the men removed the breech blocks and sights from each artillery piece and retreated southwards. In his letter Johnstone wrote that following this incident Shiel and Richardson (below) reported to him and it was noted that Richardson appeared to be 'dead beat'.

It is recorded that with a party of officers Richardson made a bid to get back to his own lines, setting off through a wood.

They had to pass through a German barrage and Richardson was hit. His fellow officers, including Dickinson, Graham, Meek and Willis carried him for two to three hundred yards, after which he was carried further on a mattress to Chaudardes, where it was decided that he was dead and his body was left by the wayside.[19]   Later, Johnstone wrote of Richardson:

"He was a gallant fellow, and did not know what fear was". [19]

Lieutenant Francis Aylmer Richardson, aged 35
'A' Battery Northumbrian Brigade, Royal Field Artillery
Died 27 May 1918

Francis was the son of the late Reverend F Richardson, Vicar of Corbridge.   He lived in Corbridge's West Park. The Hexham Courant reports that Francis' sister Miss Richardson received news that her brother had died of the wounds that he received in action that day.

Francis is commemorated on the Soissons Memorial for men who died and have no known grave.   He is also commemorated on the Acomb War Memorial, the Rolls of Honour at the Abbey and the War Memorial Hospital and at the lychgate of St Andrew's Church, Corbridge.

Western Front

June found the 1st Battalion Northumberland Fusiliers as part of the 3rd Division covering the Front near Hinges (over two miles north of Béthunc).   They were involved in the routine of trench warfare – periodic tours of duty in the Front Line followed by time in support or in reserve near Chocques.

Even in reserve there was no time for rest. Working parties were needed and men from the battalions were required to pull their weight. Involvement in carrying rations and stores to the Front led to frequent deaths from harassing fire that was constantly directed on back areas and communications. On 6 June five men from the Battalion were killed while carrying out these mundane duties. [20]

Private Frederick Abbott, Military Medal, aged 25
1st Battalion Northumberland Fusiliers
Died 6 June 1918

Fred was born in Ripon Yorkshire and was the fourth son of Mr and Mrs Abbott of Foundry Cottages, Hexham. He was a married man with a child from his first marriage. He joined the army two days after the outbreak of war, serving initially with the 1/4th Northumberland Fusiliers. During his time at the Front he had been wounded three times and when he was killed had just returned to the Front in May from a period of convalescence. In the summer of 1916 it was reported that he was in Roseneath Hospital, Broadstairs, Kent suffering from trench fever.

On Saturday 21 October 1916 the Hexham Herald reported that Fred had been awarded the Military Medal for bravery on the battlefield. This was gazetted on 11 October. At the time no details of this award were available to the local press. However, later it came to light that Fred had received his gallantry award for repelling a German bomb attack on Hill 60. Fred was the *third* son that Mr and Mrs Abbott had lost to this war. They had two further sons serving in France.

Fred is buried in Sandpits British Cemetery, Fouquereuil.

References

1. Shakespear, Lt Col. J. *Thirty Fourth Division, 1915-1919,*
   Pub: 1921, reprinted Naval & Military Press 1998.

2. Stewart, G. and Sheen, J A. *History of the Tyneside Scottish,*
   Pub: Pen and Sword Books, 1999.

3. WO 95 2828. *War Diary, 1/5th Northumberland Fusiliers.*

4. Miles, Capt. W. *The Durham Forces in the Field, 1914-18,*
   Pub: 1920, reprinteded Naval & Military Press 2004.

5. Wyrall, E. *Die-Hards in the Great War (Middlesex Regiment),*
   Pub: 1926-1930, reprinted Naval & Military Press 2002.

6. WO 95 2615. *War Diary, 20th Middlesex Regiment.*

7. WO 95/1219. *War Diary, 1st Coldstream Guards.*

8. Wyrell E. *The Fiftieth Division, 1914-1919,*
   Pub: 1939, reprinted, Naval and Military Press 2002.

9. WO 95/2828. *War Diary, 1/4th Northumberland Fusiliers.*

10. WO 95/2477. *War Diary, 16th Northumberland Fusiliers.*

11. Cooke, Capt. C H. *Historical Records of the 16th Battalion Northumberland Fusiliers,*
    Pub: Council of Newcastle and Gateshead Chamber of Commerce, 1923.

12. WO 95/4077. *War Diary, 79th Brigade Royal Field Artillery.*

13. *Australian Official History of the First World War.*
www.awm.gov.au

14. WO 95/3077. *War Diary, 1/9th Durham Light Infantry.*

15. WO 95/2731. *War Diary, 8th London Regiment.*

16. Anon. *Post Office Rifles 1914 to 1918,*
Pub; Gale & Polden Ltd 1919.

17. Callin, Rev R W. *When the Lantern of Hope Burnt Low,*
Pub: J Catherall Hexham, 1919

18, Wyrall, E. *East Yorkshire Regiment in the Great War 1914-1918*
Pub: 1924-1927 reprinted Naval and Military Press 2002.

19. *War History of the 1st Northumbrian Bde RFA (TF) 1914-1919.*
Pub: 1927

20. Sandilands, Brig H R. *The Fifth in the Great War,*
Pub: 1932, reprinted Naval and Military 2002.

CHAPTER SIXTEEN

VICTORY IN ONE HUNDRED DAYS

"... We left our holes
And looked above the wreckage of the earth
To where the white clouds moved in silent lines
Across the untroubled blue."

Richard Aldington, *Bombardment*

Overview

First Quartermaster-General Ludendorff (Head of the German Forces), was later to describe 8 August 1919 as *'the black day of the German Army'*.

On this day the Allies deployed nine divisions, supported by no fewer than four hundred tanks, in an initial attack: Australian, Canadian and British troops all were used. During the nights when the attacking units were gathering the Germans persistently shelled the assembly area and on 7 August they destroyed a number of tanks. Near Morlancourt a localised German action pushed the Front line back by five miles, taking a large number of British prisoners. However the Germans were still unaware of an impending attack.

The attack began at 4.20am on 8 August when the artillery laid down an intense creeping barrage. By the end of that day the Allied forces had captured the towns of Harbonnières, Caix and Fresnoy, an advance of over five miles. This breakout from Amiens laid the foundations for the advances over the next one hundred days – and led ultimately to victory.

Advances on the South Bank of the Somme

On 6 August the King inspected the 5th Battalion Border Regiment. Three days later the Battalion took up position near Warvillers, (south of the River Somme and three miles north of Bouchoir, a town on the main Amiens to Roye road) in preparation for an attack on a stretch of the railway running between Hattencourt and Fresnoy.

Very heavy machine gun fire met the initial advance on 10 August, forcing the troops to deploy into sections and advance in snake formation. They found that the wire had not been cut properly, resulting in the death or injury of many soldiers. No further advances were made on 11 August and the battalion was relieved on 12 August during which relief Captain Harrison was mortally wounded.[1] During this attack the Borderers lost two officers and eighteen men.

Captain Brian Charles Harrison, aged 40
11th Battalion Border Regiment
attached 5th Battalion Border Regiment
Died 12 August 1918

Brian was born in August 1878, the eldest son of Charles Augustus and Julia Elizabeth Harrison of Beacon Grange, Hexham. His father was churchwarden at the Abbey. Brian was educated at Aysgarth School where he was appointed Head Boy. He later attended Sedbergh School, Eton and Trinity College, Oxford. By the beginning of the war Brian was a master at Sedbergh School.

He obtained a commission in the newly raised Lonsdale Battalion of the Border Regiment, and was sent to France

in 1915. He was wounded in July 1916, on the first day of the Battle of the Somme – the Lonsdale Battalion advanced from Authuille Wood for an attack on the Liepzig Salient and came under heavy machine-gun fire from the Nord Werk on the battalion's right flank. On that day the battalion suffered over five hundred casualties. Brian was wounded again during the St Quentin Offensive in the spring of 1917; he was mentioned in dispatches in December 1917. Whilst overseeing the relief of the battalion on 12 August Brian was wounded accidentally, a wound which proved to be fatal.

Brian is buried in Rosières Communal Cemetery Extension.

The Advance in Picardy

Battle of Albert: 21 – 23 August 1918

On 21 August the Allies made a large-scale attack along a Front from Albert to Arras. In the north (Arras) the Third Army commanded by General Sir Julian Byng was used, and in the south (Albert), the attack was undertaken by elements of the Fourth Army under General Sir Henry Rawlinson. The advance across the old Somme Battlefield would involve troops from three divisions: the 17th, 21st and 38th.

The 2nd Battalion Lincolnshire Regiment transferred to the 21st Division as part of the Third Army in February 1918 and they were involved in the battle to recapture the town of Albert. For the 21st Division the attack was centred on the area around Grandcourt. At 5.45am on 21 August the 2nd Lincolns captured Beaucourt sur Ancre with relatively few casualties. They continued their advance in dense mist towards the railway line on the north bank of the Ancre.

Later in the afternoon part of the 2nd Lincolns ('A' and 'D' companies) were relieved by Northumberland Fusiliers and marched to Acheux-en-Amienois; a large number of men in these companies were suffering from the effects of gas. The two other companies ('B' and 'C') holding the outpost line were ordered forward, with 'C' Company on the right hand side of the advance. They passed through the Front held by the 1st Lincolns and consolidated a position in a sunken road which eventually was enfiladed by direct machine gun fire, rifle and trench mortar fire from Grandcourt. Enemy soldiers were also able to get around the left flank of 'B' Company. During these incursions by German troops Lieutenant Walton was killed. The War Diary reports the date of Walton's death as 21 August, but databases show it as 22 August.[2, 3]

Lieutenant George Pears Walton, aged 29
1/4th Battalion Northumberland Fusiliers
Attached 'C' Company
2nd Battalion Lincolnshire Regiment
Died 22 August 1918

George Walton was the youngest son of John Pears J P and Frances Mary Walton of Acomb High House and Green Ends, Alston. He was educated at Sedburgh School, where he was Head of his house and a prominent member of the rugby team. Subsequently he went to Durham College of Science. He spent a few years in Canada and on his return in 1912 helped in the management of the family's interest in Messrs Walton and Cowper's lead and coal mines. He played as a forward for Tynedale Rugby Club and was a key player when the team won the Northumberland Senior Cup in 1914.

He enlisted in the Northumberland Fusiliers as Private in December of 1914. The London Gazette of 11 May 1915 records George's promotion to 2nd Lieutenant, (23rd April, 1915). A plaque in St John Lee Church records that Lieutenant Walton was killed in action at Beaucourt-sur-Ancre whilst attached to the Lincolnshire Regiment. It also records that he had been seriously wounded on 16 September 1916 at High Wood on the Somme when a bullet caused a severe fracture of his right arm. After a long period of convalescence he had returned to the Front in June 1918, and was attached to the Lincolnshires.

A letter from his commanding officer to his brother Mr J C P Walton of Greens End, Alston, described how George was killed:

> *"Your brother was killed in action during the present British advance. He was hit on the 22nd August after the battalion had been through some very hard fighting and whilst his company was advancing to take a most important enemy position."*

George is buried in Queens Cemetery, Bucquoy, Pas de Calais.

His headstone contains the following inscription:

TO LIVE IN HEARTS
WE LEAVE BEHIND
IS NOT TO DIE

He is also commemorated at Tynedale Rugby Club, now at Corbridge.

The 6th Battalion East Kent Regiment was temporarily attached to the 35th Infantry Brigade to assist in an attack on Méautle (south of Albert). For this attack, to the north were troops of 18th Division and to the south those of 47th Division.

The East Kent was assigned to capture the second objective, which was conditional on the 7th Norfolk securing the initial objective.

During the early hours of 22 August, the assembly points for the attack were heavily shelled by German gas shells. Nonetheless, at 4.45am the attack went on and achieved all of its objectives by 8.35am.

The Battalion War Diary reports that eleven heavy machine guns and fourteen prisoners were captured during this action. Battalion casualties for the attack were: one officer killed and two wounded. The other ranks suffered five killed (of whom William Oswald was one), twenty nine wounded, thirty missing and one gassed. The writer reports these as *"very slight"*. [4]

Private William Oswald, aged 26
6th (Service) Battalion, (The Buffs) East Kent Regiment
Died 22 August 1918

William was born in Fullwell, County Durham in 1892. He was a married man living with his wife at the Red Lion in Widehaugh.

Although he lived in Hexham at the time he initially enlisted in Blaydon, joining the 1/4th Battalion Durham Light Infantry. He was subsequently transferred to the Buffs. Before the hostilities he was employed at Widehaugh Gardens.

William is buried in Méaulte Military Cemetery, near Albert.

On 23 August the 13ᵗʰ Royal Fusiliers moved up for an attack on the German Front Line which lay to the west of the town of Bapaume. The attack followed a creeping barrage. The left flank met considerable opposition from a German strongpoint in the brickworks – for a time it was feared that the attack would fail due to the heavy opposition it encountered. Groups of fusiliers managed to work their way around the flanks of the brickworks and they eventually quenched resistance from this German position, taking sixty prisoners. The two companies on the right flank met little resistance and a large number of German prisoners were returned to the rear.

As the attacking troops clambered up the sides of the railway embankment they ran into fierce rifle and machine gun fire; an intense struggle followed during which the attacking forces used trench mortars. They managed to scale the eastern bank of the cutting and to intensify their fire. At this point the Germans appeared to have lost heart and so began to surrender in large numbers. The Battalion Diary records that the attack appears to have come as a surprise to the Germans; when they cleared out the dugouts in the walls of the cutting:

> "there was ample evidence of a meal that had just been prepared and hot coffee was steaming on the tables".

Nearly three hours after the start of the attack, troops from the 1/1ˢᵗ Hertfordshire Regiment took up the challenge. Later in the afternoon the Royal Fusiliers contended with heavy fire from the enemy as they pushed forward for a second time, and it was realised that no further progress could be made without the support of artillery or tanks.[5]

During the day the Battalion took over five hundred prisoners for a total cost of one officer and thirty three other ranks killed (of whom Robert Plant was one), although this does not include figures for wounded or missing in action.

Private Robert Sidney Plant, aged 19
13th (Service) Battalion Royal Fusiliers
Died 23 August 1918

Sidney was born at Sandhoe. He was the second son of Mr and Mrs Plant of the Hermitage Cottage, Hexham. For some time as a boy he was a chorister at Stagshaw Church. After leaving school he was employed as under-chauffeur by Mr Noble of Sandhoe House. He was also employed for a year at the Motor Department of Elswick Works, Newcastle.

Sidney enlisted in the Services on Easter Monday 1917, his eighteenth birthday. He had been rejected earlier because he was under age. Initially he was attached to Motor Transport at Grove Park where he passed his examinations as a qualified driver. Subsequently he was transferred to the Royal Fusiliers and was sent to France in February 1918.

Sidney is buried in Aichiet-le-Grand Communal Cemetery Extension. He is also commemorated on the Rolls of Honour in the Abbey.

In the middle of August the 15th Battalion Durham Light Infantry was involved in a series of actions on the old Somme Battlefield, recapturing ground which had been lost to the Germans in their Spring Offensive (see Chapter Fifteen). During the evening of 23 August the battalion, together with the Kings Own Yorkshire Light Infantry and the East Yorkshire Regiment, was ordered to occupy high ground south of Miraumont. By midnight they had taken this high ground and they held it throughout the next day (24 August) in spite of the fact that at one point they were completely surrounded by the enemy. On 25 August the battalion moved into Boom Ravine and was held in Divisional Reserve.

On 26 August the 15th Battalion formed up on high ground west of Le Sars in preparation for an attack north-eastwards towards Ligny-Thilloy (a mile south of Bapaume). The attack was held up by heavy machine gun fire, partly because the advancing troops were unable to keep up with the protective creeping barrage. During the evening the 15th Battalion repulsed a German counter-attack. The action continued until the evening of 27 August when the Durham Light Infantry was relieved.[6, 7]

During this period of action the 15th DLI suffered the following casualties:
Officers: 7 killed, (of whom William Charlton was one) 1 taken POW and 9 wounded.
Other ranks: 56 killed 186 wounded and 26 missing.

Lieutenant William Godfrey Charlton, aged 20
15th Battalion Durham Light Infantry
Died 26 August 1918

William was the younger of the two sons of John and Anne Fenwick Charlton of the School House, Seaton Deleval, formerly of Hexham. William's father, John, was Head Master of Seaton Deleval Council school. William was the Grandson of Mr G F Hedley of Quatre Bras, Hexham. William's older brother, George, was killed in 1916 whilst serving with the South Wales Borderers (see Chapter Nine).

Before the war William was employed by Lloyds Banking Company at North Shields. After enlisting he trained with the *Inns of Court Officer Training Corps*. In 1916 (aged eighteen) he was severely wounded but he

returned to the Front in June 1918, to be killed two months later.

William is buried in Warlencourt British Cemetery, near Bapaume.

The Second Battle of Bapaume
31 August – 3 September 1918

Both the 5th and 2/4th Battalions of the Kings Own Yorkshire Light Infantry (KOYLI) as part of 1st Midlands Brigade (187 Brigade 62 Division) were part of an advance against German positions near Courcelles, (northeast of Bapaume) which began on 25 August.

On 25 August the 2/4th KOYLI based west of Ervillers attacked in an easterly direction to the north of Mory. This attack was held up because the other units involved in the attack had not been able to take and hold their own objectives. During the afternoon the battalion was subjected to an intense barrage of high explosive and gas shells followed by a counter-attack by the Germans. The men of 'D' Company charged a section of the advancing Germans and took a large number of prisoners. As a result they were able to make contact with the Guards Brigade. On the next day (26 August) the KOYLI came under intense machine gun fire making further movement forward slow and difficult. However, when they had reached a forward position it was found that the other battalions on their flanks had lagged behind, with the result that their position was not secure.

During the morning of 27 August the battalion was again ordered into the attack, with the 5th KOYLI on the right and the Guards to the left. The attack moved forward behind a moving barrage which according to the War Diary '...*was splendidly laid*'.

On the right of the battalion front, 'C' Company reached its objective with scarcely a casualty. However to their left 'D' Company encountered heavy machine gun fire. The Guards also came under intense fire, which delayed their advance, as did 5th KOYLI on the right. Later in the day they made a strategic withdrawal so that the gains made across the Front could be consolidated. During the night of 27/28th August the battalion was withdrawn and relieved by the 8th West Yorkshire Regiment.[8]

The death-count for the attack was one officer and thirty-three other ranks killed, of whom Michael Donnelly was one.

Private Michael Edward Donnelly, aged 21
2/4th Battalion King's Own Yorkshire Light Infantry
Died 27 August 1918

Michael was born in Benwell, the son of Edward and Elizabeth Donnelly of Princess Street, Newcastle. He enlisted in Hexham and was initially with one of the Tyneside Irish Battalions before being transferred to Yorkshire Light Infantry.

Michael was killed in action and was buried in the HAC Cemetery, Ecoust-St-Mein.

On 25 August the 5th King's Own Yorkshire Light Infantry advanced and occupied the village of Mory, (approximately 3 miles north of Bapaume) and also a valley which ran to the south of the village. The advance continued during the following day taking high ground to the southeast of Mory. On 27 August the advance continued and 'D' Company attacked the Sugar Factory west of Vaulx-Vraucourt, taking a large number of prisoners. The War Diary reports that these were from the German 5th Grenadier Regiment. During the early hours of the next day the battalion was relieved by the 1/5 Devonshire Regiment.[9]

The attack cost the lives of one officer and thirty-four other ranks, of whom John Robson was one.

Private John Robert Robson, aged 19
'D' Company, 5th (Service) Battalion
King's Own Yorkshire Light Infantry
Died 27 August 1918

John was born in Hexham, the only son of John and Elizabeth Robson of Eastgate. Before enlisting he was employed as a gardener by a Mrs Russell. Initially he did his basic training with the West Yorkshire Regiment but was subsequently transferred to Yorkshire Light Infantry.

John was killed in action and was buried in Gomiécourt, South Cemetery.

On Saturday 7 September, the men of the 1st Royal Berkshire (99th Brigade 2nd Division) were positioned in trenches between Demicourt and Hermies, southwest of the city of Cambrai and west of the Canal du Nord. These trenches were being shelled heavily by the Germans. During the early morning the battalion moved eastward to establish a forward position on the banks of the canal. To counteract this movement, the Germans attacked these new positions on three occasions. During the last of these the Germans were able to force the British from some of their forward positions, killing or wounding a number of the defenders including Henry Gibbin.[10]

Private Henry Gibbin, aged 23
1ˢᵗ Battalion Royal Berkshire Regiment
Died 7 September 1918

Harry was born in Corbridge. He was the husband of Johanna Gibbin of Holy Island, Hexham. Before enlisting with the Northumberland Fusiliers in April 1915 he was employed by Mrs Hewitt as a cartman. Subsequently he was transferred to the Royal Berkshire Regiment and was killed in action.

Harry is buried in Vaulx Hill Cemetery, near Bapaume.

The Second Battle of Arras

On 23 August, the 1/14ᵗʰ London Regiment (168 Brigade 56 Division) attacked the village of Boiry-Becquerrelle, five miles south of Arras. The Regimental History reports that the attack was made over completely unfamiliar ground, but was successful in its outcome. During the attack 'A' Company skirted the south of the village and 'C' Company the north. The other companies provided support. At 4am the assembled troops were subjected to a gas shell barrage, which caused them to wear their respirators for the next two hours. A short bombardment preceded the British attack, which followed a creeping barrage. By 6am they had cleared the village and captured a German trench on the far side. By this time the German artillery had begun a heavy artillery barrage which prompted heavy responsive fire by the British battalions, but this did not prevent them going on to capture the German reserve position which lay a further half mile to the east of the village.[11, 12]

During this action nearly thirty men were killed, including Cuthbert Smith, together with a hundred other casualties suffering from the effects of gas and other wounds. In the early hours of the next morning the battalion was relieved by elements from 167th Brigade.

Private Cuthbert Smith, aged 20
1/14th Battalion City of London Regiment
(London Scottish)
Died 23 August 1918

Cuthbert was born in Mickley Square and was the son of Sergeant-Major John William DCM and Mrs Catherine Smith of Hencotes. Cuthbert was killed in action and is buried in Henin Communal Cemetery Extension, Pas de Calais.

In the early morning of 24 August the 1/2nd Battalion London Regiment moved towards the Front Line from their bivouac area near Basseux. The initial destination for their attack was the Boiry Reserve Trench and Boiry Works, a German strongpoint which had been captured by elements of the 168th Infantry Brigade on 23 August. The idea was to strengthen the position in anticipation of a German counter-attack. During the night the Germans fired a large number of gas shells into the area held by the battalion.[13]

Private John Kirkland, aged 19
1/2nd Battalion City of London Regiment
Died 24 August 1918

John Kirkland was born in Bellingham and was the oldest son of George and Edith Kirkland of Kingsgate Terrace, Hexham. Before his war service he lived in Wylam and was employed as a clerk at the local station. On enlisting aged eighteen he was at first attached to the

2nd **Reserve Cavalry Regiment. He went to France at the end of March 1918.**

John was killed in the action described above and is buried in Summit Trench Cemetery, Croisilles.

The following inscription is found on his headstone:

UNTIL THE DAY BREAKS

The 1/4th Gordon Highlanders were part of the Highland Division (51st) who played an important part in the attacks made on the German Lines in late August. These encounters were known officially as the *Battle of the Scarpe*, (first phase of the *Second Battle of Arras*). From 26 August during five days of intense fighting the strongpoints of Rouex, Greenland Hill and Plouvain were captured.

On 28 August at 6.30am the Gordon Highlanders attacked Greenland Hill behind a creeping barrage and were able to report its capture by 8.00am. The Battalion Diary reports that resistance was feeble and that more than ninety German prisoners were taken. In the afternoon the Germans shelled the newly obtained trenches relentlessly, a bombardment which continued for the next several days, resulting in mounting casualties, including Edward Baty.[14]

Corporal Edward Joseph Baty, aged 22
1/4th Battalion Gordon Highlanders
Died 31 August 1918

Edward was born in Hexham in 1895. He was the adopted son of Mr and Mrs J Campbell of Quatre Bras, Hexham. They were informed at first that their son had

been wounded between 29 – 31 August. Later it was confirmed that he was killed in action.

Edward is commemorated on the Vis-en-Artois Memorial for the missing.

Battle of Cambrai: 8 - 9 October 1918

On 5 October the 12/13th Northumberland Fusiliers (NF) were positioned west of the Canal du Nord near Banteux. The War Diary states that the battalion was reinforced by a new draft of men which consisted of a number of officers and eighteen other ranks. The next day they moved off very early, crossing the Canal du Nord and taking up a position in the Hindenburg Line, east of Bantouzelle. Even though the battalion was still officially in reserve, the Battalion Diary records that three men were wounded during this manoeuvre. On 7 October the battalion moved up to a position behind the Beaurevoir Trench in preparation for an attack on Walincourt-Selvigny the next morning. This attack on 8 October went in at 6am and by late evening the fusiliers had gained their objectives. Casualties for the day were three officers killed, (included in this number were two of the officers who had joined on 5 October) and thirty-two other ranks killed, including John Wilkinson. The next day the battalion was 'leapfrogged' by elements of the 7th Division who took on the battle with the retreating Germans.[15]

Private John William Wilkinson, aged 22
12/13th Battalion Northumberland Fusiliers
Died 8 October 1918

John was born in Ovingham and was the son of William and Elizabeth Wilkinson of Shaw Well Farm, Corbridge.

He was killed in action and is buried in Prospect Hill Cemetery, Gouy. Gouy is situated eleven miles south of Cambrai.

Pursuit to the River Selle

On 10 October the 13th Durham Light Infantry as part of the 74th Brigade were detailed to occupy the high ground to the northeast of Le Cateau-Cambrésis. The attack started at 5.30am without a preliminary artillery bombardment. By 10am the attack was held up by machine-gun fire coming from positions southwest of the village of St Benin. On their right American troops were also held up west of St Souphet. Consequently 13th Battalion were ordered to take St Benin and they did so, attacking through a heavy hostile artillery barrage. They took the village with ferocious hand-to-hand fighting and established a forward Line beyond the River Selle. During the night and all of the following day the battalion's position was bombarded with German gas shells. Late in the evening of 11 October the 13th Durhams were relieved and they withdrew to Honnechy. Since the beginning of the month the battalion had seen the deaths of four officers and one hundred and nine men, of whom George Irwin was one.[7]

Private George Irwin, aged 21
13th (Service) Battalion Durham light infantry
Died 11 October 1918

George was born in Hexham in 1898 and was the son of William and Mary Irwin of Bells Yard, Gilesgate Bank. George is buried in Escafourt Communal Cemetery near Le Cateau-Cambrésis.

Final Advance in Picardy

The 9th Cheshire (19th Division, 56th Brigade), reached the Front on the night of 2/3 November, near Sommaing (northeast of Cambrai and half way to Valenciennes). On 3 November they attacked the village of Jenlain, (southwest of Valenciennes). Initially the attack was held up by enemy machine-gun fire. Some time during the day, a platoon forced its way into the village, at which point the German defenders withdrew eastwards. The Regimental History notes that this attack was carried out under heavy artillery fire not only from the Germans, but also from their own side. They maintained the attack the next day.[16]

On 7 November the battalion took part in an attack on Bellignes, which achieved all of its military objectives. The War Diary has a great deal to say about the British artillery barrage, which made the attack into *a very difficult and dangerous proceeding*.[17]

This engagement is officially named *The Passage of Grande Homelle,* the *Homelle* being the name of the river to the west of Bellignes. The casualties for this attack were nine officers wounded and twelve NCOs and men killed, of whom Thomas Craig was one. One hundred and thirty-two men were wounded.

Private Thomas Brown Craig, aged 35 years
9th (Service) Battalion Cheshire Regiment
Died 7 November 1918

Thomas was born in Garrigill, Cumbria, but had lived for most of his life in Hexham. He was the son of William and Tamar Craig. Before the hostilities he served his apprenticeship with Messrs W A Temperley and Co of Beaumont Street, Hexham where he had been promoted to cashier. He was a well-known cricketer who played

for Hexham and had captained the side.

Thomas is buried in Cross Roads Cemetery, Fontaine-au-Bois.

Final Advance in Flanders

The *Fourth Battle of Ypres* officially opened on 28 September. The Allied forces in Flanders consisted of twelve Belgian Divisions (under King Albert) in the north and ten British and six French Divisions in the south. The advance began where the British Front Line had been in June 1917 (before Passchendaele). On 28 September the British regained Wytschaete and advanced up to six miles in places. However, as in the summer of 1917 the rain simply fell and continued to fall – incessantly.

On 1 October, the 7th Seaforth Highlanders (27th Brigade 9th Division) formed up in front of the village of Slypscapple, (Slijpskapelle) about six miles east of Ypres to attack the Menin-Roulier railway. At 6.15am, after a brief barrage, the attack was launched under the cover of a smoke barrage using 'B' and 'C' companies with 'A' and 'D' companies in reserve. The Menin to Rouliers (Roeselare), railway, north of Ledeghem was reached successfully and after a brief pause the advance continued under increasingly enemy resistance. The fire came especially from fortified German pill boxes, which the enemy tried to hold at all costs. It was later found that these fortified positions were in fact the last line of defence in the Flanders sector.

The Highlanders eventually captured Ledeghem and patrols then pushed forwards towards Rolleghem Cappelle, but they suffered serious hostile machine-gun and sniper activity and the battalion was eventually withdrawn to consolidate a position along the railway line.[18]

Casualties for the attack are recorded as four officers and twenty three other ranks killed (of whom William Baird was one) and four officers and sixty-nine other ranks wounded.

Private William Baird, aged 40, Military Medal
'C' Company 7th Battalion Seaforth Highlanders
Died 1 October 1918

William was born in Dumfries, Scotland. He was the son of Mr and Mrs Baird of Kirton, Dumfries. He was a married man whose wife's address is recorded as Workington Hall, Cumberland. William was initially in the Gordon Highlanders, before being transferred to the Seaforth Highlanders. The Battalion War Diary for October 1918 lists the name of William Baird as a recipient of the Military Medal, presumably posthumously.

William's name appears on a number of War Memorials in the Hexham area, including those at Acomb and Wall, although details of his life are rather sketchy and his connection with the area unclear.

William is buried in Dadizeele, New British Cemetery, north of Ypres.

References

1. Wylly, Col H C. *The Border Regiment in the Great War,* Pub: Gale and Polden Ltd 1924.

2. WO 95/2154. *War Diary, 2nd Lincolnshire Regiment.* 3.

Simpson, Maj-Gen C R. *History of the Lincolnshire Regiment 1914-1918,*
Pub: 1931, reprinted Naval & Military Press 2002.

4.   WO 95/1860. *War Diary, 6th East Kent Regiment.*

5.   WO 95/2532. *War Diary, 13th Royal Fusiliers.*

6.   WO 95/2161. *War Diary, 15th Durham light Infantry.*

7   Miles, Capt W. The Durham Forces in the Field 1914-18, Pub: 1920, republished Naval & Military Press 2004.

8.   WO 95/3091. *War Diary, 2/4th King's Own Yorkshire Light Infantry.*

9.   WO 95/2086. *War Diary, 5th Battalion King's Own Yorkshire Light Infantry.*

10. WO/95/1371. *War Diary, 1st Berkshire Regiment.*

11. WO/95/1266. *War Diary, 1/14th London Regiment, (London Scottish).*

12. Lindsay, Lt-Col J H. *London Scottish in the Great War,* Pub: 1926, reprinted Naval & Military Press 2002.

13. WO 95/2960. *War Diary, 1/2nd London Regiment.*

14. WO 95/2886. *War Diary, 1/4th Gordon Highlanders.*

15. WO 95/2155. *War Diary, 12th/13th Northumberland Fusiliers.*

16. Crookenden, Col A. *Regimental History of the Cheshire Regiment in the Great War,* reprinted Naval & Military Press 2005.

17.   WO 95/2079. *War Diary, 9th Cheshire Regiment.*

18.   WO 95/1765. *War Diary, 7th Seaforth Highlanders.*

HEXHAM ABBEY.

Thanksgiving Services

FOR

CESSATION OF HOSTILITIES,

Sunday, November 17th, 1918.

ORDER OF SERVICES.

Morning, 11.	Evening, 6-30.
God Save The King.	God Save The King.
Procession, Hymn 379.	Procession, Hymn 166.
Psalms 46, 150.	Psalm 9.
Lesson.	Lesson.
Te Deum : Stanford in B Flat.	Deus ... ... *Noble.*
Creed.	Creed.
Anthem : "I will sing" *Sullivan.*	Anthem : "God is our hope" *Greene.*
Prayers.	Prayers.
Hymn 165.	Hymn 165.
SERMON BY THE RECTOR.	SERMON BY THE RECTOR.
Hymn 166.	Hymn 379.
Hallelujah ! ... *Handel.*	Te Deum : Huntley in E flat.
Blessing *Stainer's Amen.*	Blessing *Stainer's Amen.*

CHAPTER SEVENTEEN

WESTERN FRONT 1918

"Poppies whose roots are in man's veins
Drop, and are ever dropping"

Isaac Rosenberg, d.1918, *Break of Day in the Trenches*

Overview

The 1st West Yorkshire Regiment (18th Brigade) was based in the Dickebusch sector, south west of Ypres. On the night of 8 – 9 August the 1st Battalion was involved in a local action against the German Front Line trenches. This attack was timed to coincide with another local attack carried out by the 2nd Durham Light Infantry and other elements of the 41st Division on the right (west). Both attacks started at midnight on a very dark night indeed. The aim of the attack by the West Yorkshires was to drive the enemy from the forward crest of the Viestraat Ridge, a position they had held for some time. They had been using it as an observation point to direct accurate shelling of Allied rear area communications.

The attack by the West Yorkshires failed because they met stubborn resistance from the 8th German Division. However, the other attack to the west by the DLI was much more successful. West Yorkshire casualties for the night included: three officers wounded, one taken prisoner; other ranks three killed (of whom Arthur Lowes was one), forty one wounded, six missing and two taken prisoner.

311

Private Arthur Lee Lowes, aged 20
1ˢᵗ Battalion West Yorkshire Regiment
(Prince of Wales's Own)
Died 9 August 1918

Arthur was born in Acomb. He was the youngest son of Robert Parker and Alice Lowes of Meadow Terrace, Hexham. Before he enlisted on his eighteenth birthday he worked as a clerk with Messrs Fell & Co Ltd at their Wentworth Nurseries; he lived in Acomb. He went to the Front in October 1917 and was killed in action in August 1918.

Arthur is buried in Kemmel No 1 Cemetery, south of Ypres.

The 2ⁿᵈ Scottish Rifles were part of 20ᵗʰ Division, which was responsible for the defence of the Avions Sector, south of Lens. In September 1918 there was speculation that the Germans were preparing to withdraw from Lens; as a result the British were sending out numerous night patrols into No Man's Land to assess the accuracy of this speculation. This resulted in heavy shelling of No Man's Land by the vigilant Germans.

On 9 September a patrol set off into No Man's Land led by Second Lieutenant Millar; it ran into considerable resistance from a German forward observation post. The following night (10 October) a further patrol was sent out under Lieutenant D Graham, whose objective was to destroy this troublesome forward observation post. However, the Germans had second-guessed the British and they ambushed the British patrol. In the ensuing fight one man was killed, nine others were wounded including Lieutenant Graham. A further man was recorded as missing presumably killed.[2]

As a result of these raids the Germans shelled the Allied positions relentlessly, killing William Summers. It was not until after 6 October that the Germans withdrew from this sector of the Western Front.

Private William Summers aged 20
2ⁿᵈ Battalion Cameronians (Scottish Rifles)
Died 10 September 1918

William was the youngest son of Matthew and Elizabeth Anne Summers of Kingsgate, Hexham. He was a junior chorister at the Abbey and was also a member of the Guild of Bellringers. At the onset of hostilities he was working as an assistant under Mr Cunliffe at W H Smith & Sons at Hexham Station.

In August 1914 William enlisted with the local Battalion of the Northumberland Fusiliers and went to France with them in April 1915. He was involved in the battalion's baptism of fire at the *Second Battle of Ypres* when the Germans made a determined attack to push the Allies out of Belgium. However, it was discovered that William was under age and he was sent home. In October 1916 he rejoined the Forces and was stationed in Ireland until August 1917. After this he was posted to France with the Highland Light Infantry and was later transferred to the Scottish Rifles. He saw action at *Ypres* (1915) *Arras* (1917) and *Kemmel Hill* (1918).

William was leaving the trenches with a working party when part of the trench system was hit directly by an enemy shell. He died instantaneously along with three other comrades; a corporal was also seriously wounded. In his letter to Mrs Summers the Scottish Rifles' Chaplain wrote:

"I wish to express my profoundest sympathy with you in your heavy bereavement and pray that God will comfort and strengthen you in your great sorrow. Your boy has given his life in a great cause and his will be a hero's grave."

He is buried in Sucrerie Cemetery, Albain-Saint-Nazaire. The following words are carved at the foot of his headstone:

THE SOUL REDEEMED IS IN THE HAND OF GOD

References

1   WO 95/1618. *War Diary, 1st West Yorkshire Regiment.*

2.   WO 95/2117. *War Diary, 2nd Cameronians (Scottish Rifles).*

CHAPTER EIGHTEEN

THOSE WHO DIED AT SEA

"We will frighten the British Flag off the face of the waters and starve the British People until they, who have refused peace, will kneel and plead for it".

Kaiser Wilhelm II of Germany, 1 February 1917

Overview

During the years leading up to the Great War, Britain's position as a world power was demonstrated by the size of her navy – the Senior Service. Kaiser Wilhelm II of Germany began to challenge British supremacy by embarking on an aggressive policy of building a great number of *capital* ships. There are no formal criteria for capital ships, but they are recognisable as important warships, those with the heaviest firepower and armour; a capital ship will generally be the leading ship in any fleet. When the Kaiser enlarged his country's nautical power, the British Government responded by building a comparable number of new warships.

When war was declared a number of German capital ships were at large in the oceans of the world. These warships began to cause disruption to Allied shipping and to threaten the transportation of troops from the British Empire to Europe. Most noteworthy was the SMS Emden which roamed the Indian Ocean sinking or capturing up to thirty Allied merchant ships and bombarding Madras, damaging its oil tanks. Eventually, on 9 Nov 1914, the Australian Light Cruiser HMAS Sydney caught up with the Emden, forcing its captain to ground his vessel. In the Pacific Ocean, there was similar disruption and danger from German ships; worse still, they inflicted the first defeat on the British Navy for over a century (*Battle of Coronel,* 1 November 1914). The victorious German fleet eventually sailed into the Atlantic where it was caught and eventually destroyed by the British Navy, (*Battle of Falklands*, 14 November 1914). This loss of German ships in the Atlantic effectively ended the wider, global threat to the Allies from the German Fleet.

Closer to home, as the Great War began the British Navy was ordered to blockade Germany in an attempt to force the Germans into surrender. It was evident that a local blockade of each German port would be very dangerous for the blockading ships which would undoubtedly be subjected to bombardment from coastal batteries. Instead, Britain used a combination of converted merchant ships, Royal Navy vessels and minefields to enforce blockades to the north and south of the British Isles where the Atlantic Ocean enters the North Sea. However, this still allowed the German Fleet freedom to roam *within* the North Sea, as shown by the raids made on the ports of Hartlepool, West Hartlepool, Whitby and Scarborough, on 16 December 1914. These attacks resulted in one hundred and thirty seven deaths, mainly civilians.

The Navy was also involved in the Dardanelles in 1915, with disastrous results (see Chapter Five).

In the North Sea a number of clashes took place between the British and German Fleets, particularly the *Battles of Dogger Bank* (24 January 1915) and *Jutland* (31 May 1916). At *Jutland* German ships sank more British ships than did the British sink German vessels, but the British fleet inflicted considerable damage on many of the remaining German ships. Both sides had expected victory; neither side could claim it, although the Kaiser did so at a later date. Nonetheless, the German fleet left the scene of the battle never to venture again from its home ports during the war.

Submarines

Of greater concern to the Allies was the threat from the German submarine fleet, because Britain relied heavily on imports to feed its population and to supply its 'war machine'. Submarine warfare against merchant vessels during the early stages of the war was conducted according to the rules of war. Ships would be stopped, crews allowed to take to the lifeboats and then the ship would be scuttled – although naval vessels were always fair game. It was not long before this relatively civilised behaviour was abandoned in favour of the unrestricted sinking of merchant and hospital ships.

Torpedo hitting a merchant ship.

In February 1915, the Kaiser declared the sea around the British Isles a war zone – from 18 February, Allied ships in the area would be sunk without warning. British ships hiding behind neutral flags would not be spared, though some effort would be made to avoid sinking vessels that were clearly neutral. In August over 168,000 tons of Allied merchant shipping was sunk. The sinking of neutral ships, including the *Lusitania* and the *Arabic*, involved the death of many American civilians which unsurprisngly led to strained diplomatic relations between Germany and the USA; the

Kaiser revoked his order for unrestricted submarine warfare – for the time being. However, even with restrictions attacks by German submarines continued to have a damaging effect on merchant shipping. In the last months of 1916 they sank one hundred and fifty four merchant vessels. The situation in Britain was becoming desperate. Admiral Sir John Jellicoe said that if things continued to worsen Britain would have to sue for peace by summer 1917. Early in February 1917 the Kaiser once again declared unrestricted submarine warfare:

"We will frighten the British Flag off the face of the waters and starve the British People until they, who have refused peace, will kneel and plead for it".

As a response the British Government began a poster campaign in an effort to persuade people to conserve food. One slogan stated:

"I am the crust. When you throw me away or waste me you are adding twenty submarines to the German Navy. Save me and I will save you."

In April 1917 the losses to Allied shipping from German submarines exceeded 860,000 tons, with comparatively few submarines lost in reply. In late April the admiralty introduced a much-needed convoy system which began to reduce these unsustainable losses, but it was not until the middle of 1918 that the level of merchant ship losses fell below 300,000 tons.

The submarine war had the effect of driving Britain to undertake one of the most notorious land battles of the war, *Third Ypres* or *Passchendaele*, in an attempt to break the German Line and to capture the submarine bases at Blankenberghe and Ostend.

The Dead of 1915

On 3 February 1915, HMS Clan MacNaughton foundered in heavy seas off the north coast of Ireland. She was an armed merchant cruiser from the 10th Cruiser Squadron and was commanded by Commander Robert Jeffreys RN. The ship was built on the Clyde in 1911 by Alexander Stephen and Sons and was steam propelled with a gross tonnage of 4985 tons. She had a crew of two hundred and sixty one men, of which no survivors were found.

On a visit home before joining his new ship Percy Biggs, a seaman who served and died on the Clan MacNaughton, told his niece that the ship had been a merchantman, designed to carry heavy cargo in the hold and nothing on deck. He was sure that now that she had nothing in the hold and heavy guns on the deck she would be very unstable; if they met heavy seas she would turn turtle. He wrote:

> *"you will never hear of us again, we will be taking tea on Davy Jones' Locker".[1]*

He was right.

Engine Room Artificer Ernest Temperley Baty, aged 27
Royal Navy Reserve HMS Clan MacNaughton
Died 3 February 1915

Ernest was the eldest son of William and Dorothy Baty of 16 Tynedale Terrace, Hexham, who also had two other children, a son and a daughter. He had served his time to be a seagoing engineer and at the outbreak of war was an engineer with the Prince Line. Early in 1914 he volunteered for naval service and at the outbreak of hostilities had been appointed as an engine room artificer (mechanic).

In his younger days he was an active footballer and for

319

several seasons he played fullback for Northern Star in the West Tyne League. In March 1915, Hexham Parish Magazine reported:

> *"Ernest Temperley Baty has laid down his life for his country. His great sacrifice will receive abundant reward in a more blessed world of peace and joy. To that world there is no more sea of separation."*

Ernest is commemorated on the Chatham Naval Memorial.

The Dead of 1917

The merchantman SS (Steam Ship) Kwasind was on a voyage from Bilbao to Hartlepool with a cargo of iron ore when it hit a floating mine off Southwold, Suffolk. This had been laid by the German mine-laying submarine UC4. Twelve lives were lost.

The ship was built in 1894 and at the time of her sinking was owned by the Arctic SS Company Limited, which was in turn part-owned by W F Bentick-Smith of Quebec.

Ordinary Seaman William Wilson, aged 16
Mercantile Marine
Died 11 March 1917

William was the son of George William and Sarah Isabella Wilson of Prior Terrace, Hexham. He was a member of the crew of SS Kwasind registered in Quebec, (Kwasind was a friend of Hiawatha known for his strength).

William's name is on the Tower Hill Memorial, London, which commemorates the men and women of the merchant navy and fishing fleet who were lost at sea.

🐦   🐦   🐦

The Dead of 1918

HMTB (His Majesty's Torpedo Boat) No. 90 capsized in heavy weather in the Straits of Gibraltar. This ship had been built in 1895 at Yarrow with a displacement weight of 130 tons. It was armed with three 3-pdr guns and three 14-inch torpedo tubes.

Able Seaman Frederick Norman Dodds, aged 18
Royal Naval Volunteer Reserve, HMTB No. 90
Died 25 April 1918

Frederick was the fourth son of Mr and Mrs J Dodds of Prior Terrace Hexham. Before joining the Navy he was employed by the Hexham branch of the London and Newcastle Tea Company. He lost his life when HMTB No. 90 capsized in heavy weather in the Straits of Gibraltar.

Frederick's eldest brother John died after being wounded accidentally in December 1917 (see Chapter Twenty).

Frederick is commemorated on the Chatham Naval Memorial, which contains the names of 8,500 sailors who died at sea.

🐦   🐦   🐦

References

1. Private communication.

Chatham Naval War Memorial
Commemorates 8,500 sailors with no known grave from
The Great War

CHAPTER NINETEEN

THOSE WHO DIED AS PRISONERS OF WAR

"On the way we passed several POW camps and at one
camp I will always remember the sight of about twenty
'Englanders' being driven out to work, the guards having
long whips besides their rifles and lashing out at any men
who lagged behind. It was enough to make your blood boil
to see men treated like a lot of cattle, just because they were
unfortunate enough to be prisoners of war
and in their power."

Baron Richard Racey, Canadian Army, *1915 POW Diary*

Overview

During the Great War over 190,000 British and Empire
soldiers were taken prisoner by the Germans. Some of these
fellows were captured in the earliest days of the war and
therefore spent up to fifty months in captivity in camps all
over Germany. There was a misconception that the life of a
prisoner of war was simply boring and frustrating. Although
this was indeed sometimes the case, many diaries and records
show that, for all ranks, captivity under the Germans could be
a real test of endurance and physical survival. After the war a
committee was set up to investigate the treatment of Allied
soldiers in captivity in Germany, collecting data from
debriefing interviews from escapees and returning prisoners.
Oral and written testimonies bear witness to ill-treatment,
starvation, hard labour and death. It has been calculated that
one in eight of the British and Empire soldiers captured on
the Western Front died in captivity.

On 8 May 1915 during the desperate days of the *Second Battle of Ypres* (See Chapter Four) the 2nd Battalion Northumberland Fusiliers were in position near 'Mousetrap Farm' and were surrounded on three sides by the enemy. Lieutenant-Colonel H S Enderby and Adjutant Captain R Auld were taken prisoner. Both of these men suffered torture, both physical and mental, while they were in enemy hands. In his prison camp at Augustabad in Neu Brandenburg Province, Lieutenant-Colonel Enderby was forced to run the gauntlet of a hail of German rifle fire. A similar ordeal was meted out to Captain Auld. It is a wonderful thing that both of these stout-hearted men survived the war.

On 21 December 1918 an article appeared in the Hexham Herald entitled *'Murdered by Germans'*. The article outlines the experiences of Lance-Corporal J Holyoak of Sunderland who had been repatriated after four years of internment in German Prisoner of War Camps. Holyoak was serving with the 1st Battalion Northumberland Fusiliers and was taken prisoner on 25 August 1914; he described two cases of British soldiers being murdered by their German Guards:

Case One

In February 1918 Private Hughie Gault of 2nd Battalion Irish Rifles, a Belfast man, was waiting in a canteen for hot water and was ordered away by a German sentry. After a brief delay Gault was bayoneted through the right shoulder and after a scuffle he was bayoneted again, this time in the right arm. After collapsing to the floor he was bayoneted once more, in the chest; he died of his wounds two months later. Holyoak states that the German guard concerned was later promoted.

The CWGC confirms the death of Rifleman H Gault, Royal Irish Rifles, who died 1 April 1918; he is buried in Cologne Southern Cemetery.

Case Two

In September 1917 'Tiddler' Richardson, a Private in the Northumberland Fusiliers, was ordered to help load a wagon with barbed wire destined for the Front. He refused, and as a result suffered summary execution, shot by a German corporal – who was not punished for his brutality.

The CWGC confirms the death of Private H Richardson, 1st Battalion Northumberland Fusiliers who died 25 September 1917 and is also buried in Cologne Southern Cemetery.

These cases illustrate that life as a POW could be very dangerous indeed. We have no way of knowing whether those who died in captivity died simply because they had earlier been wounded in battle or, as was the case with Thomas Urwin, because they were hurt when their aircraft were brought down, or because they died from neglect or were killed by the enemy.

Second Lieutenant Thomas Alexander Urwin, aged 21
Royal Flying Corps
Died 15 January 1918

Thomas was the only son of Mr and Mrs T H Urwin of Shaftoe Leazes, Hexham. He was educated at St Bees School, Cumberland and at the age of eighteen he enlisted in the Royal Engineers. During the period between attestation and active service he was able to pass preliminary medical examinations at Edinburgh University. He was hoping eventually to qualify as a dentist, following in the footsteps of both his father and grandfather. Thomas transferred to the Royal Flying Corps and received a commission, after which he went to France in October 1917. On a flight over enemy territory on 12 January 1918 Thomas's aircraft was brought down. Initially his parents were informed simply that he had been taken prisoner by the Germans. However, they later received a letter from Edward Long of the *Comité Internationale de la Croix Rouge, Agencie Internationale des Prisonniers de Guerre* in Geneva, explaining that their son had died of his wounds. The following report appeared on a list dispatched from Berlin:

> *"15 February 1918: Urwin, Thomas Alexander, Second Lieutenant R.F.C., born 15 May 1897 Newcastle upon Tyne; died 15 January 1918, in field hospital Bohain from shot wound leg and concussion of the brain; buried in the military hospital at Bohain Grave 274."*

Thomas is now buried in Prémont British Cemetery.

The 8th Battalion Machine Gun Corps (MGC) was attached to the 8th Infantry Division. The Machine Corps 'A', 'B' and 'C' Companies were attached to 23rd 24th and 25th Infantry

Brigades respectively. On 22 March the division arrived in the Rosières Harbonnières area and moved eastward towards the Canal de la Somme. On 24 March the Germans attacked the Canal de la Somme Line and were able to cross the river at Fointaine Les Pargny and at Béthencourt-sur-Somme. At dusk the divisional defensive line had retreated westwards towards Morchain and Potte. On the left of this line 'A' Company of the MGC came under great pressure but they were able to hold their position.

On 25 March the Germans attacked at dawn and the division was forced to fall back to the west of Omiécourt. The War Diary of the MGC reports that in the evening 'C' Company had run out of ammunition and that the remnants were reduced to fighting with rifles as infantry. During the night the battalion fell back to a position in front of the village of Chaulnes, but by 9am (26 March) the Germans had penetrated this Line. A new Line was established between Vrély and Rosières to the north. At this point all of the MGC companies received a fresh supply of ammunition.

This Line was held throughout 27 March, but during the night and early hours of 28 March the Germans made several concerted attacks. As a result the 8th Division retreated and dug in near the village of Caix. This Line was soon penetrated but a valiant effort by the defenders re-established it. At midday they received orders to fall back to Moreuil as part of a general retirement. During late March the 8th Division was forced to retreat over a distance of more than twenty five miles, reaching a point only sixteen miles from Amiens.[1]

Second Lieutenant John Miller Emerson, aged 21
8th Battalion Machine Gun Corps (Infantry)
Died 8 April 1918

John was born on 18 February 1897 in Hexham and was the eldest son of George Edward and Charlotte Emerson of the George and Dragon Inn, Market Street. He was

 educated at Queen Elizabeth Grammar School. Before the hostilities he was employed as a clerk at Barclay's Bank at their Quayside Branch in Newcastle. He was also a junior chorister at the Abbey. John was a dedicated golfer and had won the Newton Challenge Cup which was a prestigious prize at the Tynedale Golf Club. He was also a finalist for the Bankers' Trophy.

He enlisted with the Northumberland Fusiliers in the early months of 1916 and was attached to the 1st Battalion. After a brief time at the Front with the Northumberland Fusiliers, John was selected for a commission and returned to England for training at the Officers Training Corps. He received a commission with the Machine Gun Corps and went to France in October 1917. He was fortunate enough to be at home in Hexham for his twenty-first birthday in February 1918.

On 28 March, John's parents were informed that he had been wounded and that he was missing. In late April they were informed by the Red Cross Society that he was a prisoner of war. Finally on 12 August they received information from the War Office, based on reports from the Red Cross in Geneva, that John had died in a German Field Hospital at Rosières of wounds to his thigh, and had been buried in the Hospital Cemetery.

Today, John is commemorated in Heath Cemetery, Harbonnières.

On 27 March the 2nd Battalion Lienster Regiment, as part of the 47th Brigade, was in a position to the east of the village of

Proyart, which is south of the River Somme and north of the town of Harbonnières.

The Germans advanced against Proyart at 8am and at first they were repulsed. However, later in the morning, after receiving further reinforcements, the Germans managed to get around the left flank of the 47th Brigade through a gap between it and the 48th Brigade to the north. At 10am the 47th Brigade was forced to retire to the south. Thus, the gap that existed earlier in the day between these two brigades widened still further.

Private William Hogg, aged 36
2nd Battalion Leinster Regiment
Died 15 April 1918

William was the second son of Mr and Mrs Hogg of Prior Terrace, Hexham and was born in Allendale. He was a married man with six children of which the eldest was just thirteen. Before enlisting he was employed as a cartman for Fenwick's Dye Works Ltd. Originally he enlisted in the Northumberland Fusiliers but was later transferred to the Leinster Regiment. He was reported missing on 27 March 1918. Weeks later a report was received through the Red Cross from a German POW hospital that he had died of his wounds. On 27 May, his brother George also was reported as being a prisoner of war. All five of the Hogg brothers played their part in the Great War. The memorial in the Abbey Gardens records Private W Hogg's regimental affiliation as 1/4th Northumberland Fusiliers.

William is buried in Valenciennes (St Roch) Communal Cemetery.

By April, the 18th Northumberland Fusiliers had left the Somme and were in the area near Armentières. They had suffered extensive gas shelling. On 9 April the Germans had launched an offensive in this area called Georgette (see also Chapter 15). At 4am the Fusiliers were 'stood to' and later that morning they were detailed to destroy the bridges over the River Lys once all the Allied troops had crossed. Until mid afternoon a group of Fusiliers on the German side of the River managed to keep the Germans at bay. However at 4pm they received orders to retire across the river destroying the remaining footbridge behind them. As the Fusiliers were withdrawing towards the river the Germans let loose a heavy machine gun barrage. A small rearguard action allowed a lot of the men to cross the river, but the Germans had broken through unobtrusively and were behind those remaining, who at this point were carrying two of their wounded. The remnants of the defensive force were forced to surrender. After a short interrogation the prisoners were escorted toward Erquinghem. At a wayside dressing station, the wounded men were given some medical attention and were left with their captors.[3, 4]

Private Michael Reed, aged 41
18th Battalion Northumberland Fusiliers
Died 21 June 1918

Michael was born in Allendale and was the husband of Ellen Reed of Back Street (St Mary's Chare) Hexham. Before enlisting he worked as a mason's labourer. Initially Mrs Reed received a postcard through the Red Cross from Michael saying that he was a prisoner of war in Stargard Hospital, that he was in bed and that he hoped to be 'up and about soon'.

Although the War Office originally posted Michael as being wounded and missing on 10 April, it was later reported that he died of his wounds when a prisoner of war in Germany.

Michael is buried in Berlin South-Western Cemetery.

On 27 May the Germans launched their third offensive, code named Blucher (see Chapter 15) along the Chemin des Dames Ridge in the Champagne Region of France.   The subsequent battle is known as the *Third Battle of the Aisne*. At the time of the offensive, four divisions of the British IX Corps, of which the 50th Northumbrian Division was part, were in the Front Line.   The 1/4th Battalion East Yorkshire belonged to its 150th Brigade and was involved in the desperate fighting which effected the devastation of the 50th Division.[5]

Private John William Norman Wilkinson, aged 20
1/4th Battalion East Yorkshire Regiment
Died 12th August 1918

John was born in Hexham, the son of Mr and Mrs M Wilkinson of Crescent Avenue.   Before joining up he worked as a clerk for the North Eastern Railway Company.   He enlisted in Hull and was originally in the East Riding Yeomanry, a cavalry regiment.   Subsequently he was transferred to the 1/4th Battalion East Yorkshire Regiment.   He was posted as missing on 27 May.   In early August 1918 the Hexham Herald reported that his parents had received a postcard through the Red Cross stating that he was uninjured.   Subsequently the German authorities notified his parents that he had in fact died in August.

John is buried in Chauny Communal Cemetery, British Extension.   This large cemetery was made for the burial

of remains brought in from the battlefields of the Aisne, including numerous bodies from German cemeteries.

References

1. WO 95/1702. *War Diary, 8ᵗʰ Battalion Machine Gun Corps.*

2. WO 95/2308. *War Diary, 2ⁿᵈ Battalion Leinster Regiment.*

3. WO 95/3451. *War Diary 18ᵗʰ Battalion Northumberland Fusiliers.*

4. Shakespear, J. Lieut-Col. *Historical Records of the 18ᵗʰ (Service) Battalion Northumberland Fusiliers.*
    Pub: Council of the Newcastle and Gateshead Chamber of Commerce, 1920.

5. Wyrell E. *The Fiftieth Division, 1914-1919*
    Pub: 1939.   Reprinted, Naval and Military Press 2002.

CHAPTER TWENTY

THOSE WHO DIED AWAY FROM THE FRONT

The broken heroes from afar
Are soothed at last to rest ...
... like some angel star
She guards at God's behest.

Sergeant J A Barton NF of Hexham, *The Night Nurse*

Overview

The care of wounded soldiers would begin only yards behind the fighting, at Regimental Aid Posts (RAPs), found in either support or reserve trenches. These aid posts were manned by the Battalion Medical Officer, his orderlies and the battalion's stretcher-bearers (drawn from the battalion's musicians). The facilities were primitive – they could afford only basic first aid. From here the wounded were passed down the chain to an Advanced Dressing Station (ADS).

Members of the Royal Army Medical Corps (RAMC) were attached to Divisions and were known as Field Ambulances; they manned the Advanced Dressing Stations. Each Division had three Field Ambulances, one to each Brigade. Although an ADS was better equipped than an RAP, it still could provide only a limited range of treatments. Wounds could be dressed and a limited range of emergency operations performed. It is unsurprising, therefore, that many of the ADSs would have an adjacent cemetery. Some of these burial grounds still exist today, for example the Duhallow ADS Cemetery, Ypres, which was in operation from July 1917. From an ADS the wounded would be passed down the line to Casualty Clearing Stations (CCS).

Casualty Clearing Stations were large and well-equipped; their role was to retain all serious cases that were unfit to travel further and to treat them for their wounds. Soldiers with relatively minor injuries were treated and returned to the Front, others were evacuated. A typical CCS could accommodate up to a thousand casualties and would be based as close as possible to a railway line or a canal.

At a CCS, complex operations such as amputations were performed. Some carried specialist units dealing in nervous disorders, skin diseases and infectious diseases. They could also care for cases of general sickness including trench foot, venereal disease and trench fever. RAMC personnel manned these stations.

From the CCS the wounded would be sent by rail or canal barge to hospitals in France or to an embarkation port for shipment to the UK – an injury that necessitated time back in the UK was known as a *blighty* case. If a soldier managed to get as far as a hospital there was good chance that he would survive. These hospitals were located near the army's principal bases such as Boulogne, Le Havre, Rouen, Le Touquet and Etaples and contained up to 1040 patients. However in 1917 many were enlarged so as to offer up to 2500 beds. RAMC personnel including female nurses staffed the hospitals – Vera Brittain was one of these brave women, and an account of her experiences can be read in her outstanding autobiography, *Testament of Youth*.

Wounded soldiers who were well enough to be moved often travelled to the UK for treatment in British hospitals. If they survived – and after medical board review – they were shipped back to France, sometimes to their original unit, but not always. As explained earlier in this book, if a man died in either the CCS or in hospital it is not always a simple matter to find out where he was when he received his fatal wounds.

Apart from those detailed below there are several other men recorded earlier in this book who also died in hospitals away from the Front. The time and place of the fatal injuries of these soldiers are known *exactly*, hence their particular positions in the book.

The Dead of 1914

Sapper Robert Robson, aged 42
1ˢᵗ Division Signal Company, Royal Engineers
Died December 1914

Robert was born in Hexham and was the second son of Mr Robert Robson, for many years parish clerk at Hexham. He was a married man who left a widow and two children who lived in Alexander Road, Gateshead. His brothers John and Joseph of Robson Printers (the original of today's company, printers of this book) received the news of his death in a letter sent by a fellow soldier.

As a boy Robert found employment in Hexham Post Office and during the early 1890s he moved to the General Post Office in Newcastle where he was employed until the outbreak of war when he volunteered his services as a telegraphist. He had acted in a similar role during the South African War and it was reported that he had twice been captured by the Boers.

The unofficial report from the Front stated that Robert was wounded in the back by shrapnel and also received a bullet in the leg. He died of his wounds in a base hospital.

Robert is buried in Boulogne Eastern Cemetery.

The Dead of 1915

Corporal Shoeing Smith James Henry Robson, aged 23
'A' Squadron, 1ˢᵗ Northumberland Hussars
Died 8 February 1915

James Robson was born in Hexham and was the son of Mr and Mrs George Robson of Lane House, Hexhamshire. He had served his time as a blacksmith with Mr Ellerington of the Shire. Following this he worked for Mr H Oxley in Hexham and then for Mr Brown in Haydon Bridge, with whom he was employed on mobilization. He had been a member of the Territorial Cavalry Regiment for over three years.

In a letter to his parents from France, Lieutenant Robson reported:

> " Corporal Robson died in hospital at St Omer as a result of Scarlet Fever... I can only add that his loss will be greatly felt by all who knew him and worked with him."

James is buried in Longuenesse (St Omer) Souvenir Cemetery.

The Dead of 1916

For the attack on the 22 – 23 July the 3rd Field Company Australian Engineers was attached to the 1st Division Australian Infantry. The History of the Royal Australian Engineers states: [1]

> *"The attack, which was linked to the second phase of the Somme offensive, followed the final bombardment soon after midnight on 22-23 July. By 2.30am the new front line had been reached, and work on the defences was in hand, the 1st, 2nd and 3rd Field Companies being helped by the 5th Field Company from the 2nd Division and the 13th from the 4th Division. Soon however, daylight came, and aimed shell fire commenced...*
>
> *Gradually, during the 23rd and 24th July, much of the northern part of Pozières was occupied, in spite of intense shelling of all troops in the forward positions and also in the area behind... The 1st Division had captured nearly all of its objectives. Its casualties, moderate in the first assault on the southern half of the village, had begun to mount when the enemy artillery was repositioned: and thereafter the infantry and the associated units in the forward area had suffered under shell fire of an intensity never experienced in Gallipoli. It was plain by the 25 July that the next stage of the attack required fresh troops. The 1st Division was relieved by the 2nd ..."*

Sapper Ernest Wallace, aged 25
3rd Field Company Australian Engineers
Died 19 September 1916

Ernest was the fourth and youngest son of Henry Wallace of Hexham and (later) Wylam. Before going to South Australia in 1913 aged 21, he had been educated at the Sele School in Hexham. His sister also travelled to Australia and was listed as his next of kin under her married name of Saint. Ernest was an enthusiastic footballer who played centre-forward for Hexham

Athletic. He was also playing for Newburn when they won the Northern Alliance. 'Down Under' he worked as a bricklayer, living with his married sister in Kirkcaldy, South Australia.

In December 1914 he enlisted in the Australian 10th Infantry Regiment and initially saw service in Egypt, but soon was sent to Gallipoli. He was present at the Suvla Bay landings in August 1915, transporting ammunition under heavy fire. He spent a long time in hospital with severe dysentery. When the call came for volunteers for the Royal Engineers he returned to Egypt to become a Sapper. He next saw action on the Western Front where he was severely wounded, sustaining injuries which weeks later would lead to his death. His left arm had to be amputated and he was also suffering from severe wounds to the head and back.

Ernest died in a military hospital in Boulogne and is buried in Boulogne Eastern Cemetery.

The 1/4th Northumberland Fusiliers as part of the 149th Brigade were heavily involved in the first day (15 September 1916) of a major attack called *Flers-Courcelette,* (see Chapter Eight) in which the Fusiliers suffered a significant number of casualties.[2]

Private John Fox, age unknown
1/4th Northumberland Fusiliers
Died 21 September 1916

John was born in Dumfries, but enlisted with the Territorial Battalion in Hexham. His details show that he died from his wounds.

John is buried in Flatiron Copse Cemetery, Mametz.

Flatiron Copse was the site of an ADS (Advanced Dressing Station) which was established soon after the capture of Mametz Wood on 14 July 1916. The associated burial ground remained in operation until this area was recaptured by the Germans in March-April 1918.

The Dead of 1917

Private William Coulson, aged 33
1/4th Battalion, Northumberland Fusiliers
Died 27 January 1917

William and his wife lived in Holy Island, Hexham. Before he enlisted he had worked for Mr Charlton as a slater for over twenty years. His wife was notified that he had died of natural causes.

William is buried in Albert Communal Cemetery Extension.

The four Battalions of the Tyneside Irish (24th, 25th, 26th and 27th Battalions of the Northumberland Fusiliers) were all involved in the action which began on 9 April and was known as *The First Battle of the Scarpe*, named after a river to the south of Arras. For the period of the battle (9 – 14 April) and in the following days the 24th Northumberland Fusiliers lost three officers and sixty-five men.[3]

Lance Corporal James William Kelly, aged 27
24th Battalion (Tyneside Irish) Northumberland Fusiliers
Died 18 April 1917

James was the son of George and Margaret Kelly. George and his wife lived in Burn Lane, Hexham with their young child. He had been employed at the Gem Cinema in Hexham but when he enlisted he was working for Messrs Bell and Sons in their wool warehouse. He was also a well-known footballer who had played for a number of local sides. He joined up in October 1914 and went to the Front in December 1915. He was involved in many battles on the Somme and had survived the appalling massacre of 1 July 1916, the *First Day of the Somme*. He died of his wounds in one of the Military Hospitals around Boulogne.

William is buried in Etaples Military Cemetery.

On 26 October 1/5th Northumberland Fusiliers (149th Brigade) were involved in the battle known as *Second Passchendaele (Third Ypres)* (see Chapter Fourteen).[2]

Private John Walker, age unknown
1/5th Battalion Northumberland Fusiliers
Died 1 November 1917

John was a married man who left a widow and two children. They lived at Diamond Terrace, Hexham. He was born in Cumberland, and had worked as a farm labourer for Mr Graham of Coastley. At the time of enlisting he was employed by Messrs Hunter (traction engine proprietors) of Hexham, as a steam wagon driver.

John died of wounds received in action and is buried in St Sever Cemetery Extension, Rouen. Rouen was a centre for a number of military hospitals, which were stationed around the southern outskirts of the city.

❧   ❧   ❧

On 30th November the Northumberland Hussars were attached to 12th Division and were involved in the *Second Battle of Cambrai*. A German offensive had driven a wedge into the Division's weak right flank and the Hussars' task was to establish a defensive line between 6th Queens Regiment at Vaucellette Farm and the 55th Division at Piezières. They managed this during the late afternoon although the expected attack didn't materialise. However, the Hussars came under heavy shelling during the following morning and withdrew that evening (1st December).[4]

Private John George Dodds, aged 26
1/1st Northumberland Hussars
Died 1 December 1917

 John was born in Newcastle and was the son of John Dodds of Prior Terrace. Before the hostilities he was employed at the Black Bull in Corbridge and he joined up at the beginning of 1915. He was deployed to France in February 1917. He was one of four brothers who were serving the King either ashore or afloat.

Casualty records for this period relate that George was wounded accidentally. He is buried in Tincourt New British Cemetery which was a centre for casualty clearing stations during the year March 1917 – March 1918, after which the Germans reoccupied the village. John's younger brother, Frederick, died at sea in 1918. (see Chapter Eighteen).

❧   ❧   ❧

The 1/4th Battalion Northumberland Fusiliers were involved in the eighth phase of the *Third Battle of Ypres* which was known as *Second Passchendaele* and was fought between 26 October and 10 November, when the village of Passchendaele fell. At 5.40am in pouring rain the 1/4th Northumberland attacked behind a creeping barrage. Roll call that night revealed the truly terrible losses suffered by the 1/4th, which were:

Officers and men, 38 killed, 161 wounded and 66 missing (most of these would be dead). These figures represent *more than half* of those who had gone into action.[2, 5]

During December 1917 and January 1918 the 1/4th Northumberland Fusiliers were involved in the defence of the Front Line near Passchendaele.

Private William Charles Love, aged 25
1/4th Battalion Northumberland Fusiliers
Died 19 February 1918

William was born in Hexham and was the son of the late William Easterby Love and Alice Love of Gilesgate Bank, Hexham. He is buried in Wimereux Communal Cemetery.

On 24 March the 1st Battalion Coldstream Guards together with the 2nd Battalion Grenadier Guards were in the Front Line near the village of Hamelincourt, between Arras and Bapaume. In the evening the Germans took the village of Erviliers to the southwest but were later evicted by the Irish Guards. Later the Battalion, was ordered to dig a new trench facing southeast as the situation on their right was considered critical. During the afternoon, after receiving a series of conflicting orders, the battalion was ordered to retire to a line east of Adinfer into a trench system – a system that turned out to be non-existent – and had to spend the night digging in. Confusing orders had left the neighbouring 31ˢᵗ Division in their original position and so the Guards were left with their right flank exposed or 'in the air' as it was known.

In the afternoon of 26 March the German artillery was very busy and the villages of Hamelincourt and Moyenville were severely battered by shells. The bombardment continued well into the evening.

Guardsman Herbert Nicholas Fogg, aged 29
2ⁿᵈ Battalion Grenadier Guards
Died 31 March 1918

Herbert was born in Hexham. He was the husband of Robina Fogg of Southey Street, Gateshead. He died of wounds received in action, and is buried in St Sever Cemetery Extension Rouen. Rouen was a centre for large number of military hospitals

Private Charles Edwin Mason, aged 26
10ᵗʰ Battalion (Princess Louise's)
Argyll and Sutherland Highlanders
Died 4 April 1918

Charles was born in Knaresborough, Yorkshire, and was the only son of Mrs Mason of Foundry Lane, Hexham. Before he enlisted in the regular army in 1909 he had worked as a farm labourer in Humshaugh and Wark.

It is reported that he had been wounded no fewer than nine times during his Great War service and had also been gassed. After the ninth occasion he was transferred to working on the land in France. Ironically (and very sadly) it was while he was engaged doing this peaceful work that he was kicked by a horse, dying from his injuries some time later in a military hospital in Rouen. This was a curiously tragic end for one who had passed a long, dangerous and arduous military service at the Front.

Charles is buried in Boisguillaume Communal Cemetery Extension, Rouen.

On 22 March the 1/8th Argyll and Southern Highlanders faced the full force of German Storm troopers during the opening phases of the spring offensive on the Somme. They held a forward position northwest of St Quentin, in front of the village of Vermand. In a number of rearguard actions during 21 – 24 March the battalion had over a hundred men killed as well as a large number wounded. It is assumed that William Oliver was wounded during this period of intense and confused action and that he died later of his wounds.[7]

Private William Oliver, aged 42 years
1/8th Battalion Argyll and Sutherland Highlanders
Died 14 April 1918

William was a married man with three young children, living in Cockshaw when the war began. He had been born in Jedburgh but had lived in Hexham for many years.; he was a stonemason by trade. He enlisted in late 1916 with the King's Own Liverpool Regiment but was later transferred to the Argylls. William first went to France in early 1917 and a couple of weeks before he died he was home on leave, returning to the Front as late as 3 April. Records show that he died of his wounds.

William is buried in Longuenesse (St Omer) Souvenir

Cemetery.   St Omer was the site of many hospitals during the war.

❧   ❧   ❧

The 1ˢᵗ Battalion East Kent was based in the area around Westhoek, (approximately 2½ miles east of Ypres) between 15 and 23 April. In the previous week the battalion had been reinforced by a draft of two hundred and fifty men (presumably Private Robinson was one of these men). On 17 April the battalion position was heavily shelled and Company Sergeant Major Field and thirteen men of other ranks were wounded.

Further south the German offensive had captured the Messines Ridge and Kemmel Hill. On 23 April the battalion moved back to the ramparts of Ypres.[8]

Private George Sydney Robinson, aged 19
1ˢᵗ Battalion (The Buffs) East Kent Regiment
Died 26 April 1918

George was born in Hexham, the youngest son of John William and Elizabeth Ann Robinson of South Park. He was educated at St Bees and Durham School and at seventeen he joined the Officers Training Corps. He enlisted into the 'Buffs' (East Kent Regiment) at Lincoln's Inn, London, and was transferred to the Front in March 1918. George's parents were informed that he had been 'wounded in action' on 17 April; they were told that he had received injuries to the left hand and both legs and was lying in a base hospital. Subsequently he died of these wounds.

George is buried in Haringhe (Bandagehem) Military Cemetery near Ypres.

One of George's brothers, Captain John Wilfred Robinson, was killed on the Somme on 15 November 1916, see Chapter Eight. His eldest brother, Lieutenant Colonel F Robinson DSO, was in hospital in Oxford at the time of his brother's death, recovering from wounds received in the German offensive of early March.

The 234th Battalion Machine Gun Corps was attached to 4th Infantry Division.

Private John Heenan, aged 22
234th Battalion Machine Gun Corps
Died 30 April 1918

John was born in Crawcrook, Newcastle and was the son of Michael and Margaret Heenan of Ryton-on-Tyne. Initially on the nominal roll of the 1/4th Battalion Northumberland Fusiliers, he transferred to the Machine Gun Corps. The Hexham Herald reported that John's uncle Mr R J Conkleton of Pearson's Terrace received the news that John had died of his wounds in the 18th General Hospital, Cameria, France.

John is buried in Etaples Military Cemetery.

The 15th Battalion Lancashire Fusiliers (a 'Salford Pals' Battalion) were part of the 96th Brigade involved in the defence of Mount Kemmel during the second German offensive (operation Georgette) in the spring of 1918. During 17 April elements of the 15th 18th and 19th Lancashire

Fusiliers drove off a number of aggressive German attacks. These violent days cost the brigade ninety-four men, and it is believed that Hugh Brown (below) was wounded during the action of 17 April. On 18 April the Brigade was replaced by French troops in the Front Line and the Fusiliers took over the duties of digging trenches at the rear of the hill. On 25 April the Germans attacked the hill on a broad Front and by 7.30am they had triumphed, affording their forces uninterrupted views over the southern section of the Ypres Salient.

Lieutenant Hambord who was captured on the slopes of the hill, later wrote:

> " ... as soon as the barrage lifted the French went forward in large parties some fifty strong, to surrender to the advancing Germans...."

Corporal Hugh Brown, aged 20
15ᵗʰ Battalion Lancashire Fusiliers
Died 29 May 1918

Hugh was born at Ballantrae, Ayrshire and was the son of William and Margaret Brown of Quarry House Farm. Although initially with the Royal Field Artillery he was transferred to the Lancashire Fusiliers. His parents received word that he had been dangerously wounded in the head and was at a clearing station in France. In March 1918 the 29ᵗʰ and 56ᵗʰ Casualty Clearing Stations were established at Gezaincourt. Hugh died of his wounds in one of these Stations.

Hugh is buried in Bagneux British Cemetery, Gezaincourt.

During late April and early May 1918 the 1ˢᵗ Battalion Essex Regiment was stationed three miles west of the Front Line near the village of Gommecourt (eight miles north of Albert).

During the German offensive on the Somme (see Chapter Fifteen) the Germans were unable to recapture this particular part of the old Somme battlefield of 1916.

The men of the Essex Battalion spent their time in a three stage rotation system: on the Front Line, in Divisional Reserve and at rest. The War Diary shows that much of their time away from the Front was spent working on improvements to the defence systems.

On the night of 1 – 2 May they moved into the Front Line east of Bucquoy to relieve the 8th Battalion Somerset Light Infantry. Their main task was to improve the level of defence in this sector. Throughout the next few days the men were bombarded by heavy shells and had to endure incessant sniping, resulting in a number of casualties: the Battalion Diary records two soldiers killed and five wounded by 5 May.

On 8 May the men of the Essex Regiment, in cooperation with 13th Rifle Brigade, made a localised advance into No Man's Land. The Germans responded with heavy artillery fire which caused a number of casualties. One officer was killed and one wounded; five other ranks were killed and seven wounded.

Private Joseph Watson, aged 27
1st Battalion Essex Regiment
Died 8 May 1918

Joseph was born in Hexham, the second son of Joseph and Ellen Watson of Haugh Lane. He was married to Margaret and they lived in Bywell Terrace, Seaton Sluice, Northumberland. Initially he served in the Norfolk Regiment but was transferred to the Essex Regiment. He was wounded in action and was transferred to a Casualty Clearing Station near Doullens.

Joseph is buried in St Amand British Cemetery. His

older brother, George, was killed 7 May 1915, see Chapter Four.

During late June the 12th Battalion Northumberland Fusiliers were enjoying a lengthy period of rest, recreation and training. This respite lasted until they were ordered to relieve the Anson Battalion of the Royal Naval Division on 24 July. Their training involved firing practice with rifles and Lewis Guns and improving their signalling techniques, especially communications with aircraft. Second Lieutenant Tully joined the battalion on 22 June at Grandcourt and was actively involved in these training sessions. [11]

Second Lieutenant Richard Latimer Tully, aged 19
1/4th Battalion Northumberland Fusiliers
Attached 12th Battalion Northumberland Fusiliers
Died 22 July 1918

Richard was the second son of James Edward Tully JP and Mrs Tully of West Quarter, Hexham. He was educated at Aysgarth School Yorkshire and afterwards at Charterhouse and had gone up to Cambridge where he underwent his army cadet course. In September 1917 he enlisted in the 1/4th Northumberland Fusiliers and subsequently obtained a commission on 30 January 1918. He went to the Front in late April 1918.

Richard died of virulent pneumonia at a base hospital following a successful operation to correct injuries accidentally received whilst playing football.

Richard is buried in Bagneux British Cemetery, Gezaincourt.

In late September the 1st Northumberland Fusiliers, (1st Division, 9th Brigade) were involved in action east of Bapume. On 14 September they were in Front trenches near Havrincourt when they were attacked by German infantry. They repulsed this and a number of smaller attacks with resolution, but the cost to the battalion was seven men killed and forty-two wounded. In the days that followed further casualties resulted from enemy artillery attacks. Later in the month the 1st Northumberland Fusiliers were involved in the capture of Flesquières Ridge (five miles east of Cambrai). Casualties reported for this action were four officers killed and two wounded, with twenty-six men from other ranks killed, one hundred and thirty-four wounded and thirty-five missing.[12]

Private John Edward Robson, aged 30
1st Battalion Northumberland Fusiliers
Died 13 October 1918

John was born in Newcastle upon Tyne and was a married man and the father of two children; at the outbreak of war they lived in North Terrace, Hexham. Before joining up he was employed by Hexham and Acomb Cooperative Society as manager of the Acomb Branch. He was the second son of William Robson of Broad Gates, Hexham. Before being transferred to the Northumberland Fusiliers he served with the King's Own Yorkshire Light Infantry.

Two weeks before his death, his wife had received word that John had been seriously wounded in action and was lying in a Casualty Clearing Station in France. In fact John's injuries were so severe that they necessitated the amputation of both legs. Sadly, following the amputation of his legs he eventually died in the Casualty Clearing Station.

John is buried in Grenvillers British Cemetery, which was the site of the 34th, 49th and 56th Casualty Clearing Stations. John is commemorated also on the Roll of Honour in the Abbey, and also in Trinity (Primitive Methodists) Church.

In September and October 1918 the 1st Battalion West Yorkshire Regiment (6th Division, 18th Brigade) was involved in actions against the German defensive line known as the Hindenberg Line, to the east of Peronne. The 6th Division were involved in the following officially recognised actions:

Battle of St Quentin Canal	*29 September – 2 October*
Battle of Beaurevoir	*3 – 5 October*
Battle of Cambrai	*8 – 9 October*

Private Charlie Conkleton, aged 19
1st Battalion (Prince of Wales's Own)
West Yorkshire Regiment
Died 21 October 1918

Charlie was born in Hexham and was the youngest son of Thomas Conkleton of Haugh Lane, Hexham. On 12 October the Hexham Herald reported that Charlie had been wounded and was in the 1st Australian General Hospital, Rouen with shell wounds to his left leg. He died nine days later. Charlie was the second son that the Conkleton family had lost during the Great War, (see Chapter Fourteen).

Charlie is buried in St Sever Cemetery Extension, Rouen, which was a centre for Allied hospitals.

References

1. McNicholl, CBE. Maj-Gen R.R. *History of the Royal Australian Engineers 1902-1920.*

2. Wyrell E. *The Fiftieth Division, 1914-1919*
   Pub: 1939, reprinted, Naval and Military Press 2002.

3. Sheen. J. A. *History of the Tyneside Irish,*
   Pub: Pen and Sword, 1998.

4. Pease. H. *The History of the Northumberland (Hussars) Yeomanry.*
   Pub: Constable and Company Limited, 1924.

5. WO 95/2826. *War Diary, 1/4t^h Battalion Northumberland Fusiliers.*

6. WO 95/1215. *War Diary, 2nd Battalion Grenadier Guards.*

7. WO 95/1944. *War Diary, 1/8th Battalion Argyll and Sutherland Highlanders.*

8. Private Communication

9. Stedman. M. *Salford Pals*
   Pub: Pen and Sword

10. WO 95/2537. *War Diary, 1st Battalion Essex Regiment.*

11. WO 95/2155. *War Diary 12th Battalion Northumberland Fusiliers.*

12. Sandilands. Brig. H R. *A History of the 1st and 2nd Northumberland Fusiliers 1914-1918.*
    Pub: St Georges Press 1938 reprinted Naval and Military Press 2001.

CHAPTER TWENTY ONE

THOSE WHO PERISHED IN OTHER FOREIGN THEATRES OF WAR

"... There shall be
In that rich earth a richer dust concealed;
A dust whom England bore, shaped, made aware,
Gave, once, her flowers to love, her ways to roam ..."

Rupert Brooke, *The Soldier*

Overview

As suggested in Chapter One, the Great War of 1914 – 18 is commonly known as the First *World* War, but many of us nonetheless associate that global conflict chiefly with the horrors of the Western Front, with the Somme and with Passchendaele.

However, British and Empire forces fought and died in many other parts of the world in defence of the British Empire, and as Jon Davies says in his foreword, many of the young men who marched away were leaving their home parishes for the first time. As related in Chapter Five, they fought the Turks in 1915 on the Gallipoli Peninsula; they fought in Mesopotamia (present day Iraq and Iran) and in Egypt and Palestine. They battled and died in Greece (against the Bulgarians and the Austrians) and in Italy (against the Austrians and the Germans) from late 1917. Further, troops were involved in Africa against German colonial troops and in the Caucasus against Germans, Turks, and eventually Red Russian forces. Soldiers were also involved in the defence of India and in the capture of the German territory of Tsingtao in China.

353

Egypt and Palestine

The Turks and their German Allies saw the Seuz Canal as being an important strategic prize in their effort to win the war and to challenge the British Empire in India. With this in mind the Turks attacked British forces on the banks of the canal in February 1915. The British easily repulsed this attack and no further attempts were made on Suez during 1915 as both sides needed to commit their reserves to Gallipoli. Early in 1916 the British garrison, which included troops from Australia and New Zealand, began to move into Palestine with the intention of forming a defensive line one hundred miles east of the canal, although progress towards this was slow.

Also at this time, the Turks (under the German commander Kress von Kressenstein) were building up forces for an attack on the east bank of the canal. By June the Turkish and Arab forces, 16,000 strong, had gathered on the Sinai-Palestine border awaiting the arrival of machine-guns and heavy artillery. In response, the British deployed their forces in fortified positions about twenty miles east of the canal to the west of the town of Romani. These forces consisted of the British 42nd and 51st Divisions along with the Anzac Horse Brigades (including the 3rd Australian Light Horse).

On the night of the 3rd/4th August the Turks attacked the British Lines south of Romani, which were defended by the Australians. Initially the Turks did capture part of the town, but they found it hard to achieve much more than this because the Australian forces put up such a stubborn fight. Eventually the Turks were forced to retreat to El Arish, sixty miles to the east, closely followed and harassed by the Allies. Although the Turks claimed that they were victorious their losses were very significant and by December the British forces had cleared the Turks from the whole of the Sinai Peninsula.

Sergeant Benjamin Disraeli Alexander, aged 28 years
3ʳᵈ Battalion Australian Light Horse
Died 9 August 1916

Benjamin Alexander was the youngest son of Joseph and Catherine Alexander of The Leases, Newcastle upon Tyne. He was born in Hexham in 1887 and was educated at Battle Hill School. After leaving school he was employed first at the North Mail Office in Hexham. He then moved to Pontefract in Yorkshire, where he found employment as Head of Clerical Staff for the Cooperative Wholesale Society. In October 1914 he left England for Tasmania, where he worked for Mr Weston, a well-known fruit grower of The Springs, Exeter, Tasmania.

He joined the Australian Light Horse in early 1915 and later in the year was promoted to Sergeant. On leaving Australia on 23 November 1915 these Australian troops were initially destined to go to Europe. However, attacks by the Turks on the strategically important Suez Canal kept the Australian troops in Egypt, where Benjamin was killed.

Benjamin is buried in Kantara War Memorial Cemetery, Egypt.

India and the North West Frontier

1918

For the British, the security of India was vital to the successful conclusion of the war. When war was first declared the bulk of the regular army in India was withdrawn and replaced with partly-trained Territorial divisions, whose role was to maintain control of three problem areas, these being: general internal security, the North West Frontier and Burma. The Mountain Batteries, to which Richard Telfer belonged, were used in the North West Frontier Region. Turkey entered the war in

October 1914 with a proclamation of Jihad (see Chapter Five, Gallipoli), and Britain was understandably very concerned about the loyalty of its Indian Muslim troops; as it turned out they never became a problem. Turkish and German agents worked hard to persuade the Emir of Afghanistan to go to war. This he refused to do, although his successor did so after the Great War was over. However, some of the renegade Afghan tribes, such as the Mahsuds in Waziristan, did attack British positions with the help of German and Turkish agents in 1917, but they were resolutely forced to sue for peace.

Gunner Richard Dalzell Telfer, aged 38
1ˢᵗ Mountain Battery, Royal Garrison Artillery
Died 5 June 1918

Richard was born in Acomb in 1880 and was married in Durham in 1907. Before he enlisted in Spennymoor, he worked as a grocer in Great Lumley. Richard's death was recorded as 'died' rather than 'killed', which generally meant that a man perished as the result of sickness rather than being killed in action.

Richard is commemorated on the Karachi 1914 – 18 War Memorial which contains the names of those who served in garrisons and died in Pakistan (formerly India) and who are buried in civil and cantonment cemeteries.

Salonika

In October 1915 an Anglo-French force landed at the Greek port of Salonika (now known as Thessalonica), to provide military assistance to the Serbs who were under attack from German, Austro-Hungarian and Bulgarian forces. However, this assistance arrived too late to save the day. The French insisted that Allied forces should remain in Greece, although the British were less than enthusiastic about waging war in this arena.

During 1916 the Allies mounted some highly aggressive campaigns, resulting in the eventual defeat of the Bulgarian Army and in its subsequent surrender on 30 September 1918.

However, quite apart from the dangers of battle, malaria and dysentery proved to be the major drain on manpower during this campaign. The British alone suffered over half a million 'non-battlefield' casualties.

In London the War Department relegated this campaign to the status of 'low priority'. As a result, assistance to the fighting men was rendered by voluntary organisations such as the Scottish Women's Hospital founded by Dr Elsie Maud Inglis and the Young Men's Christian Association (YMCA).

1916

Sapper Robert Elliott, aged 34 years
2/1st (Northumberland) Field Company Royal Engineers
Died 2 November 1916

Robert was the son of Henry and Alice Elliott of Newbrough and was married to Meggie Elliott of Rye Terrace. They had two children. He was a joiner by trade having served his apprenticeship with Messrs Herdman. An accomplished cyclist, he had won a number of prizes for racing and was for many years a member of the Falstone Club. Robert joined the Royal Engineers in February 1915 and saw action at the Battle of Loos and in Egypt before going to Salonika. Records report the cause of death as 'died', which means that Robert probably died of illness rather than as a direct result of being in action. Robert is buried in the Struma Military Cemetery, Kalokastron, north east of Thessalonica.

1918

Civilian Mr Charles Guthrie, aged 40
Young Men's Christian Association
Died 17 July 1918

Charles Guthrie was the second son of Mrs Guthrie of St Wilfrid's Road, Hexham. Charles was a joiner by trade and under the sponsorship of Canon Savage he and another courageous man went out to Salonica to erect Y.M.C.A. huts. He died in hospital from severe dysentery.

Charles was the secretary of the Hexham Branch of the Amalgamated Society of Carpenters and Joiners. He was also the Hon Sec of the Tynedale Lodge of the Ancient Order of Foresters and was a member of Hexham's Unionist club.

Charles is buried in Salonica (Lembet Road) Military Cemetery.

The Caucasus

In late 1917 the British established a military force (39th Brigade) under Major-General L C Dunsterville, who gave his name to his brigade – the Dunsterforce. Their objective was to maintain the independence of a group of nations including Georgia, Armenia and Azerbaijan. It was hoped that this would prevent the invasion of India via Persia by a joint Turkish and German Army. Dunsterville was a Russian-speaking officer, who many think was the inspiration for the eponymous hero of Rudyard Kipling's 'Stalky and Co'.

The initial force was created using élite units of British, Australian, Canadian and New Zealand troops and was based in Hamadan in Western Persia. It was equipped with a fleet of seven hundred and fifty transport vehicles. The situation was complicated by the fact that by the time this force was operational the Russians had been forced out of the war and the new Russian army was being run by revolutionary (Red) troops. In their first campaign the Dunsterforce was confronted by a force of three thousand Red Russian troops and was forced to retire. Meanwhile the Germans with their Turkish allies (supported by some of the local tribes) had occupied the Georgian capital Tiblisi and had threatened Baku in Azerbaijan. In June the force captured Enzeli on the south-west shores of the Caspian Sea. By this time the Dunsterforce had increased to include three battalions of non-revolutionary (White) Russian troops and had occupied Baku.

On 26 August about one thousand Turks attacked 'Dirty Vulcan', which was held by a company of the 7th Battalion North Staffordshire. The Staffordshires suffered heavy casualties and were obliged to withdraw and form a new defensive Line, and it was reported that they were able to defend this new position. The battalion lost forty-four men on this day, of whom Joseph Boswell was one.

Private Joseph Boswell, aged 25
'A' Company, 7th Battalion Prince of Wales's
(North Staffordshire Regiment)
Died 26 August 1918

Joseph was born in Gateshead in 1894, the son of Joseph and Janet Boswell of King's Gate Terrace. In November 1917 he wrote to his mother telling her that he was convalescing in hospital in Amaria. Touchingly, he also wrote that he wished that he could be at home to 'play billiards with his father'. In January 1919 the Hexham Courant reported that Private Boswell had been killed in action in Mesopotamia. In correspondence with his parents the Office of War Records reported that Joseph was buried in the British Cemetery at Baku on the west coast of the Caspian Sea.

NORTH STAFFORDSHIRE REGT.
MAJOR   LANCE CORPORAL
HAVELOCK B. A. J.   JARRATT A. G.

CAPTAIN   PRIVATE
SPINK E. M.   ACKROYD A.
                        BOSWELL J.
LIEUTENANT   BRADSHAW A.
RUSSELL R. G.   BROWN A.
                        ELLERY R. J.
COY. SJT. MAJOR   MURRAY A. R.
HOLMES A. E.   OAKES J.
                        RALSTON J.
CORPORAL   RUSSELL G.
BLOOR G. T.   STAFFORD G.
                        WOOD E.

The Commonwealth War Graves Commission stated that Joseph was commemorated on the Haidar Pasha Memorial, in a remote suburb of Istanbul. However, after a fruitless search for his name in this cemetery the author reported that it was not there and the Commission checked and revised its records accordingly. Joseph is actually commemorated on the Baku Memorial, Azerbaijan, as his parents were told. The author has not, so far, verified this in person!

In September 1918 a force of fourteen thousand Turks threatened Baku and the Dunsterforce wisely withdrew to their base at Hamadan, accompanied by large numbers of Armenian refugees. After the Armistice in 1918 the force returned to Baku as an occupying force, from where the forces were eventually repatriated.

CHAPTER TWENTY-TWO

THE FLU EPIDEMIC OF 1918

Before I had left Vittel, the flu epidemic of 1918 had taken,
I think, as heavy a toll of our troops as any battle with the
Germans had done.

Edmund Wilson, *The Army 1917-1919*

Overview

Early in 1918 large numbers of soldiers began to complain of
being ill with symptoms such as sore throats, headaches and
loss of appetite. Although the illness was highly contagious,
it lasted for only a few days and was nicknamed the "three day
fever". Doctors were unable to identify the causes of the
illness, but eventually attributed it to a new strain of
influenza. Soldiers at the Front gave it the name of Spanish
Flu, but there is no evidence that the virus originated in
Spain. Throughout the early months of 1918 soldiers
continued to be infected by the virus, but death from the
illness was a very rare occurrence.

However, in the summer of 1918 the symptoms of those
becoming ill became increasingly more severe. Of those who
contracted the virus, about twenty percent of cases further
contracted bronchial pneumonia or septicaemic blood
poisoning, which generally led to their death. Others
developed heliotrope cyanosis which was identified by the
bluish condition of the sufferer; this resulted in death within
a few days.

All of the different forces on the Western Front were affected
by this virus. On the British mainland the first cases of what

became an epidemic occurred in Glasgow in May, from where it quickly spread to other towns and cities.

Private Alfred Thomas Andrew Noble, aged 19
53rd Training Reserve Northumberland Fusiliers
Died 29 October 1918

Alfred was born in Hexham and was the youngest son of Mr and Mrs Andrew Noble of St Andrews Road. Before joining up in early 1918 he worked for Messrs Wm Robb and Sons. At the time of his death from pneumonia (resulting from influenza) he was undergoing basic training in the Midlands.

Alfred is buried in Hexham Cemetery.

Private 2nd Class John Thomas Hogg, aged 37
Royal Air Force
Died 31 October 1918

Thomas was the husband of Mrs Ruth Hogg of Tyne Green. Before enlisting he was employed as a cartman by Messrs Fairlam of Battle Hill. He died of pneumonia (resulting from influenza) at Blandford Military Hospital in Dorset.

Thomas is buried in Hexham Cemetery.

Private John (Jack) Baty, aged 28
3rd Battalion Royal Fusiliers (London Regiment)
Died 2 November 1918

Jack was born in Hexham and was the eldest son of the late Isaac and Elizabeth Baty of Jubilee Buildings. He served his time as a blacksmith with his uncle, William Baty. Before joining up he was working at Settlingstone Mines. He was a popular playing member of St Patrick's Football Club along with his brother. Jack was an ex-Territorial and, as did many others, he enlisted with the local Northumberland Fusiliers within the first week of the war. He was attached to the Transport Section and went to France in April 1915. Later in the war he was transferred to the Royal Fusiliers. In early October 1918 he received a slight facial wound. On 29 October Jack was admitted to the Canadian General Hospital, France, suffering from influenza, which then developed into pneumonia.

Jack is buried in Mont Huon Military Cemetery, Le Treport.

Private Fred Hall, aged 23
Royal Army Medical Corps
Died 3 November 1918

Fred was the son of Thomas and Rose Hall of the Cottage, Shotley House, Shotley Bridge, Durham. Before the war he was employed as chauffeur to Mr H Pele of Duke's House, Hexham.

In 1915 he went to France as a driver of the "Bambrough" (sic) one of a fleet of ambulances sent out to France from the Tynedale District for service with the Northumberland Fusiliers. Late in 1917 this ambulance was transferred to Italy where British forces were fighting the Austrians alongside the Italians. Having contracted severe influenza, Fred died of pneumonia in the 24th Stationary Hospital, Cremona, Italy.

Fred is buried in Cremona Town Cemetery, Italy.

Private Joseph Young, aged 29
7th Divisional Mechanical Transport, Army Service Corps
Died 10 November 1918

Joseph was born in Hexham, the son of William and Elizabeth Young of Skinners Arms Cottage. He was posted to France in late 1916 and was attached to the Army Service Corps in support of the 7th Division. This Division saw action at Passchendaele in the autumn of 1917, after which it was transferred to Italy. Joseph died in hospital of influenza.

Joseph is buried in Bordighera British Cemetery, Italy.

CHAPTER TWENTY THREE

THOSE WHO DIED AT HOME

"We have done well; we like to hear it said.
Say it, and then, for God's sake, say no more."

A P Herbert, *After the Battle*

Overview

Not everyone on our various war memorials died overseas or
in military hospitals. Some men had joined up and were in
training but had never reached the battlefield when they died.
Others were engaged in military work in this country and met
their deaths in some tragic accident, as was the case with Henry
Lockhart (below). Still others returned injured and broken
from battle and died some time later. Sad to say there are some
men about whom there was very little information to be found
– the circumstances of their deaths appear to be irrecoverable.
For this chapter I have traced as much data as was possible, and
however brief the record, every soldier is included.

The Dead of 1915

Corporal Henry King Lockhart, aged 32 years
Motor Cyclist Section, Royal Engineers
Died 19 June 1915

Henry was the second son of Colonel Lewis Charles
Lockhart and the late Anne Higginbottom of Summerrods
Rigg. Henry was educated at Alnmouth, Uppingham and
Exeter College Oxford, where he achieved an MA. He
served his articles as a solicitor in Newcastle and London

and was admitted in 1907. He became a partner in his father's firm in 1909.

Henry was an expert and enthusiastic motorist and motorcyclist who on enlisting decided to use these skills when he joined the Colours in January 1915.

Henry was interested in athletics and was a keen hockey player, playing regularly with the Tynedale team. He was a skilful golfer winning many tournaments over the Hexham course.

Henry met his death as the result of a motorcycle accident near Hitchen in Hertfordshire, whilst serving with the Royal Engineers. He had been due to go out to the Front in a matter of weeks.

Henry is buried in the family plot in Hexham Cemetery.

❦   ❦   ❦

Private James William Riley, aged 46
1/4ᵗʰ Battalion Northumberland Fusiliers
Died December 1915

James's death was reported in the Hexham Herald on 1 January 1916. It records only that he died at Turner's Yard, Hexham. The notice of death states:

> *"Fortified with the rites of the Holy Church on whose soul, sweet Jesus, have mercy."*

James's death is not recognised by the Commonwealth War Graves Commission and no record of his burial can be found in Hexham Cemetery.

❦   ❦   ❦

The Dead of 1916

Private Robert Wilson, aged 36
1/4th Battalion Northumberland Fusiliers
Died 6 August 1916

Robert was born in Hexham and from his age it would appear that he rejoined the local Territorial Battalion at the onset of hostilities.

Robert is buried in Hexham Cemetery.

The Dead of 1917

Able Seaman William Maclachlan, aged 23
Royal Navy
Died 18 January 1917

William was the second son of Mrs Maclachlan of Gilesgate, Hexham. He joined the Navy at the age of fifteen in 1908.

On Saturday 27 January 1917, The Hexham Herald reported William's death with the following orbituary:

"At the outbreak of war he was allocated to HMS Queen Elizabeth and was involved in the fighting in the Dardanelles. He volunteered for mine sweeping duties and was lucky not to be killed when his vessel was destroyed killing eight of the ten-man crew. He was rescued following ten hours in the water. After the Helles landings he was wounded. His comrades presented him with a compass bearing the inscription 'Sunday, April 25th, 1915, Dardanelles'. During the landing of troops at Suvla Bay on the peninsula he rescued

an Army Officer, who died the following day. For his efforts his brother officers presented William with the dead officer's sword in recognition of his bravery.

Following his involvement at Gallipoli he studied and passed all his examinations in torpedo gunnery and also wore the cross guns. As a result he was transferred to the torpedo section of the British North Sea Battle Squadron. This squadron fought at the Battle of Jutland (May 31 – June 1 1916). His ship was sunk and he spent a considerable length of time in the North Sea, which appears to be a major contribution to his death. Whilst in hospital he was awarded the King's Badge.

After a stay in hospital he came to Hexham and died in January 1917. He was buried in Hexham Cemetery on Sunday 21st. The Reverend A. H. Jackson conducted the service."

William was invalided home after spending time at both Chatham and Haslar Naval Hospitals. William's death was reported in the Abbey Parish magazine but for some reason it is not recognised by the Commonwealth War Graves Commission; perhaps they were never told of it by his family. He is buried in Hexham Cemetery along with three others in an unmarked grave.

Drummer John Scott Snowball, aged 19
1/4th Battalion Northumberland Fusiliers
Died 1 April 1917

John was the son of Mr and Mrs Michael Snowball of Kingsgate Terrace, Hexham. He died of illness at his home in Hexham.

John is buried in Hexham Cemetery.

Private Robert Smith, aged 32
1/4ᵗʰ Battalion Northumberland Fusiliers
Died 2 July 1917

Robert was the third son of Mr and Mrs Robert Smith of Woodbine Terrace, Hexham. He was born in Nether Warden. He left a widow and child who lived in St Andrew's Road, Hexham. He was a member of the Hexham Territorials who were mobilized in August 1914. He spent a substantial part of the early days of the war on garrison duties on the Isle of Man and died a matter of weeks before he was due to go out to France. Whilst travelling from the Isle of Man to Catterick Barracks, Yorkshire, he became seriously ill. He died two weeks later in Catterick Bridge Hospital. His body was transported back to Hexham.

John is buried in St Michael's Churchyard, Warden.

Gunner John Robert Dodd, aged 35
Durham Brigade Royal Garrison Artillery
Died 11 October 1917

John was born in Hexham, the son of Thomas and Catherine Dodd. He enlisted in South Shields and died of his wounds having been sent back to the United Kingdom. It was impossible to trace where John was serving at the time of his injury.

John is buried in Hexham Cemetery.

Private Richard Dalzell Oliver, aged 23
Army Cyclist Corps
Died 22 November 1917

Richard was the youngest son of Thomas and Elizabeth Oliver of Beaumont Street, Hexham. He enlisted with the local battalion of the Northumberland Fusiliers and went to France in April 1915. In that month he was involved in the desperate fighting around Ypres at the time when the Germans first used gas warfare. At some point he was transferred to the Army Cyclist Corps. In December 1916 he was invalided to England suffering from ill health. He was expected to return to active duty after a period of convalescence but apparently he suffered a relapse and died in the Second Eastern General Hospital, Brighton. His older brother was also serving in France.

Richard is buried in Hexham Cemetery.

The following inscription is found on his headstone:

HE GAVE HIS LIFE
FOR US

Pioneer John Edwin Bruntlett, aged 20
50th (Northumbrian) Signal Company Royal Engineers
Died 25 December 1917

John was born in Skegness and was the eldest son of George and Mary Bruntlett who had formerly lived in Hexham but at the time of his death were living in Rodham Terrace, Stanley, County Durham. In civilian life he was employed as a clerk on the North Eastern Railway. The Hexham Courant of 22 September 1917

reported that John had been dangerously wounded in the face and eyes and was at a CCS in France. Obviously he was well enough to be moved to England, but unfortunately he died on Christmas Day in St George's Hospital in London, of wounds received in action on 12 September.

John is buried in Stanley New Cemetery. He is also commemorated at St Aidan's United Reformed Church in Hencotes. The commemoration tablet was previously in the English Presbyterian Church in Battle Hill, which was demolished in 1954.

The Dead of 1918

Private John Robson, aged 24
36th Battalion Northumberland Fusiliers
Died 10 January 1918

John Robson was the only son of John and Hannah Robson of Market Place, Hexham. Before enlisting at the onset of hostilities he was employed by his father, who was a merchant tailor. He was also a member of Hexham Unionist Club. He went to France in April 1915 with the 1/4th Battalion Northumberland Fusiliers and saw action at the *Second Battle of Ypres*. During 1917 he was wounded in the elbow, which not surprisingly incapacitated him for active service. As a result he was transferred to duties at home in the UK. On New Years Day 1918 he was admitted to Surrey

House Military Hospital in Margate suffering from Pneumonia, from which he died.

John is buried in Hexham Cemetery.

Major Surtees Atkinson, MC, aged 30
Royal Field Artillery
Died 7 February 1918

Surtees was the second son of John Atkinson JP of Newbiggin near Hexham and was married to Margaret Atkinson of Bootham Grange, York. He served in France from the very beginning of hostilities. Surtees was mentioned in Sir John French's final list for 'gallant and distinguished conduct in the field', which was published by both the Hexham Courant and the Herald on Saturday 8 January 1916. The London Gazette of 29 December 1916 confirmed that (as a Captain) Surtees was awarded the Military Cross. He died on the operating table at a Hospital in Leeds whilst undergoing routine surgery.

Surtees was buried with full military honours at Fulford Cemetery in York.

Regimental Quarter Master Sergeant
Andrew George Richardson, aged 43
1/4th Northumberland Fusiliers
Died 21 June 1918

Andrew was born in Gateshead in 1874. He joined the Northumberland Volunteer Battalion as a bugler, before the establishment of the Territorial Regiment. With the establishment of the Territorial Regiments in 1906 he became a Non Commissioned Officer and travelled to

France in 1915. He fought in the harrowing *Second Battle of Ypres* and indeed saw service in all of the conflicts that involved I/4th Northumberland Fusiliers. During the winter of 1917 – 18 he was admitted to the Lord Derby War Hospital in Warrington, Lancashire suffering from a nervous breakdown (shell shock). This hospital had over a thousand beds for mental patients. Later he returned to Hexham, but it appears that his condition deteriorated and he spent time in hospital in Morpeth, where he died.

For many years before the war, Andrew was the landlord of the Bush Inn, an old established hostelry (sited where we now have the Council Chambers for Tynedale District Council). The Bush had previously belonged to his father. At his death his family were residing at St Wilfrid's Road.

In those days Andrew played rugby as a fullback for Tynedale Rugby Club. Latterly he qualified as a county referee. He was also interested in coursing and acted as a 'slipper' at local meetings. He was a member of the Hexham Unionist Club; on the day of his funeral the club's flag flew at half-mast in his honour. His wife and son laid a wreath, which bore the following inscription:

UNTIL THE DAY BREAKS

Andrew was buried with full military honours, including the firing of three volleys over his open grave in Hexham Cemetery. The bearer party were Drummer J Urwin, Private R Pearson, Private H Addison and Private J Jewitt, all Northumberland Fusiliers based in Hexham. Andrew is not recorded in the Commonwealth War Graves listing, but his private family gravestone may be found in Hexham Cemetery.

Private James William Rowell, aged 35
'A' Company 1/4th Battalion Northumberland Fusiliers
Died 13 July 1918

James landed in France in April 1915 with the first batch of men from Hexham and was involved in the attack on the German trenches on 26 April during the *Second Battle of Ypres*. It was during this battle that the Germans first used chlorine gas as an offensive weapon. The Hexham Courant of Saturday 29 May 1915 listed James as being one of the battalion's injured. Three years later, on 17 July 1918, the Courant reported that James Rowell of Mills Yard, Hexham, had died of wounds which he had received in action. James is buried in an unmarked grave in Hexham Cemetery. His death is not mentioned on the Commonwealth War Graves list.

Engine Room Artificer
Anthony Ritson Bell Pearson, aged 31
Royal Navy
Died 23 September 1918

Anthony was born in Hexham in October 1886, the son of Mr and Mrs A Pearson of Kingsgate Terrace. He joined the Navy as a boy in 1900. Anthony was recommended for promotion to Engine Room Artificer in December 1916. He was invalided from the service suffering from tuberculosis in October 1917 and died a year later.

His name appears on Hexham's War Memorial, but he is not commemorated on the Commonwealth War Graves list of the fallen. The date of his death is taken from the Roll of Honour published by the Hexham Courant, Saturday 1 November 1919. A search of Hexham Cemetery records shows that he is buried within the cemetery and his date of death is confirmed.

The Dead of 1919

It is hard to overstate the importance – and difficulty – of maintaining the necessary supplies to support a war of this magnitude. The logistics needed careful planning and a great deal of hard work. A single mile of Front required 1934 tons of supplies each day. In most cases, existing rail tracks ended miles away from the Front Lines, so stores of food and ammunition were carried by a time and labour consuming transport system – from trains to lorries and then onto horse and cart. By 1916 a solution to this problem was found in the building of narrow gauge tramways to link the standard railways to the trenches. By 1917 it was decided to use standard gauge tracks all the way there.

Canada, a developing country, had established a considerable rail network – the Canadians had constructed more miles of track than had any other Allied nation. For this reason they were asked to provide skilled workmen to play a leading role in the construction and operation of railways on the fighting Fronts. Many of the first recruits came from the Canadian Pacific Railway Company.

In October 1916 the 1st Canadian Construction Battalion crossed over the English Channel to France and was renamed the 1st Battalion Canadian Railway Troops. During the battle of Passchendaele the Canadians laboured under appalling conditions to keep the supply lines open when the tracks were severed by enemy shellfire on average a hundred times per day. Until the end of the war all railway construction and maintenance was carried out by Canadian troops; eventually over 19,000 troops were involved in this work at any one time.

Sergeant Thomas William Burn, aged 31
1st Battalion Canadian Railway Troops
Died 2 February 1919

Thomas was born in Hexham in 1887 and was a

shoemaker by trade before he emigrated to Canada. It appears that he attended Trinity Methodist Church in Beaumont Street as his name appears on its War Memorial. He was married to Eva Burn of MacDonald Street, Mimico, Ontario. He joined up in January 1916 and records his occupation as shoemaker. He was a small man with a fair complexion and blue eyes.

Thomas is buried in Hexham Cemetery.

From 12 –14 April 1918, the 1st Battalion Royal Scots Fusiliers were in action north of Béthune (1½ miles). Early in the morning of 12 April they took up a defensive position east of La Bassée Canal (Canal d'Aire) north of the drawbridge at Avelette. This Line was later extended towards the village of Locon and along the road towards the village of Les Lobos. During the middle of the morning the Germans shelled the Royal Scots' position and later that morning attacked the Line from the area around the Bois de Pacaut. In the afternoon, German troops managed to get around the righthand side of the Scots' defensive position and were able to pour rifle and machine-gun fire from the right and from behind, injuring and killing many soldiers. Eventually the Scots were forced to withdraw towards La Bassée Canal where they took up a position to protect the road bridge across the canal which led towards Hinges from Le Cornet-Malo. During all of this time German troops continued to attack their defences from the north using heavy machine-gun fire and trench mortars positioned near Vert Bois Farm. The action on 12 April carried on well into the night with the Germans continuously getting behind the lines of defence, forcing withdrawal southwards towards Béthune. A further Front Line east of La Bassée Canal and west of the Canal de la Lawe was established late that night. On 13 April the Germans contented themselves with shelling the Royal Scots' positions. Late on 14 April the Battalion was replaced at the Front by the Kings Own Yorkshire Light Infantry.

Casualties for this action were:

Officers: 2 Killed, 3 wounded and 2 missing.

Other ranks: 8 killed, 166 wounded (of whom Private Victor Bathgate was one) and 149 missing.

Private Victor Bathgate, aged 20
1ˢᵗ Battalion Royal Scots Fusiliers
Died 28 April 1919

Victor was born in Hexham and was the son of Mrs Elizabeth Bathgate of Dean Street Hexham. Originally Victor enlisted in the forces when he was fifteen and was sent back from France, because of his age. Victor was wounded on 16 September 1916 during an attack on the Somme whilst serving with the 1/4ᵗʰ Northumberland Fusiliers. After convalescence he initially joined the Highland Light Infantry but was later transferred to Royal Scots.

On 12 April 1918 he received gunshot wounds. The Hexham Courant reported that he was dangerously wounded in the back and was in hospital in Sheffield. His mother had already lost a son, Rifleman James William Banks, a regular soldier who had served in India before the war, (died May 1915). A year later, after no fewer than fourteen operations, Victor died with his mother at his bedside.

Victor was laid to rest in Hexham cemetery with full military honours. The following words from the Gospel of John are found on his headstone:

GREATER LOVE
HATH NO MAN THAN THIS
THAT A MAN LAY DOWN HIS LIFE
FOR HIS FRIENDS

Sapper James William Dodds, aged 34
5ᵗʰ Provisional Company
Died 9 November 1919

James was the son of Jane and the late Alexander Dodds.

James is buried in Hexham Cemetery

The Dead of 1920

Private George Basil Porteous, aged 36
Royal Defence Corps
Died 1 February 1920

Basil was born in Northumberland, the son of George and Isabella Porteous of Deneholme, Hexham. He was married to Cecilia and lived in St Wilfrid's Road. He was a cartwright by trade.

In early 1917 the Hexham Courant reported that Private George Basil Porteous of the South Wales Borderers had been wounded in the left shoulder by shrapnel. Subsequently he was transferred to the Royal Defence Corps whose role was similar to that of the Home Guard in World War Two. Basil died of endo-carditis

Basil is buried in Hexham Cemetery.

The Enigmatic Private Brown

The name of Private W H Brown Durham Light Infantry appears on the War Memorial. An extensive search of both the Commonwealth War Grave Site and Soldiers who Died in the Great War did not reveal any information about this casualty.

Private William Harry Brown, aged 22
1/6th Battalion Durham Light Infantry
Died 13 October 1917

The above information was obtained from the Roll of Honour published in The Hexham Courant, Saturday 1 November 1919. The name is also found in Roll of Honour published in the December 1918 Abbey Parish Magazine under Harry Brown. A roll of Honour was not published in 1917.

When men have not been mentioned on the central databases (see Chapter Twenty Three), it appears to indicate that the soldier in question may have been discharged from the army and died a short time later, usually in the United Kingdom. There are no records of burial at Hexham Cemetery. Extensive searches of both the Hexham Courant and Hexham Herald did not produce any clues to his identity.

Death Plaque (also known as the 'Dead Man's Penny') were made of bronze. These were given to the families of soldiers and sailors who died or were killed by any means including natural causes between 4th August 1914 and 30th April 1920.

12cm diameter

Approximately 1,150,000 plaques were produced.

William Summers (top row far left) with his family.
See page 323

CHAPTER TWENTY-FOUR

HEXHAM REMEMBERS

"… dedicated to the glorious memory of the men of
Hexham who laid down their lives in the
Great War 1914 -1918"

From the plinth of the cross in the Abbey grounds.

As the war came to an end in November 1918, in cities towns
and villages all over the British Isles people started to think
about how best their community could build a lasting edifice
to commemorate the huge number of soldiers, sailors and
airmen who had lost their lives during the Great War. Field
Marshall Earl Haig issued a public statement expressing his
personal thanks to:

> "…all ranks of the Army and non combatant and auxiliary
> services, including the many thousands of women, who by
> devoted work in many capacities have assisted the victory
> of our arms so that generations of free people, both of your
> own race and all countries, will thank you for what you
> have done."

The people of Hexham, as was the case in countless other
towns across the country, felt the need to demonstrate their
particular thanks in the form of stone and mortar. Early in
1919 a War Memorial Committee was set up to explore the
options for Hexham's commemoration. The committee was
made of thirty people and was chaired by Mr James T Robb.
Mr John A Baty (Lloyds Bank Chambers) acted as Honorary
Secretary, whilst Mr W W Cornish (Lloyds Bank) acted as
Honorary Treasurer.

Following a number of public meetings it was announced by the War Memorial Committee that Hexham should remember its War heroes in two ways:

A Cottage Hospital.
A Monument, which would be erected in some central position, on which the names of the men could be recorded.

It was readily acknowledged that a large sum of money was needed to implement these plans, to be raised by public subscription. The committee estimated that the figure required lay in the region of £15,000, and in order to find this sum they organised a number of fundraising events, including simple house to house collections. A handbill to inform the public of the committee's ideas used the following appeals:

'The Committee desire to urge most strongly that the present appeal is not based upon the ordinary grounds of charity and philanthropy, rather an opportunity is furnished for a public Thankoffering (sic) to those who have given their lives for us.'

'We ask you to consider how deep is your debt to those who have fallen and to make your contribution an indication of your gratitude to our gallant men.'

In February 1919 the Committee announced that they had

secured (for £12,000) *St Wilfrid's*, a Victorian house with extensive grounds, to convert into a memorial cottage hospital. In the 1880s the house had been owned by Richard Gibson, a solicitor and agent for Lambton's Bank. In 1919 it was owned by Nancy, the widow of Colonel Jasper Gibson, also a solicitor.

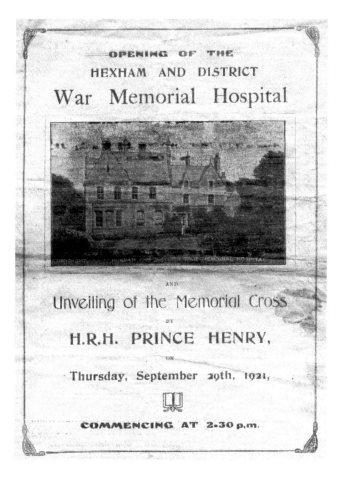

On 24 July 1921 a United Service was held in the Abbey Grounds and a collection made for the hospital. This money is believed to have been used to help fund the equipment for the hospital. When it opened it consisted of a male ward (six beds), a female ward (six beds) and a ward for children (four cots), together with an operating theatre and X-ray facility.

The County Council Clinic was also on the site, with an entrance on Eastgate. Having served the town well, the memorial cottage hospital (having been in the hands of the NHS) was finally closed on 1 April 1995, to be demolished at a later date. *Gibson's Field* housing development now stands in its place.

The Hexham War Memorial Cross.

The Committee also decided to erect a memorial cross in the Abbey Grounds. The style of cross chosen was the one which had been designed by Sir Reginald Blomfield RA and had also been selected by the then Imperial War Graves Commission for erection in the British cemeteries in France and Belgium. It was erected by William Cresswell, sculptor and monumental mason of Argyle Terrace, Hexham, using Portland Stone. The names of the fallen were cut into the plinth after the dedication ceremony. Over time the names have had to be re-cut and re-painted.

In his capacity as Honorary Secretary of the War Memorial Committee, Mr John A Baty published a Roll of Honour as the basis for the names to be commemorated on the cross. This list appeared as a supplement to the Hexham Courant on Saturday 11 November and included the following appeal:

> *'Relatives and Friends are requested to intimate to Mr John A Baty, the Hon Sec., Hexham War Memorial committee, or to Mr M Green any misdiscription or omission in the above.'*

The list contained 216 names including residence, age and date of death. Some of these names did not eventually appear on the Hexham Memorial. Further names were added and a new list appeared in another supplement to the Hexham Courant on 1 October 1921 which listed initials, surname, rank and regimental affiliation and contained 222 names.

The inscription on the plinth of the cross reads:

> THIS CROSS AND S WILFRID'S
> WAR MEMORIAL HOSPITAL
> ARE DEDICATED TO THE
> GLORIOUS MEMORY OF THE
> MEN OF HEXHAM WHO LAID
> DOWN THEIR LIVES IN THE
> GREAT WAR 1914-1918

The opening of the Hexham and District War Memorial Hospital and the unveiling of the Memorial Cross took place on Thursday 29 September 1921. These duties were carried by H R H Prince Henry (Harry), third son of King George V and Queen Mary, who later became the Duke of Gloucester; it was Prince Henry's first official ceremonial duty. A baby girl born in Hexham that day was named Henrietta after the Royal visitor. Hexham was *en fête*, and the Courant of the day described in lavish terms the beautiful floral displays which festooned virtually every business premises in the town!

Prince Harry's first duty of the day was at the hospital where he was welcomed by the Chairman of the Memorial Committee. After a guided tour of inspection, the Prince duly opened the Memorial Hospital using a fabulous gold key designed and made by Reid and Sons of Newcastle, and bearing an enamelled Arms of Hexham. Prayers were given by the Reverends J E McVitie and J V C Farquahar and the vote of thanks was proposed by the High Sheriff, Clarence D Smith.

After this the Prince's party travelled to the Abbey Gardens by way of Eastgate, Fore Street and Beaumont Street where he was met at the Benson Memorial Gate by General Sir Loftus Bates CB KCMG DSO. The Prince inspected a Guard of Honour drawn from the 1/4th Northumberland Fusiliers, Northumberland Hussars and Ex Service-Men. After the Memorial Cross had been unveiled, the Last Post was sounded and the Reverends Farquahar and McVitie said some prayers. Following this the Royal party were taken on a tour of the Abbey.

On 8 October, The Hexham Courant featured a picture of Prince Harry with Lord and Lady Rayliegh (Beaufront Castle), the rector and the verger, Lady Constance Howard, Captain Stannyforth, Mrs Dugdale and the Hon Mrs Lascelles.

When the Prince, his retinue and the civic dignitaries had gone on their way, the pristine war memorial began immediately to serve the function for which it was intended. Relatives and friends whose loved ones had laid down their lives for their country approached the cross and reverently placed their wreaths or their posies of flowers. Many of the messages left with these tributes are heartbreakingly simple:

In sorrowful remembrance of our dear son,
Percy Robson RND

In loving memory of our three sons, Harry, Fred and
Tom Abbott

In loving memory of our dear son, Pte Isaac Reay

In saddest remembrance of George Pearson

*In proud and loving memory of Second Lieutenant
J M Emerson*

In affectionate memory of my pal, Sam Morris

In loving remembrance of Daddy

As well as pride, many of those who tarried, bereft and miserable at the foot of the cross, must have felt within their hearts anger – indeed fury – at the senseless waste of it all. Passionate pride and joy in Britain's victory was always in tension with outrage and bitter regret at the appalling squander of human life. This became the tenor of much of the best known poetry that came out of the Great War. Siegfried Sassoon, for example, described the Menin Gate memorial as a *"pile of peace-complacent stone"*, and stated that he would understand if its nameless men should *"deride this sepulchre of crime"*. [1] But the men who marched away in Hardy's poem [2] went to the field [of battle] *ungrieving*, knowing that they would regret it for ever if they did not respond to England's need:

> *Her distress would leave us rueing*
> *Nay, we well see what we are doing,*
> *Though some may not see...*

Hence the faith and fire within them, the inner source of the steadfast courage and selfless heroism shown by these fallen men of Hexham, described in this book. For my part, I simply honour them.

Alan Isaac Grint
May 2006

References

1.   Siegfried Sassoon. *On Passing the New Menin Gate*.

2.   Thomas Hardy. *The Men Who March Away*.

The Beaumont Street Memorial Archway, entrance
to the Abbey Gardens, with the Memorial Cross
in the background.
See Chapter Twenty Four.

APPENDIX

WAR MEMORIALS OF HEXHAM 1914–1918 WAR

As well as the two civic memorials – the Memorial Cross in the Abbey Gardens and St Wilfrid's Memorial Hospital, erected as we know by the people of Hexham to commemorate the men who fell in the Great War – there are a number of other tributes to men who paid the ultimate sacrifice. Some of these commemorate a large body of men, some are a tribute to work colleagues or members of a congregation, still others are a personal tribute to the loss of a loved one.

Beaumont Street Arch

This memorial was dedicated to the honour of the 1/4th Northumberland Fusiliers by Mr J T Robb as a private thanksgiving that his three sons returned from the war. A late 17th or early 18th Century stone gateway, originally erected at the entrance to the White Hart Inn on the east side of the south end of Fore Street, it was moved at the expense of Mr Robb in 1919 to its present site at the entrance to the Abbey Gardens. (Robb's department store now occupies the site on which it originally stood).

The arch features two bronze plaques, one on each side of the opening, dedicated to the 4th (1/4th) Northumberland Fusiliers who served in the war; they do not commemorate any named soldiers. One of the plaques commemorates the major actions in which the local Territorial Battalion fought.

Trinity Methodist Church, Beaumont Street (1)

The brass memorial plaque was unveiled 3 October 1920 by Lieutenant-Colonel J Ridley Robb during a memorial service conducted by the Reverend J Griffen Hodson. It bears the names of twenty-eight members of the Trinity Wesleyan Methodist Church who lost their lives. All but two of the men are also commemorated on the Abbey Memorial Cross. These two names are listed on memorials outside the town.

Trinity Methodist Church, Beaumont Street (2)

This brass plaque commemorating ten men of the Primitive Methodist Church and School was initially hung in the Central Primitive Methodist Church, which was then at the corner of Battle Hill and Beaumont Street (now the Community Church), and was removed to the Trinity Methodist Church when the Primitive church closed for worship on 28 December 1952. All of the men are also commemorated on the Memorial Cross.

St Aidan's United Reformed Church, Hencotes (1)

This memorial was unveiled on 2 January 1921 by Col E P A Riddell, CMG, DSO accompanied by the Rev. J E McVitie and Mr William Robertson. It commemorates seventeen members of the congregation of the English Presbyterian Church on Battle Hill. The memorial was originally hung on the west wall in the English Presbyterian Church, but was removed for storage to the Church hall on Hencotes when the church was demolished in 1954, pending the building of a new church. By 1959 the congregation decided that they could not afford the rebuilding of a new church, so the hall was adapted to become the permanent church, which was rededicated in October 1960. All but one of those on this memorial is also on the Abbey Memorial Cross. He is commemorated instead on the Corbridge memorial.

St Aidan's United Reformed Church, Hencotes (2)

This plaque commemorates six members of the Congregational Church, which was on Battle Hill, all of whose names appear on the Memorial Cross. The memorial was lost when the Church was closed in 1967 and subsequently demolished in 1967. In 1997 the memorial was found again during the renovation of the Hexham Community Centre and was later re-hung in St Aidan's United Reformed Church.

St Mary's Roman Catholic Church, Hencotes

This memorial, which takes the form of an altar to the Sacred Heart and a brass plaque, contains the names of thirty-five men. It was unveiled by the Bishop of Hexham and Newcastle in January 1920. It was commissioned by the congregation and cost £260 to erect. All but three of the men are also commemorated on the Abbey Memorial Cross. The other three are to be found on memorials in outlying villages.

Salvation Army Citadel, Market Street

A Roll Call of those who died between 1914 and 1918 is made at the Salvation Army's Remembrance Day Service. The Roll is based on a paper list and contains eight names. All but one name is also found on the Abbey Memorial Cross.

Roll of Honour, Hexham Abbey

A Roll of Honour is situated on the east wall of the War Memorial Chapel (now known as the Lady Chapel) in the centre of the north transept aisle. It was dedicated on 2 February 1936 and bears two hundred and forty-seven names. Many of the names are to be found also on the Abbey

Memorial Cross, others are to be found on the memorials of outlying villages and towns.

War Memorial Chapel, Hexham Abbey

A chapel in the centre of the north transept aisle was dedicated in February 1936 by the Bishop of Newcastle to the men of Hexham who died in the Great War. The memorial includes an altar and various furnishings.

Sanctuary, Hexham Abbey

Two candlesticks were commissioned from Mr Temple Moore to commemorate twenty-four men of Hexham Abbey parish who had died between 1914 and some time in 1915.

Stained Glass Window, Hexham Abbey

Dedicated to those who served in the RFC and RAF during the Great War.

Church Hall, East End Methodist Church, Leazes Terrace

This memorial commemorates only one individual, Private John Kirkland, and was originally erected in the Church. When the new church was opened in 1936, the brass plaque was left in its original position as his family felt that this was the building with which John was familiar.

Memorial Hospital – Roll of Honour Boards

These wooden boards, dedicated to the men of Hexham who laid down their lives, were initially hung in the War Memorial

Hospital in Eastgate. When the hospital closed in April 1995 they were sent to Hexham General Hospital for temporary storage and were re-erected in the new hospital when it opened in July 2003.

Roll of Honour, Hencotes TA Centre

This memorial is a copy of a special supplement commissioned by the Hexham Herald and printed in gilt on art paper. It commemorates the members of the 1/4th Battalion Northumberland Fusiliers who responded to the call in August 1914.

Hexham Middle School, Fellside

In July 1923 a plaque was erected in the original hall of the Queen Elizabeth Grammar School at Fellside. It was commissioned by the Queen Elizabeth Grammar School Old Boys' Association and records the names of seven masters and one hundred and five scholars who fought in the war, of which sixteen died. The plaque gives details of the date, age and location of those who died. Only three of those who died appear on the Abbey Memorial Cross. Some are to be found on the memorials of outlying villages and towns.

Queen Elizabeth High School, Whetstone Bridge Road

When the new school was opened in 1965 a memorial to the fallen from the 1939-1945 War was removed from the Queen Elizabeth Grammar School at Fellside and brought to the new building. A new Great War plaque was made to match the style of the 1939-1945 War plaque, incorporating only the names of those who died. The original plaque from the Great War was left in Fellside School when it became the Middle School, because that was the building familiar to those who were commemorated.

393

The Sele County First School, Hexham.

In the main entrance of the school is a bookcase which was given by the old boys to commemorate their fallen comrades. No individual names are given.

Tynedale Rugby Football Club, Tynedale Park, Corbridge

In 1920 the Rugby Club, then based on the east side of Hexham, (Dene Park), raised a subscription list to provide a memorial. They bought an old army hut to remember their dead and turned it into a pavilion for the club. A brass plaque listing the names of the fallen was erected in the clubhouse. The President of the Northumberland Rugby Union, Mr H I Welford, officially opened the pavilion in January 1921. The plaque was moved to the new club house when the team occupied its new ground. The memorial lists the names of forty-nine men who played for the club and lost their lives; the civic Memorial Cross also bears the names of thirty two of these, the others are to be found on the memorial in Corbridge and on other local monuments.

Hexham Golf Club, Spital Park, West Road

A Brass plaque commemorates sixteen members of the Club who died in the Great War. It was originally erected in the former Clubhouse (now Princess House) on the West Road. It was re-erected in its present position in 1954. The Abbey Memorial Cross contains twelve of the names found on the golf club memorial.

Post Office Sorting Office, Bridge End Industrial Estate, Hexham

This memorial was erected in May 1922 in memory of the men who were connected with the Hexham Postal Depot,

394

which covers a large geographical area. It contains eighteen names from 1914 -1919 and three names from 1939 -1945. The memorial was originally erected in the Post Office in Market Street, opposite St Wilfrid's Gateway (now Hadrian House, Tynedale Council). The memorial was moved in 1963, when the new public Post Office Counter was opened on Battle Hill. When this was moved to Robbs Store, the memorial was moved to the Post Office enquiry counter in the rear of the Battle Hill building. When this too closed in November 1999, the memorial was moved to the new facility at Bridge End Industrial Estate. Of the eighteen Great War names only seven are found on the Abbey Memorial Cross.

Portable Holy Communion set, Hexham Abbey

On Easter Sunday 1919, the parents of William Richard Thew, their only son, presented to Hexham Abbey an engraved portable Holy Communion set in his honour. The set consisted of a stopped flagon, chalice and wafer paten.

Memorial to Captain Reginald Head, Hexham Abbey

A marble memorial plaque hangs in the Abbey commemorating the deaths of John Oswald Head, died July 1914 aged 85 and Captain Reginald Head, died April 1915 aged 30 (see Chapter Five). It was erected by Dorothy Head, wife of the first and mother of the second.

'Sammy', Fusiliers Museum, Alnwick

The 1/4th Battalion Northumberland Fusiliers adopted Sammy the dog as a regimental pet when he joined them (uninvited!) at the train station in Hexham and subsequently landed with them in France in April 1915. At the *Second Battle of Ypres* he was wounded and gassed during the fighting. Sadly, he was killed accidentally during firing practice in late 1916. His body was returned to England and the fusiliers paid for a taxidermist to preserve his remains. Until 1996 Sammy stood in his glass case in Hencotes TA Centre, but he was latterly removed to the Regimental Museum in Alnwick.

GLOSSARY OF MILITARY TERMS

Army Structure:

Division (e.g. 50th Northumbrian Division)
A Division was a self-contained unit of approximately 18,000 men comprising infantry, artillery, engineers, medical, transport and signals units. Within the Division, the infantry was divided into three Infantry Brigades.

Infantry Brigade (e.g. 149th Infantry Brigade)
In 1914 an Infantry Brigade consisted of 4 Battalions sometimes coming from different regiments. Due to manpower shortages, by early 1918 the four battalion system was reduced to three. In 1914, an Infantry Brigade would consist of over 4000 men.

Battalion (e.g. 1/4th Northumberland Fusiliers)
A Battalion was the basic tactical unit of the British Army in 1914 and at full strength contained 1,007 men of whom 30 were officers. The highest ranking officer was a Lieutenant-Colonel. In 1914 a machine gun section was also attached to a Battalion which quickly increased in size. When going into action Battalions would leave behind a number of men, intended to form the nucleus for rebuilding the battalion in the event of heavy casualties. Each battalion was split up into five sections: the Battalion Headquarters and four companies.

Company
Companies were usually designated by the letters 'A' through to 'D', although there were exceptions to this, who used the other end of the alphabet and the Guards who were numbered '1' through to '4'. At full complement each company consisted of 227 men and was commanded by either a Major or a Captain. Each company was divided into four platoons.

Platoon

Each Platoon consisted of either 53 or 54 men under the leadership of a Lieutenant or Second Lieutenant. Furthermore each platoon was subdivided into four sections, each made up of twelve men under a Non Commissioned Officer (Sergeant or Corporal).

Other terms:

Bite and Hold
By 1917 it was realised that the 'Great Break' through was a highly unlikely event and that allowing the infantry to surge forward in many cases led to their destruction. General Herbert Plumer, in command at Messines and saviour of Passchendaele, was instrumental in developing the bite and hold attack. He favoured limited objectives: no more than 1000 yards gain (the bite), using a creeping barrage to give a curtain of fire behind which the infantry attacked. On gaining their objective the barrage would be maintained whilst the attackers had time to consolidate their new position (the hold).

Creeping Barrage
A creeping barrage was designed to give a curtain of artillery fire just ahead of advancing infantry. It would creep forward in advance of the attack: a rate of 60 yards per minute was commonly adopted. When deployed successfully it was very influential to the outcome of an attack and would reduce casualties enormously. However, if the infantry was unable for one reason or another to keep in contact with barrage then its effects on the attack were minimal.

Enfilade Fire
Enfilade fire is a military concept to describe rifle, machine-gun or artillery fire which can be directed against the enemies' position along its long axis. A trench is enfiladed if the enemy can fire down its length; an attack is enfiladed if

enemy fire can be directed across the line of the attack, rather than from the front.

Redoubt

These were heavily defended positions built in the early years of the war as integral positions within the German Front Line. They were sited to give all-round fire and were often sited with other redoubts so that interconnecting fields of fire could be developed. The concept was further developed in the Hindenburg Line. In late 1917 and early 1918 the idea of the Redoubt was adopted by the British, partly to alleviate the problem of the reduced umber of troops available for duty.

Sap

A shallow, heavily disguised narrow trench which was cut ahead of the Front Line into No Man's Land. It was also referred to as a listening post. The occupants of a sap were expected to keep a close watch for any signs of enemy activity, such as mining, preparations for a gas attack or enemy wiring parties. Duty in a sap was considered a dangerous posting, as both sides would launch raids to eliminate these forward positions.

GENERAL BIBLIOGRAPHY

Books

1. Evans, M. M. *Passchendaele and the Battles of Ypres 1914-18*
    Pub: Osprey 1997.

2. Farndale, Gen Sir M. *History of the Royal Regiment of Artillery Western Front 1914-1918*
    Pub: Royal Artillery Institution 1986.

3. Farndale, Gen Sir M. *History of the Royal Regiment of Artillery The Forgotten Fronts and Home Base 1914-18*
    Pub: Royal Artillery Institution 1988.

4. Hart, P. *The Somme*
    Pub: Weidenfield & Nicolson, 2005.

5. Keegan, J. *The First World War*
    Pub: Hutchinson, 1998.

6. Middlebrook, M. *First Day on the Somme*
    Pub: Penguin, 1971.

7. Middlebrook, M. *The Kaiser's Battle*
    Pub: Penguin, 2000.

8. Prior, R. Wilson T. *Passchendaele*
    Pub: Yale University Press, 2002.

9. Sheffield, G. *The Somme*
    Pub: Cassel, 2003.

10. Westlake, R. *British Regiments at Gallipoli*
    Pub: Pen & Sword, 1996

11. Westlake, R. *British Battalions on the Somme*
Pub: Pen & Sword, 1994.

Newspaper Sources

Hexham Courant 1914 to 1921

Hexham Herald   1914 to 1921

St George's Gazette 1914 to 1918

Soldiers' Death Details

CWGC (Commonwealth War Graves Commission)
www.cwgc.org

Soldiers who died in Great War, CD-Rom Version 1.
Naval & Military Press

Internet Sites

1/4th Battalion Northumberland Fusiliers
www.4thbnnf.com

1/7th Battalion Northumberland Fusiliers
www.fairmile.fsbusiness.co.uk

Long, Long Trail, British Army in the Great War.
www.1914-1918.net

Long, Long Trail, Forum.
www.1914-1918.net

Australian War Memorial
www.awm.gov.au

Canada and the Great War
www.thegreatwar.ca

Old Front Line, Battlefields of WW1
http://battlefields1418.50megs.com

First World War. Com
www.firstworldwar.com

National Archives
www.nationalarchives.gov.uk

The London Gazette
www.gazettes-online.co.uk

INDEX OF SOLDIERS

INDEX OF SOLDIERS

INDEX OF SOLDIERS